Whistleblowing

THE LEARNED SOCIETY OF PRAXIOLOGY

PRAXIOLOGY:
The International Annual of Practical Philosophy and Methodology Vol. 18
WHISTLEBLOWING: IN DEFENSE OF PROPER ACTION

Whistleblowing

In Defense of Proper Action

Praxiology: The International Annual of Practical Philosophy and Methodology

Edited by

Marek Arszułowicz and Wojciech W. Gasparski

Transaction Publishers
New Brunswick (U.S.A.) and London (U.K.)

This book is printed on acid-free paper that meets the American National Standard for Permanence of Paper for Printed Library Materials.

Library of Congress Catalog Number: 2010024212
ISBN: 978-1-4128-1120-0
Printed in the United States of America

Library of Congress Cataloging-in-Publication Data

Arszułowicz, Marek.
Whistleblowing : in defense of proper action / Marek Arszułowicz and Wojciech W. Gasparski.
p. cm. -- (Praxiology ; 18)
Includes bibliographical references.
ISBN 978-1-4128-1120-0 (alk. paper)
1. Whistle blowing. 2. Business ethics. I. Gasparski, Wojciech. II. Title.

HD60.A77 2010
174--dc22

2010024212

Contents

Editorial

Wojciech W. Gasparski
Kozminski University
Warsaw, Poland

Praxiology, like a grammar, is about the correct conduct of humans, i.e., about human action: grammar is verbal communication, praxiology is human action in general. Its mission is to deliver a dictionary, a conceptual apparatus, and rules, practical directives ("ortho-graphy") of proper actions towards purposes, i.e., states selected by actors because of their values. It is noticeable, however, that grammar is one thing—an ideal, and the practice of human actions is another. There are a great many actions proper in terms of all praxiological characteristics, but also many, too many, human actions improper from a praxiological point of view as well as from a moral perspective. Some of them are mistakes because of so-called practical errors (*errare humanum est*), others are simply wrong deeds performed deliberately by crafty fellows (ill will). Correction of misbehavior needs identification of what causes such conduct, which is the more difficult the more hidden are the assumptions taken for granted of the action in question. In such cases occurring in economic life, the way suggested by experienced analysts is whistleblowing.

The praxiological literature has not covered this controversial issue so far. The topic is discussed mainly by lawyers and ethicists, chiefly in relation to business activities and interrelations between business and public and/or local administration, also with the world of politics. This volume is the first time a book has been dedicated to the issue of disclosing some of the practical errors and wrongdoing considered under the praxiological (action theory) umbrella with an obvious link to ethics. Both praxiology and ethics are parts of practical philosophy as it was nicely formulated by Mario Bunge [1989]. Thus writes the philosopher:

> Axiology is centrally concerned with the good, ethics with the right, and action theory with actions that are both efficient and right. Now a right action is one that promotes the good, whereas a wrong one promotes evil. Hence the good is in every regard—conceptually, biologically and technically—prior to the right. Not that the ability to discriminate good from bad suffices to sort out right from wrong. Whereas the former ability is presumably possessed by all animals, only animals possessing a modicum of moral sensibility, intelligence, imagination and social experience can tell right from wrong and, moreover, plan right and efficient actions. (Bunge 1989, 5-6)

That is why this book was designed to accompany previous volumes published in the series of praxiological inquiry. Economics and its "engineering"—business—are rooted in praxiology. Human actions related to economic/business conduct should be effective and efficient (the "double E") according to praxiological right-criteria. But these criteria are of secondary order in the sequence of norms that should be taken into account. The primary norm is ethicality (the "third E") which defines the endo- and exo-morality of economic/business activities on the basis of the axiological good-foundations presupposed for the area of human actions in question (Gasparski 2009, 234).

The editors of this volume believe that this book, composed of articles on whistle-blowing written from different angles and presenting a variety of experiences will add new value to both praxiology and ethics related to economic activity in its social and global context. The issues, problems, and questions raised by the international group of eminent scholars in their contributions to the book harmonize with the contemporary debate induced by the present economic crises which have uncovered the practical errors and hypocrisy of the actors responsible for the leadership and management of, mostly, financial institutions.

References

Bunge, M. 1989, *Treatise on Basic Philosophy,* Vol. 8 *Ethics,* Reidel, Dordrecht.

Gasparski, W. W., 2009, Ethical Infrastructure for Business with Special Emphasis on Poland: Designing for the Common Good, in: De Bettignies, H-C, & Lepineux, F., eds., *Business, Globalization and the Common Good,* Peter Lang, Oxford, pp. 227-250.

Introduction

Marek Arszułowicz
Business Ethics Center, Kozminski University
Warsaw, Poland

When the law of "qui tam" (*qui tam pro domino rege sequitur quam pro se ipso*) was introduced in the Middle Ages into social life, the police were weak, there were no reliable means of communication, science was poorly developed, and the economy could offer the masses nothing but hard work and little reward. One might conclude that such conditions created a good background for corrupt practices and to counteract them any successful tool would be more than welcomed. Then the idea of whistleblowing emerged. Since that time the landscape of social and scientific life has changed dramatically. We have conquered the moon, democracy has made its way into various nations offering its fruits to many, we have unlocked the power of the atom, we have overcome the distance via quick communication, we have even discovered the physical dimensions of the universe. But have we become equally successful in conquering the human mind by shaping and modeling it in a way that it can produce only good fruit (truth, honesty, and wisdom)? Or are we still too weak to raise the smallest matter—the energy of the human mind? Do we still need whistleblowing to deal with malpractices in modern world?

Eminent scholars from all over the world have made an effort to create an overall picture of whistleblowing, how it is perceived and functions nowadays. The fruit of their analytical work is this book, a collection of thirteen papers that discuss the problem from different perspectives, using different methods and tools. The image of the present state of whistleblowing, emerging from this collective labor, is still blurry and inconsistent. Partially because, being still a novelty in the world of ethics, it must be shaped into a rock-solid concept accepted by a majority of scholars, and partially because it touches the ever present core of human existence: the fight between good and evil, truth and lie, surrounding the efficient organization of social life, to which no satisfying solution has been found so far. It also proves that the major concept of whistleblowing was shaken by the realities of life: the value of truth is being systematically undermined by those who possess power and riches. Truth itself is being seen as an enemy and those who carry it are likewise perceived as troublemakers. A relatively short history of whistleblowing has evoked much debate that discusses mainly the problem of: who should tell whom about what and what for.

The logic of the book allows the reader to follow the debate in a twofold manner. In the first instance, the contents are arranged in three sections: *theoretical issues, whistleblowin, and ethics, whistleblowing in practice.* The second gives freedom of confronting different authors' views in order to analyze their perspectives. The first part opens with Wojciech Gasparski's paper. It sets whistleblowing in the concept of struggle developed by Professor Kotarbinski, and suggests potentialization (a kind of warning or threat) as a lesson that can be taught by praxiology. Wim Vandekerchove analyzes a great shift from an "old model" to a "new model" of whistleblowing, that is, valuing motivation over information. This has been a burning issue, the subject of numerous heated debates. Further on Vandekerchove analyzes the False Claim Act and examines to what extent the morality is a factor is when blowing the whistle. Marek Arszulowicz criticizes the weaknesses of the whistleblowing definition and points other factors, that make whistleblowing ineffective in some countries.

The second part of the book opens with a question raised by W. Michael Hoffman and Robert E. McNulty: "when is it permissible to blow the whistle and when is it a duty?" Throughout the paper the reader may enjoy a lively debate that scientists have had with the famous De George definition and their new concept of "A Universal Dignity Theory of Whistleblowing." Tobias J.G. Louw presents the "Travelgate" case that helps to understand the ethics of whistleblowing in South Africa. Aaron Levine presents whistleblowing as treated in Jewish law. He draws implications of *Hafetz Hayyim* protocol contrasting them with secular business ethics. The contrast is derived from *imitation Dei* principle that depicts God's mercy by weakening the power of evil inclinations. Wang Nan describes the complexity of the engineering world in which a single person, not having the full picture of the whole project, may lose the sense of judging properly the upcoming danger. Here we also have an example of Chinese cultural background which is a starting point for discussing cultural differences that hinder embracing whistleblowing.

The third part of the book, for understandable reasons also the largest, transfers theory into practice. We learn from Wim Vandekerchove that legislation protecting whistleblowers is now in more than ten countries and we can follow his research in universals in whistleblowing. Guido Strack provides a very thorough picture of whistleblowing in Germany with its historical background and protection practices. David Lewis presents achievements of Public Interest Disclosure Act of 1998 in the form of practical questions and answers. His knowledge is based on research conducted at universities and local governments. A.J. Brown and Paul Latimer explore the problems of whistleblowing legislation in Australia. In the aftermath of their very deep and exact analysis of the current law they identify important issues for consideration in whistleblower regulations. Tina Uys presents the first whistleblowers of the country and discusses cultural perception impact on building whistleblowing legislation. Her comment on Peter Drucker negative reflection on whistleblowing shows how the concept has changed through time. She also makes us familiar with two names native to South Africa, very important in the whistleblowing context: *ibuntu and impimpi.* Anna Lewicka-Strzalecka shares her experience as a lecturer teaching about whistleblowing, with emphasis on understanding loyalty. Here we also have a presentation of her studies concerning Polish employee's attitude towards revealing the truth and the particular role of a manager who is perceived by employees as the role model of ethical standards. Anna Wojciechowska-Nowak presents a number of whistleblowing cases monitored by the Batory Fundation in Poland with reference to legislative limitations of the current law.

If concepts concerning whistleblowing, discussed in the book, were to be made into a list the following issues would be of interest:

- cases of whistleblowers
- concept of struggle
- cultural perception
- current legislations
- definitions
- how to teach about whistleblowing
- Jewish perspective
- rewarding
- whistleblowing history
- whistleblowing in engineering world.

Having written this far about the content of the book, let me draw reader's attention to the fact that the title "Whistle-Blowing: In Defense of Proper Action," has a double meaning. Whistleblowing is being treated throughout the debate both as the subject and the object. It defends those who reveal the truth, but as a concept it equally needs to be defended as well. The question stated at the beginning of this section "do we still need whistleblowing in the modern world?"might be answered with the help of the observed law that the more social life is developed and sophisticated the more opportunities for unethical behavior. One door opened for new human achievements opens another door for human misbehavior.

Part One

Theoretical Issues

Whistleblowing in the Light of the Praxiological Theory of Struggle

Wojciech W. Gasparski
Kozminski University
Warsaw, Poland

1. Introduction

Praxiology is about human action. It considers human action as a conscious, voluntary, purposeful human behavior. Such behavior needs means to perform the action. The means should be not only relevant but also used properly, like words when one is composing a text, whether oral or written, for communication purposes. It is grammar, orthography, and phonetics that organize language in the process of speaking and/or writing. Note that verbal communication is a kind of action, human action indeed, therefore it is reasonable to suppose that other kinds of human action are guided by their equivalents of specific grammars and orthographies. This observation encouraged Tadeusz Kotarbinski, the founding father of Polish praxiology, to coin a nickname for the discipline in question, namely a *grammar of action* (Kotarbinski 1999d, 447). He did so, as Kotarbinski himself declared in another contribution, because of the difference between his approach to philosophy and the approaches characteristic of other philosophers of the world-famous Lvov-Warsaw school of Polish philosophy; the main feature of his approach was that he took observations of reality through the "lattice of language" (Gasparski 1993). Language organization was Kotarbinski's metaphor used for understanding the rules of how other types of human action are organized. Being a logician, he—as a generalist rather than a particularist—was interested not in specific grammars of different kinds of deeds but in the universal grammar of action. One may even say that the concept of Kotarbinski's praxiology plays, to some extent, a similar role in the domain of human action that Noam Chomsky's concept of generative grammar plays in linguistics—praxiology may be considered as the generative grammar for human action. This is why other praxiologists—Ludwig von Mises for example—considered praxiology aprioristically and human action as an ultimate given (Mises 1998).

Once there is a grammar of action, the courses of actions performed by different humans are correct if they follow the rules of the grammar or incorrect if they do not. The collection of praxiological rules was located by Kotarbinski under the umbrella named "good work" (or "good labor," if you wish). This name was used in the title of Kotarbinski's treatise (published in Polish) on his praxiology; the English translation of the book lost the original title and is known as *Praxiology: The Science of Efficient Action*. An extensive summary of that—*sit venia verbo*—"ortho-praxy" (generalizing the term of ortho-graphy) is published in one of the earlier volumes of *Praxiology: The International Annual of Practical Philosophy and Methodology* (Kotarbinski 2000).

In yet another essay, Kotarbinski admitted that "organization science, managerial in its essence, and praxiology, philosophical in its character, serve jointly as a theory of good work as such. It is not necessary to add," he wrote, "that if the appeal of 'good work' is understood as a social watchword it is not sufficient to take care of efficacy only, but also to insist that the work is resourceful, i.e., efficacious in realizing justified aims." (Kotarbinski 1999c, 436). It was, in fact, an appeal to not ignore the ethical dimension of selecting the purposes of actions and the means to achieve them. This has been named the "triple E" set of orthogonal criteria linking the good with the right (Gasparski 2002).

If this is so, it is not enough to identify practical errors of a purely "ortho-praxical"[1] nature but ethical misbehavior as well. This is a kind of struggle with malfunction and wicked actions manifested in individual and collective actions performed with a moral distance between the actors, i.e., when the other party is considered not as a partner, but as a "victim" or a "non-person" (Harrison 2005, 291-308).

In many cases companies that produce goods or banks that offer so-called "innovative (toxic) financial products" treat customers in this way. Amatrya Sen, a Nobel Prize winner in economics, said recently that the "contemporary financial crisis is caused by moral crisis, for people were directed by greed and improvidence [therefore sins were committed against both "ortho-praxy" and ethics—WWG], as well as by social crises which would have been avoided if the relevant regulations were introduced beforehand" (Sen 2009), which is another practical error, in this case made under pressure from deregulation enthusiasts.

Fighting with "ortho-praxical" and moral (unethical) misbehavior is also a kind of action that needs its own means and organization. These include different types of critique, correction, education, etc. They are efficient if the unfair courses of action are identified, which in many cases is not easy to do. It seems that praxiology may offer a piece of knowledge taken from its chapter called the *theory of struggle* as a "toolbox," both intellectual and practical, supporting the fight for "good work" understood as a common good. In particular, it may shed new light on the action that consists in "informing of a wrongdoing in an organization in the hope of stopping it" known as *whistleblowing.*

Some of the main issues related to the praxiological theory of struggle are presented in this article, and a few relevant suggestions for whistle-blowing are given.

2. Elements of the Praxiological Theory of Struggle

Tadeusz Kotarbinski introduced his praxiological theory of struggle in an article devoted to the fundamental concepts of the theory (Kotarbinski 1999a). Let us overview the main concepts presented[2] in a study based on the methodological assumption of the hierarchical sequence, logical in its essence, that in the ideal system of a particular struggle theory, e.g., armed combat, competition, rivalry, etc., specific notions should be based on the conceptual apparatus of a general theory of struggle which, in the course of things, should refer to the concepts of a presupposed general theory of action, i.e., of praxiology. The efforts of the quoted author focused on the essentials of the general theory of struggle.

The first concept suggested by the philosopher is the concept of *struggle* itself. The relevant definition is as follows:

> An actor A is in a state of struggle with another actor B if: (1) A acts with the intention to perform the deed in a particular way W(A), while B acts with the intention to perform the same deed in a particular way W(B) but the course of action may not be performed in both ways; (2) actors A and B know this and act to enforce their own particular ways of performing the deed.

In other words: "Actors A and B are in a state of struggle if they want to achieve different aims taking into account what is done or may be done by the adversary if the two courses of action interfere with each other."

Such a concept of struggle is general, for it covers all kinds of struggle, such as antipathy, litigation, a parliamentary debate, a theoretical discussion, a game, a competition and so on. The generality of the theory of struggle detaches struggle from its emotional context, situating its structure closer to organization theory and economics rather than to psychology of feelings, says Kotarbinski.

Let us point out that struggle is a kind of cooperation between two or more parties engaged in an action towards a purpose. What does this mean? It means that in many cases of human action two kinds of cooperation are essential to achieve the purpose: (1) positive cooperation and (2) negative cooperation. For instance: one team of soccer players has to organize their individual actions in such a way that the team behaves like a unity, a system—this is achieved thanks to *positive cooperation* between individuals. However, one team cannot win a cup without playing a game with another team which also wants to be the winner. The two teams have to cooperate in an opposite manner and that kind of contrasting cooperation is *negative cooperation,* which is in fact a struggle. It would be good if the negative cooperation of teams, groups, individuals were performed justly, following standards of fair play. Unfortunately this is often not the case and the referees are forced to blow the whistle signaling misconduct.

The next concept of the struggle theory is *attack* considered from a purely methodological point of view, therefore free from emotional settings. Its definition is as follows: "Attack is an action of the opposing party who aims to create a state different from the existing one." For instance: during a debate actor A would like to change the opinion of another actor, B, who supports the original standpoint, defending it: actor A is an attacker while actor B is a defender. Being an attacker and a defender may change during the course of the struggle. Let us also add that attack is the beginning of a struggle which ends when one of the actors wins the struggle. Victory may be complete or partial, depending on how big a part of the original aims the attacker managed to achieve and the defender to defend.

In a great many cases there are more than two actors, even groups of actors, engaged in a struggle. Therefore the following question is very important: is it possible to be neutral being among opposite actors fighting against each other? Praxiology offers this answer: actor A participates in an action of actor B if A actively influences the outcome of the action of actor B. Therefore, actor A is taking part in a struggle between actors B and C if A is active and influences the outcome of the struggle. To be active means not only that one externally manifests one's involvement, influencing the conduct of the fighting actors, but also that one may be quasi-passive; observation or keeping an eye on the course of the actors' struggle are just examples of such quasi-passiveness. Being neutral, therefore, does not mean abstention from a struggle but a kind of participation in it. For instance, moderators of a debate are neutral not because they don't participate in the verbal fight but because they keep control over the rules of the debate, so, as Kotarbinski writes, this is an organized participation to support the benefits of all parties engaged in the struggle: "A neutral person acts and must act for she can act. Not taking part in a struggle is possible only if one is unable to take part in it" (op. cit., 158). A neutral referee should be impartial and not passive because he or she is taking part in the game to keep the game within the framework of the rules, both "grammatical" (the right) and of fair play (the good). Any excesses should be signaled by blowing the whistle, punished if necessary, and the rules ("grammar") of the cooperation restored.

The next issues of the theory are rules guiding a struggle towards its successful result. Let us assume that the struggle is conducted under pressure, writes Kotarbinski, which occurs in conditions of a compulsory or critical situation, i.e. a situation known as "there is no other choice," or a combination of both. Kotarbinski points out several rules taken from practice. Among them are: gathering of all necessary resources to prevent the other party from using its resources, a paradoxical rule of freeing one's area of activity at the expense of one's own unnecessary resources, creating compulsory situations for the enemy, creating traps, using the resources of the other party, and a few others.

In a multi-subject struggle the important factor is intensity leading to coordination of different courses of action. Coordination is often identified with organization—positive cooperation—writes Kotarbinski, who preferred to limit the understanding of this term to a whole with a hierarchical structure of elements (composition). According to such an approach, coordination leads to organization. Therefore the philosopher introduces another rule, namely to disperse the adversary's resources with the aim of disorganizing that adversary's forces. The Roman principle *divide et impera* captures the essence of the aforementioned rules.

In many cases it is not necessary to use one's resources but to show them to the adversary instead; this technique is called *potentialization.* Potentialization usually is a kind of warning or threat even. It is more efficacious than using resources, provided that words speak for potential deeds. Public relations uses this technique. One masterly use of the technique is, according to Kotarbinski, an auction: participants show each other their own forces without spending them in the course of their counterattacks or an attack by one side and defense by the other party. The most essential factor in the course of a struggle is the ability to act. That ability is limited and its scope is diminished in the course of the action up to the time point of "now or never!" says the philosopher.

The rule of accomplished facts is formulated by the cited author in the following words: "if you wish the future state of the art to be as you want it and you are able to make it that way free of any obstacles, try to do it without unnecessary delay in order to prevent it from the interference of adversaries" (op. cit., 163).

Yet another rule formulated by Kotarbinski is this: "one who wants the given state of the art to achieve particular shape in a defined period of time, should, before obstacles emerge, assure such a phase of maturity of the state in question that further evolution will prevent adversaries' attack" (ibid). This allows us to use limited resources in action for human nature is on our side. Creating coalitions is another rule of struggle, sometimes implemented in the tricky manner that one cooperates first with the weaker against the stronger and then, if necessary, wins over that weaker side.

Finally, it is important to keep the adversary in ignorance of one's intentions and resources and to know as much as possible about their intentions and resources. If necessary, one should confuse the other party, e.g., through irrational behavior, to blunt the enemy, for an adversary thinking rationally, i.e., logically, may expect us to behave in a different manner; Kotarbinski says that this is why in some cases it is so difficult to win with a layman, e.g., in chess, for the experienced player, as a rule, does not take into account the strange moves of a duffer.

Summarizing, after introducing the concept of struggle, we have characterized some of the issues that belong to the general theory of struggle originating from praxiology: the postulate of freedom of action; the dispersion of forces of the other party; rules related to concentration, coordination and organization; the role of hierarchy and highly subordinating elements in hierarchical structures; the principle of anticipation; the rule of procrastination; potentialization; tactics of "the power to decide" (or "to hold the balance"); increasing superiority through equivalent bindings; the rule of gaining knowledge about the other side while oneself confusing the adversary, and probably a few others.

It is easy to notice that some elements of the theory of struggle are similar, in a way, to the art of debate, or eristics, characterized by Arthur Schopenhauer in his book *Die eristische Dialektik* (1830). Kotarbinski acknowledged this when referring (in the preface to a Polish translation of Schopenhauer's book) to the article by Norman A. Bailey of Queens College, New York, *Towards a Praxeological Theory of Conflict* (1968). Kotarbinski wrote, however, that "eristic dialectics" is only a part of the art of debate, namely the part that is devoted to dishonest contestation rather than fighting for the truth. One may say that such a disclosure of unfair conduct is a kind of intellectual whistle-blowing, for Schopenhauer showed not only wrongdoing in processes of argumentation, but also how to defend oneself against such conduct, therefore how to fight against logical tricks and sophisms.

The general theory of struggle shows more general techniques that may be used in defense of other than logical tricks only. Thus it is time to consider the ethical dimension of struggle.

3. Ethical Consideration of a Struggle

Ethical scruples are closely related not only to struggle itself but also in many cases to the notion of struggle, something one notices in the usage of many euphemistic terms to hide the essence, praxiological essence, of this kind of human action. By the way, "whistleblowing" is a good example of eliminating the negative connotation related to the word "denunciation" and the like (differently in different languages); despite this, it is still controversial for many.

Tadeusz Kotarbinski was not only a praxiologist but also an ethicist. Therefore it was obvious that he would raise a question related to the ethical dimension of struggle. The question reads: "Is it justified [...] to teach those, sometimes suspect, quibbles and tricks we spoke about in the above considerations? After all we have relentlessly discussed means useful to the aims, like 'the end justifies the means'. This is pure Machiavellism, is it not!? [...] A procedure ideal as a technique of action might be at the same time dishonorable from an ethical point of view. And the lesson of such conduct is taught here" (Kotarbinski 1999b, 197). Isn't this an argument against the general theory of struggle?

The cited author offers counterarguments to set our minds at rest. He assures us that nobody is encouraged to act in this way. Discovering the techniques that are used in the form of a norm was done for stylistic reasons. "*Homo sum, human nil a me alienum puto,*" said Terentius. If this is so, it is understandable that all aspects of human action should be clarified with scholarly precision.

Knowing *that* as related to human action does not ultimately mean it is suggested as knowing how. In one case it is useful to know how to defend oneself from the wrongdoing of others, in another—to prevent potential misbehavior. In both cases the crucial thing is good will. "The world of tricks as a subject of cognitive reflection is as interesting as the world of animal behavior, like the construction of nests by birds, or more generally the world of technical beauty studied cognitively and aesthetically similarly to studying with relish the construction of the animal body, of an innocent butterfly or a predacious weasel," writes Kotarbinski (ibidem).

It would be good to know all the techniques of misbehavior, and probably there are specialists who are busy with this, to gather knowledge on the "masterpieces." Knowledge is one thing; good or bad application of that knowledge is another. A knife may serve as a tool for cutting bread, as a surgeon's lancet for saving somebody's life, or as a murder weapon in a killer's hand. It is not the knife, however, that should be blamed for wrongdoing, for the knife is a tool. It is not the struggle techniques that should be blamed for fights, for they are descriptions of the tool-character, but the actors who use them with wrong intentions.

> it is necessary to know discreditable catches to be able to give them up deliberately. Energy calls for selecting the most plausible means to the accepted aims, honor forces us to withdraw from aims achievable only through ignoble means. But the truth is that ethical admissibility or inadmissibility of particular means depends on what the struggle is for, and what is the real threat during the struggle. (Kotarbinski 1999b, 198)

Concluding his ethical considerations related to the struggle theory and its application in practice, Kotarbinski quoted the comment of Marcus Aurelius that "the art of life is more like the art of struggle than the art of dance"[3] (*Meditations,* book VII: 102; quoted after Kotarbinski 1999b, 198).

4. What Can Whistleblowing Learn from Praxiology?

First and foremost, whistleblowing can learn from praxiology that it constitutes cooperation, negative cooperation by its nature. A person who notices wrongdoing in an organization is acting against that misbehavior but not against the organization itself, unless the organization as a whole is set up for unjust purposes and the whistle-blowing insider does not want to be considered one of the wrongdoers. In such a case the whistle-blower is acting in the interest of the organization and/or of a broader social and/or natural environment, i.e., the external stakeholders of that organization. If whistleblowing is, in praxiological terms, a kind of negative cooperation, it is a struggle against the wrongdoing identified by the whistleblower with the intention of eliminating the disclosed misbehavior. It is, therefore, a defense rather than an attack, defense against the bad practices of corrupted actors whose misbehavior should be considered, from the struggle theory point of view, as an attack on the proper function of a given organization.

Next, being familiar with the struggle techniques and their rationale, a whistleblower can more easily identify elements of the techniques used by wrongdoers and point them out as the grounds for his or her critique. Whistleblowers may also engage appropriate struggle techniques to protect themselves from a counterattack by the corrupted actors.

Finally, although whistleblowing is a defensive measure, it is perceived by many, mostly by those that the whistleblowers criticize, as an attack through the disclosure of secret information about the criticized conduct in the organization. Such a situation forces whistle-blowers to follow the advice that the theory of struggle calls potentialization or—to quote the Roman proverb—*si vis pacem para bellum,* not to end up fighting against the organization's wrongdoing but to prevent a counterattack, by demonstrating that the position of the whistle-blower is not weak and vulnerable as a defender of demanded change from wrong to right conduct in and/or by the organization.

5. Conclusion

Philosophy does not provide immediately useful outcomes, what is useful is to study pieces of philosophical inquiry, said Kotarbinski. Doing so allows one to broaden the scope of one's understanding of the area of interest. Studying the praxiological theory of struggle, one is able to acquire the relevant conceptual apparatus to analyze human action in the kind of manifestation that is characteristic of negative cooperation. Thus, one may ask if the quotation from Herbert Spencer's treatise (viz. my article [Gasparski 1994]) is still valid: "Mankind has eventually gone right after trying all possible ways of going wrong; the wrong-doings being habitually checked by disaster and pain, and death" (1880).

I am afraid that the truth is contained more in the following quotation from a book by Charles Arthur Mercier, one of the first British praxiologists: "The significance of pain is that it is the equivalent in consciousness of some action which is tending to destroy the organism, and it is difficult to evade the impression that its origin and persistence are due to its giving a readier and more effectual warning to the whole organism of destructive agents affecting any part than material process could. Until it had attained intelligence enough to foresee the effects of acts no organism would make any effort to avoid disintegration, if disintegration were unattended with pain" (Mercier 1888). Whistleblowing is painful for organizations, companies, corporations and other institutions probably for the same reason. Many, too many, are wise after the event despite the warning offered by this quotation from over a century ago.

Let us conclude these reflections with yet another quotation, this time from the twentieth century's *fin de siècle*: "Whistle blowing should [...] alert corporations to what can and should be done if they wish to be both moral and excellent. When corporate structures preclude the need for whistle blowing, they protect both workers' rights and the public's good" (De George 1995, 241). This would be real potentialization.

Notes

1. I introduce a new term, "ortho-praxical," instead of "ortho-practical," to avoid misunderstanding. The former refers to "ortho-praxy" while the latter is commonly understood as non-theoretical.
2. The overview gives an account of the issues presented in Kotarbinski's essay (1999a).
3. The quotation may also be read: as: "The art of living resembles wrestling more than dancing" (Marcus Aurelius, 1992, Meditations, transl. A. S. L. Farquharson, Knopf, New York).

References

Bailey, N. A., 1968, Toward a Praxeological Theory of Conflict, *Orbis,* XI no. 4 (Winter), pp. 1081-1112.

De George, R. T., 1995, *Business Ethics,* 4th Edition, Prentice Hall, Englewood Cliffs, NJ.

Gasparski, W. W., 1993, *A Philosophy of Practicality: A Treatise on the Philosophy of Tadeusz Kotarbinski,* Societas Philosophica Fennica, Helsinki.

Gasparski, W. W., 1994, Some Whys and Wherefores in the Failure of Social System Design, *Systems Practice,* Vol. 7, No. 6, pp. 687-697.

Gasparski, W. W., 2002, Effectiveness, Efficiency, and Ethicality in Business and Management, in: Zsolnai, L. & Gasparski, W.W., eds., *Ethics and the Future of Capitalism,* Transaction Publishers, New Brubswick (USA)—London (UK), pp. 117-136.

Harrison, M. R., 2005, *An Introduction to Business and Management Ethics,* Palgrave MacMillan, Houndmills.

Kotarbinski, T., 1999a, Basic Concepts of the General Theory of Struggle (originally published as "Les idees fondamentales de la theorie generale de la lutte," *Philosophia,* Beograd, 1936, Vol. 1:1/4, pp. 196-214) in: . T. Kotarbinski's *Collected Works: Praxiology* Part One (in Polish), Ossolineum Publishers, Wroclaw, pp. 153-166.

Kotarbinski, T., 1999b, From the Issues of the General Theory of Struggle, in: T. Kotarbinski's *Collected Works: Praxiology* Part One (in Polish), Ossolineum Publishers, Wroclaw, pp. 166-198.

Kotarbinski, T., 1999c, Multiplicity of sources for the good work appeal (originally published in 1969), in: T. Kotarbinski's *Collected Works: Praxiology* Part One (in Polish), Ossolineum Publishers, Wroclaw, pp. 434-436.

Kotarbinski, T, 1999d, The sources of general problems connected with an issue of action efficacy (originally published in 1971), in: T. Kotarbinski's *Collected Works: Praxiology* Part One (in Polish), Ossolineum Publishers, Wroclaw, pp. 437-447.

Kotarbinski, T., 2002, The ABC of Practicality, in: L. V. Ryan, F. B. Nahser, W.W. Gasparski, eds., *Praxiology and Pragmatism,* Transaction Publishers, New Brunswick (USA)—London (UK), pp. 25-60.

Mercier, Ch. A., 1888, *The Nervous System and the Mind: A Treatise on the Dynamics of the Human Organism,* MacMillan, London.

Mises von, L., 1998, *Human Action: A Treatise on Economics,* The Scholars Edition, Ludvig von Mises Institute, Auburn, Alabama.

Sen, A., 2009, Off with egoism!, interview by J. P. Velazquez-Gaztelu, *El Paiz* SL (8 February 2009), ref. after a Polish translation *Forum,* No 12 (23-28 March 2008), p. 25.

Spencer, H., 1880, The Study of Sociology, London (quoted after: Wiltshire, D., 1978, *The Social and Political Thought of Herbert Spencer,* Oxford University Press, Oxford).

Rewarding the Whistleblower—Disgrace, Recognition, or Efficiency?

Wim Vandekerckhove
Assistant Professor of Ethics Center for Ethics and Value Inquiry
Ghent University, Belgium

1. Introduction

Nearly all whistleblowing legislation and internal policies include a proper motive as a necessary condition for legitimate whistleblowing. One reason for this might be that this is an attempt to dispose the common objection raised against whistleblowing protection schemes that such schemes will be abused by disgruntled employees who are out for personal gain. Introducing a moral motive as a condition for protection disposes that objection. Business ethicists offer another rationale for including the moral motive. The general idea is of course that altruistic whistleblowing deserves protection—the whistleblower is the moral hero who saves society—while self-centered motivated disclosures do not. De Maria (1994) explicitly states that whistleblowing must have a moral motive; Bowie and Duska (1990), Chambers (1995) and Grant (2002) implicitly suggest it.

However, with the increasing acceptance of whistleblowing mechanisms as a way to detect and deter fraud and corruption, the idea of rewarding whistleblowers is also gaining some currency. Some examples include the False Claims Act in the U.S., which offers a financial reward to whistleblowers disclosing information about companies that fraud the government. During an OECD work group meeting on whistleblowing in 1999, labor representatives argued against including the motive or honesty of the whistleblower as a critical factor in a whistleblowing regime if the "purpose of a whistleblowing framework is to deter corruption rather than to encourage external disclosures" (OECD 2000: 9).

During a parliamentary discussion in the Netherlands, the Socialist Party tabled a list of suggestions for a better and more effective fight against fraud. One of these suggestions was to offer whistleblowers a substantial reward. Green Left called for a whistleblower fund from which whistleblowers could be paid a financial reward if they came up with hard evidence on big fraud cases (Tweede Kamer 2004: 3660-3710 and the notes on pages 3735-3737).

In 2007 the U.K. Home Office started a debate on whether citizens and employees who blow the whistle should be rewarded with a percentage of the penalties or damages paid by the wrongdoer. The debate had been initiated in the context of a Home Office review of how the Assets Recovery Agency could meet its targets of recovering £250 million a year.

Miceli and Near (1992) and Dworkin and Near (1997) describe this as a shift from an "old model" to a "new model." The "old model" valued motivation over information and viewed whistleblowing as an act of conscience and responsibility. The "new model" however values information over motivation. This new model draws it legitimacy on the consequentialist argument of efficiency. It is to the extent that whistleblowing policies are effective and efficient in generating accurate and reliable information that they are valuable. Hence, it is not the act of making a disclosure that has to be evaluated but rather the content and the potential usage of the generated information.

In short, while emphasizing and documenting the whistleblower as a moral hero might have been necessary to get the idea of whistleblower protection acceptable to policy makers, a managerial approach to the issue—including public sector management—has second thoughts about the efficiency of heroism (Vandekerckhove 2006).

This chapter examines the kind of whistleblowing that is advocated by offering rewards to whistleblowers. The first section points at the link between our focus on efficiency and our growing unease with fraud. The second section discusses whistleblowing as a source of information in that context. The third section comments on the U.S. False Claims Act. The fourth section points out some pitfalls of rewarding whistleblowers. I conclude in a balanced way, recognizing both the bright and the dark side of rewarding whistleblowers but generally warning it is not the panacea.

2. Efficiency and Fraud

Efficiency—not wasting resources in reaching organizational goals—is very central to economic reasoning and refers to organizational processes. What's more, not being efficient has a moral connotation of waste.

William Greider sees efficiency as a capitalistic virtue:

> The great virtue of capitalism—the quality that always confounded socialist critics and defeated rival economic systems—is its ability to yield more from less. Its efficient organization of production strives to produce more goods from less input, whether the input is capital, labour or raw resources (Greider 1997: 45).

One way to conceive of "organizational inefficiency" relates to the human factor necessary to enact any organizational process. A possible barrier to process innovation is regulation constricting flexibility in terms of fast changes—hiring/firing people, relocating production, and all sorts of government licensing needed in order to operate. Another source of organizational inefficiency puts private business and public sector organizations at the same side. It occurs when organizational processes and procedures show loopholes causing conflicts of interest or allowing opportunistic behavior. In other words, organizational processes might look great on paper, but they might very well not be carried out the way they are planned or intended, causing organizational inefficiencies. Two such organizational inefficiencies have gotten very high on the agenda of both governments and businesses: fraud and corruption. Fraud is the deliberate misrepresentation in order to obtain an unauthorized benefit, and as such can be considered as an inefficiency in information providing. Corruption on the other hand is an inefficiency in allocation—of goods, of services, of contracts, etc.—in the form of rent-seeking, bribery, cartels.

To define corruption as inefficiency in allocation, covers both petty corruption and grand corruption. Petty corruption is any kind of administrative corruption, for instance in the case where offering a small bribe speeds up—"greases"—bureaucratic processes. The inefficiency lies in the undue course of the process, for example going against queuing principles. Grand corruption is irregular influence in judiciary or in lawmaking, for example when a powerful lobby influences court cases or parliamentary voting on law proposals. The inefficiency there lies in the thwarting of political institutions such as democratic representation or impartial judiciary.

In one way, state monopolies are being reproached with being corrupt and serving personal interests of power hungry politicians. But in another way, it is exactly in the privatization process that corruption and fraud occurs.

Within private business too, the fear for fraud increases (see for example the annual KPMG or Ernst & Young fraud surveys). It seems that decentralization is necessary to ensure efficiency, but at the same time it increases the risk of inefficiency. Decentralized decision-making and more discretionary power to people lower in the hierarchy increases opportunities for fraud and corruption, because more people are able to cause such inefficiencies and at the same time those able to do it are less likely to get caught. Hence, decentralization calls for new ways of control. It is precisely here that whistleblowing policies as a source of information come in.

3. Whistleblowing as a Source of Information

Three factors seem important for the occurrence of fraudulent acts within organizations: (1) organizational conditions allowing fraudulent acts (both having the power to do it and weak internal control environment); (2) motivations for committing the fraud (poor liquidity position); (3) ethical attitudes indicating a possible willingness to commit an act of fraud (Loebbecke and Willingham 1988, cited in Hooks et al. 1994). Hooks et al. (1994) argue that the move towards total quality management (TQM) implies an emphasis on process controls. Therefore, auditors too might be placing more weight on the control of environment. As TQM approaches also imply empowerment and decentralization, and come in a time of computerization, Hooks et al. see difficulties for maintaining uniform accounting systems and internal control procedures. Instead, they bring forward the idea of an internal control environment, serving as the linkage between subunits, and being "in part, an operationalization of organizational culture" (Hooks et al. 1994: 88). As enhancing communication within the organization about fraudulent acts or risks is regarded as improving the internal control environment, Hooks et al. bring whistleblowing forward as a form of such an enhanced—and "upstream"—communication.

Basically, organizing is becoming too complex to keep everything under supervisory control. Moreover, if organizations are getting flatter, this simply means that superiors have more subordinates under them doing different things, being flexible, and having more job control. At a certain point in that shift, the problem of how a manager is supposed to know what is going on at the work floor, needs to be answered differently.

Whistleblowing policies can be a way to get information about what is going wrong on the work floor, can be, indeed, on the condition that they work well. Methods used to collect information about inefficiencies are only legitimate to the extent that these methods themselves show to be effective. More precisely, whistleblowing as a source of information is only justified to the extent that it generates accurate and reliable information.

Building on Hook et al. (1994), Ponemon (1994) regards three organizational factors as important for constructing an effective "upstream" communication. The first is an identified internal channel to do so. The second factor pertains to how well retaliations can be avoided and to the reward structure—financial, honor, promotion—created by the organization for truthful disclosures. The third, and according to Ponemon most important factor however is the "moral atmosphere" of the organization. The moral atmosphere of an organization is defined as that part of the organization culture that deals with ethical problems and the resolution of moral conflict. A positive moral atmosphere will have people feel free to express and discuss diversity in moral point of views. I think this is Ponemon's most puzzling factor. He writes about the "moral atmosphere" of an organization as both result of and condition for accurate and reliable disclosures: upstream communication can foster the moral atmosphere of the organization (Ponemon 1994: 118), a negative moral atmosphere will censor or block disclosures (Ponemon 1994: 124). Hence, a negative moral atmosphere tends to make whistleblowing inefficient, but at the same time, it is organizations with a negative moral atmosphere that are most in need of whistleblowing, since it is there that fraud is most likely to occur. Ponemon is aware of this paradox, but gives no answer to it (Ponemon 1994: 125, 128). Perhaps the popularity of the "proper motive" element in whistleblower protection schemes is intended as a rhetorical support for a positive moral atmosphere Ponemon aims at. But the success of the U.S. False Claims Act, to which I turn next, raises doubt about just how far we can get by worrying about the proper moral atmosphere.

4. False Claims Act

At the outset of this chapter, I noted that some important scholars on whistleblowing have noted a shift from the "old model" valuing motivation over information to the "new model" which values information over motivation. The two previous sections serve as an explanation of why this shift is occurring. Dworkin and Near (1997) see the revision in 1986 of the U.S. False Claims Act—offering financial rewards for information—as initiating that "new model."

The False Claims Act (FCA) dates from 1863 and is often referred to as the "Lincoln Law," which was originally enacted to protect the Union

Arms against fraudulent suppliers during the American Civil War, who sold sawdust for gun powder. It is based on the principle of *qui tam pro domino rege sequitur quam pro se ipso*, or *He who sues on behalf of the King also sues as well as for himself* (Bowers et al. 1999: 251). The Act establishes that anyone who sues in the name of the U.S. government in relation to fraud also sues for themselves. Basically, the idea is that the person or organization filing the law suit gets a percentage of the money the government is able to recover.

Anyone can file a *qui tam* suit, including employees of the company or agency that is defrauding the government, former employees of the company or agency, competitors, subcontractors, state and local government, federal employees, public interest groups, corporations and private citizens.

Originally, the law was hardly used by individuals because they had to bear the cost of the suit themselves. In 1943, Congress amended the law unfavorably, reducing the reward to the whistleblower who brought the suit, and providing that a person could not file a qui tam lawsuit if the government had prior knowledge of the charges. In 1986 however, Congress once again revised the FCA. The amount awarded if the information is useful and leads to a recovery of fraudulent money, was raised. The whistleblower must now bring suit under FCA and go through trial. The government then decides whether or not it joins the suit. If it does and it is able to recover money through the lawsuit, the whistleblower may receive 15-25 percent of the amount recovered. If the government decides not join, this may increase to 25-30 percent. Also, the 1986 revision allowed a qui tam case to be filed even if the government already knew about the charges.

The FCA has gained a reputation of being a very successful tool in recovering fraud. Callahan and Dworkin (2000) write that FCA reports of fraud against the government have increased from an average of 6 per year before 1986 to 450 per year in 1998. Salcido (2000) writes that the government's recoveries under the FCA have skyrocketed since its revision in 1986, totaling more than $4 billion through more than 3,000 *qui tam* cases, with the majority of those being filed against those who do business in the healthcare industry. Carson et al. (2008) calculated that for the period 1997-2001, the costs of FCA for the U.S. government were roughly $1.88 billion and the benefits (recovered fraud money) were between $26.8 billion and $97.7 billion.

The provisions of the FCA are designed to meet the motivational criteria of a reward system, namely that the reward is sufficiently large to justify the effort, that payout is sufficiently certain to justify the effort, and that the payout is timely in relation to doing the desired activity. The whole idea is getting the information. Underlying is of course the inability to control, or as Dworkin and Near describe it: "It encourages citizen enforcement of the laws when the government lacks the resources, information or ability to do it" (Dworkin and Near 1997: 10).

But that is a pragmatic argument. How can we ethically defend a whistleblowing regime that invites courageous and citizen-like behavior by appealing to personal gain; immoral in most people's perception, a-moral at best? Carson et al. (2008) offer ethical arguments to defend the FCA legislation. To objection that this law is morally corrupting by introducing selfish motives for whistleblowing, they reply that having the right kind of moral motivation is not a necessary condition of morally justified whistleblowing. The example given is an employer involved in illegal and life-threatening activities and a whistleblower motivated by malice toward that employer. The malicious whistleblower will still save many lives. Further, although external incentives can alter a person's character, they can only do so when they are applied consistently and continuously. However, Carson et al. (2008) submit, it is unlikely that one person will blow the whistle more than one time in their careers. This consequentialist reasoning is new to the ethical debates on whistleblowing and I expect it to spur further debate among business ethicists.

5. Pitfalls of Rewarding Whistleblowers

While it is easy to imagine that the altruistic motive of the whistleblower as a condition for protection can result in missing important information to save lives or correct other wrongdoing—like Carson et al. (2008) point out—offering financial rewards to whistleblowers also has double-effects. I mention three possible pitfalls of rewarding schemes.

First, in his discussion of the position U.S. government took in some qui tam actions, Salcido (2000) points out that some of these actions are targeted against a whole industry or several companies within an industry. The reason for this is that, when filing a qui tam suit, there is a financial interest to state allegations as broadly as possible and to name as many corporate defendants as possible because to do so increases the potential reward paid to the whistleblower. This is hardly the kind of "insider whistleblower" lawsuit that U.S. Congress intended to foster. In the paradigm case, the whistleblower transfers inside information to the U.S. government in exchange for a reward. This arrangement has even been conceptualized by courts as the government purchasing information it might not otherwise acquire. In industry wide, multi-defendant qui tam actions, the person bringing suit is not an employee of "the" particular defendant—hence is not a whistleblower in a strict sense. It is also typical for this kind of relators that they do not have real inside information. Therefore, Salcido (2000) argues, these actions turn the chief purpose underlying qui tam actions on its head. The qui tam provisions are supposed to operate as a mechanism under which insiders supply needed information to the U.S. government and in exchange receive a substantial reward. In industry-wide, multi-defendant qui tam actions however, the U.S. receives no useful evidence or information and still must pay a reward.

A second pitfall pertains to the moral atmosphere within organizations. Although we can question the effectiveness of emphasizing the moral motive for whistleblowing in fostering a moral atmosphere (cf. my take off Ponemon in the previous section), what is sure is that rewarding disclosures about fraud or other wrongdoing do not entail any message to employees that a moral atmosphere is wanted. At the best, rewarding schemes will not down spiral the organizational atmosphere. More likely is that, because the whistleblower is turned into a private investigator, rewarding schemes will incline the atmosphere towards a "panopticon" culture, where everyone is rewarded for registering everyone else's mistakes (Vandekerckhove 2006).

A third pitfall of rewarding schemes has to do with the characteristics of disclosures one can expect to be made. Salcido (2000) points out that FCA claims have been dismissed where relators did not provide written disclosure statements. The argument was that the disclosure requirement has the primary purpose of providing the U.S. government with enough information on the alleged fraud so that the government is able to make a well reasoned decision on whether it should participate in the filed lawsuit or allow the relator to proceed alone. Hence, the FCA does not give rewards for bare allegations contained in a complaint if these are not supported by evidence, and this evidence must be more substantive than the notion that "something fishy" is going on. Whistleblowing schemes working with the "proper motive" requirement however, are able to protect someone who raises concerns without having the smoking-gun evidence. It seems then, that the rewarding scheme might generate a higher percentage of usable information, simply because it only rewards such information—it only rewards evidence and not concerns it has to spend more time investigating. Moreover, neglecting the importance of soliciting concerns rather than allegations-with-evidence annuls the possibility of closing loopholes that might lead to future wrongdoing.

6. Conclusion

Raising concern is showing citizenship, whether that is within an organization or outside of it—and arguably even more so when one raises the concern first internally before going outside. But rewarding citizenship behavior is different from purchasing information. Whistleblowing rewarding schemes such as the FCA tend towards the latter, not the former. Hence, it is deceiving to phrase purchasing information into a rhetoric of citizenship behavior. There might very well be a good case for purchasing information on fraud—and the FCA shows that case -but these schemes come closer to *pentiti*-schemes offering repenting perpetrators or cartel members privileges and reduced sentences, then to whistleblower protection schemes aimed at breaking moral muteness in organizations (Bird 2002).

But regardless of how one wants to rhetorically position whistleblower schemes, we only have experience in rewarding whistleblowers in the context of government fraud. Most whistleblower protection legislation and schemes however cover more wrongdoing than just fraud. To suggest that a mechanism developed and positively evaluated in the context of combating fraud should be or could be broadened to other contexts of wrongdoing, shows how primordial fraud has become in our sense-making of organizational wrongdoing. Indeed, the idea that whistleblowers deserve protection has gained currency precisely because of the increased significance we have given combating fraud (Vandekerckhove 2006). But whistleblowing advocacy has also been about:

- not just fraud, but all kinds of wrongdoing within organizations,
- not just wrongdoing that has happened or is happening, but also that which is likely to happen,
- whoever is injured or threatened, not just the government.

Nevertheless, the debate about whistleblower rewarding schemes is welcome because it urges us to critically reexamine the heroic connotations we attach to whistleblowers, something that is most of the time not asked for by those who become whistleblowers. It also points out that the weakness of non-rewarding whistleblower schemes is the "proper motive" condition that applies in most of those schemes. But it is also clear that rewarding schemes are not the solution for the problems of non-rewarding schemes. Moreover, they contain pitfalls of themselves, as I have tried to show.

The crux of the matter is however, that whereas previous debates about whistleblower protection might have overplayed the morality of the whistleblower, the current debate on rewarding schemes takes morality completely out of the issue. We thereby forget that organizations themselves are an important player in any consideration of the whistleblowing issue. The rise of organizational whistleblowing procedures—urging so-called internal whistleblowing—as a compromise between moral muteness and moral heroism, or as a solution to the dilemma of being loyal to one's organization or to one's community, currently offers us a possibility to move beyond the question whether or not the morality of the whistleblower should be of concern to us. Inquiries into the morality or ethicality of human resource policies make up a huge field of research. As the implementation of internal whistleblowing procedures is beginning to surge outside of the U.S. as well, there is much more to be learned on efficiency and effectiveness of different modalities of whistleblowing schemes than whether or not we need to require moral heroism from our whistleblowers. One important question in the light of this is whether or not those who receive internal disclosures or concerns must manifest morality and if so, how to ensure that.

References

Bird, F., 2002, *The Muted Conscience: Moral Silence and the Practice of Ethics in Business,* Westport: Quorum. Bowers, J., Mitchell, J. and Lewis, J., 1999, *Whistleblowing: The new law,* London: Sweet & Maxwell.

Bowie, N. E. and Duska, R., 1990, *Business Ethics,* Englewood Cliffs: Prentice Hall. Callahan, E. S. and Dworkin, T. M., 2000, "The state of state whistleblower protection," *American Business Law Journal* 38:1, 99-175. Carson, T. L., Verdu, M. E. and Wokutch, R. E, 2008, "Whistle-Blowing for Profit: An Ethical Analysis of the Federal False Claims Act," *Journal of Business Ethics* 77: 361-376.

Chambers, A., 1995, "Whistleblowing and the Internal Auditor," *Business Ethics: A European Review* 4: 192-198.

De Maria, W., 1994, *Unshielding the Shadow Culture,* Queensland: University of Queensland.

Dworkin, T. M. and Near, J. P., 1997, "A better statutory approach to whistle-blowing," *Business Ethics Quarterly* 7:1, 1-16. Grant, C., 2002, "Whistle Blowers: Saints of Secular Culture," *Journal of Business Ethics* 39: 391-399.

Greider, W., 1997, *One World, Ready or Not. The Manic Logic of Global Capitalism,* London: Penguin Books. Hooks, K. L., Kaplan, S. E. and Schultz, J. J., 1994, "Enhancing Communication to Assist in Fraud Prevention and Detection," *Auditing* 13(2), 86-117. Loebbecke, J. K. and Willingham, J. J., 1988, "Review of SEC Accounting and Auditing

Enforcement Released," working paper (cited in Hooks et al. 1994). Miceli, M. P. and Near, J. P., 1992, *Blowing the Whistle: The Organizational and Legal Implications for Companies and Employees,* (New York: Lexington Books). OECD 2000, *Whistleblwing to combat corruption—Report on a meeting of management and trade union experts held under the OECD Labour/Management Programme,* PAC/AFF/LMP(2000)1, Paris: OECD.

Ponemon, L. A., 1994, "Whistle-blowing as An Internal Control Mechanism. Individual and Organizational Considerations," *Auditing* 13(2), 118-30.

Salcido, R., 2000, "The government declares war on Qui Tam plaintiffs who lack inside information: The government's new policy to dismiss these parties in False Claims Act litigation," <http://www.akingump.com/publication.cfm?publication_id=444> (cited July 2004).

Tweede, K., 2004, *Handelingen Tweede Kamer 2003-2004,* nr 56, Available at http://www.overheid.nl/op.

Vandekerckhove, W., 2006, *Whistleblowing and Organizational Social Responsibility,* Aldershot/Burlington: Ashgate.

My Arguments Against Whistleblowling

Marek Arszułowicz
Business Ethics Center Kozminski University
Warsaw, Poland

1. Introduction

Whistleblowing has received its world forum attention only recently, after it had been nicely packaged by American business and media people into "Business Ethics Toolbox," ready for export but unfortunately in a raw form, not ready to use. There were also *Insider*, the movie that covered the story of Jeff Wigand, *Time* magazine, which pronounced three women whistleblowers as persons of the year, American government policy with its Whistleblowers Protection Act, non-government organizations that have spread the idea worldwide; all these contributed significantly to exporting the idea of blowing the whistle when a fault is spotted. The idea of revealing the truth is as old as truth itself, but presently the world's economy is so tightly bound that hiding certain truths can cause problems for many. It can cause too many problems for too many people. Inventive skills of humankind aimed at survival have always forced people to elaborate new ways of coping with obstacles. One of those inventions is whistleblowing—a simple idea of safe depositing valuable information, collecting knowledge that can literally save lives and money.

However, "one man's meat is another man's poison." Although the system is simple, its perception in different cultures does not have to be necessarily the same. As it always happens with big theories, all that counts is a different perspective of seeing the same thing. Cultural difference is too large a subject to be squeezed into several sentences but the differences in world's perception shape minds of people. Those differences can cause misunderstanding and confusion when judging one's behavior.

The following article discusses arguments against whistleblowing. Its aim is to present what aspects of blowing the whistle can make it unacceptable for certain cultures, what hinders the process of introducing it successfully into business life, what moral dilemmas accompany the decision of blowing the whistle, what requirements shall be fulfilled to expect proper reception from employees and managers. The ideas presented are of a purely theoretical nature, with its flavor of philosophy setting open questions with various answers possible. However, the challenge should be for the benefit of whistleblowing. If it can stand the criticism and provide yet a better solution for revealing the truth the strength of the system will be undoubted. The idea of blowing the whistle is surely for a pure mind one of excellent purpose. However, men experienced with life, aware of the power of money and jealousy of their neighbors, those who witnessed hatred and isolation, those who suffered, to a small or big extend, the pain of retaliation might have cautious approach hindered by reliving bad memories triggered at the moment of making important decision. And that is the greatest weakness of the great idea: fear.

2. Definition of Whistleblowing—Does It Really Exist?

It might be surprising but there is not one definition of whistleblowing but many. All due to the fact that the term "whistleblowing" has not been defined internationally according to these same standards. The following questions are of great value in defining what deeds might or might not be qualified as to be blown whistle about. The very first concern in defining whistleblowing is the seriousness of misbehaviors, misconducts, malpractices, wrongdoings. At what point do they qualify to be treated seriously in terms of blowing the whistle? If there was an imaginary scale of "crimes," purely theoretical for the purpose of our debate, and on one end of the scale would be a minor crime of, e.g., stealing company's printing paper and at the other end of the scale would be a very serious crime of jeopardizing customers' lives, all that is in between remains vague. If there would be a point on the scale which would qualify "medium size" crimes as serious or not, who is responsible for placing that point on the scale? It would of course vary accordingly to what businesses companies perform. Therefore, there would have to be a special list of "crimes" for each and every business. Those businesses that deal with financial operations only would set money frauds as the most dangerous. Those which deal with building and constructions would set safety measurements first. Food producers would care about life and health of their customers. The lists would be endless. The problem is that there cannot be a definition with endless lists. Therefore, if the definition must be redefined accordingly, we naturally come back to the very first question: who is going to grade the "seriousness" of crimes.

Another weak point in defining whistleblowing is its ultimate output. When successfully introduced into company's life, do we expect whistleblowing to be public or confidential? Do we really want all company's serious crimes made public hence lowering its market credibility or confidential and solved within company's capability? The former is damaging for innocent company's employees the latter is very often impossible since it might concern top managers who would prevent all actions. And here naturally comes the question of: what is whistleblower's real contribution? What is his/her real job? Depositing information or taking active part in counteracting company's negative actions?

Faced with giant problems, whistleblowers are scared enough when they realize the consequences of witnessed wrongdoing. Would it not be enough to expect that they deposit their knowledge safely? Or must it always end up in a court? In other words what are the expectations concerning whistleblower's involvement in a crime they only witnessed? Do they really have to put at risk their job career, family life, personal feelings in order to prove their point? Or can it be done in a more secure way leaving the battle to "proper" people and institutions?

To what extent whistleblowers agree to be involved in just case, depends vastly on their cultural background. Seeing culture as a kind of software implemented on a hard disc of a brain, it is natural to expect different perception of the importance of revealing the truth according to country, religion, education. As a matter of fact whistleblowing is nothing more or less than revealing the truth. Meditation of truth entails the meditation of lies, and these two direct thoughts towards notion of good and evil. Once we try to find out why people would reveal the truth, hence doing something good and noble, we must also find the answer to the question why people do bad things in the first place. The concepts of good and evil, truth and lie vary in different cultures. It is a concept of powers that drive our lives, the role of a single person in a society. Either the single person is capable of changing the world or the world cannot be changed at all, therefore it must be left to its own course of action with the conclusion "nothing can be done."

And finally, here comes the very core of whistleblowing. Do we expect whistleblowing to be a duty or a natural free will impulse of a good citizen reacting to misbehavior? Pushed into the area of law environment whistleblowing loses its freshness and potential. Regular whistleblowing ends up in auditing which is a form of controlling. However, the real danger very often lies behind audited documents with the purpose of not being revealed. It is very often the knowledge outside documents that is crucial. To reveal it, there must be no obligation. The idea of whistleblowing is that of being a preventing power. If we want to prevent a catastrophe we naturally aim at not allowing something to happen. Law deals with crimes, that is, with something that *did* happen. How then can we expect of something that *will not* happen to be within the realms of law? If then lawful institutions cannot take any action until the crime is committed, who is trustworthy enough to take the deposit of truths whistleblowers witnessed?

Maybe whistleblowing belongs to the group of undefined expressions, those which when thought only are clear but when attempt is made to define them the true meaning is lost.

3. Personnel

People are the most important asset of each and every company. The same rule, of successful business world, must be also applied when projecting successful whistleblowing. The attention must be drawn to the personnel responsible for and involved in depositing the truth, setting processes into motion, protecting source of information, disseminating the idea, as well as to lawmakers, managers, fellow employees. What is the role of each group mentioned, who is responsible for which part of the process? The complex project requires good preparation.

Whistleblowing entails voluntary or compulsory engagement of many people: managers, owners, family, courts, media, proper institutions, lawyers, sometimes police. The question is: who is the leading power of whistleblowing or rather who should play the role of a leader? In whose interest would it be to implement procedures of early misconduct signaling? For the purpose of this paper whistleblowing shall be divided into three stages. The first is pre-whistleblowing, the second whistleblowing in action, the third post-whistleblowing. Pre whistleblowing period is time, when all company's duties are performed excellent but the policy of company's whistleblowing procedure is being presented and implemented. All for the sake of emergency situations to make employees aware of the steps they should take in revealing the truth. Who, at this stage, is most interested in implementing that procedure? The obvious answer is the owner of the business since a company's loss is the owner's loss. What about those cases when an owner is involved in any kind of unethical behavior? What about companies with no direct owner? Who should speak in the name of stockholders, customers, employees who might indirectly suffer the consequences? Who then shall promote the idea, provide help and security, counsel actions?

Whistleblowing in action is the stage when the truth has been disclosed, voiced, deposited. The whole process is in motion. Legal advice is what people expect most at the point of taking important decision. The U.S. legal system has evolved qui tam cases lawyer who specialize in whistle-blowing trials. Can citizens in different countries enjoy such luxury? If not, the problem of legal advice and support is open. The help might be expected from non government organizations whose mission is spreading the idea of ethical workplace, fair business, fighting with injustice. But they do not represent lawyers whose occupation is defending people. They can advice but not act.

Post whistleblowing stage is the period when the case is closed regardless of its output. Whistleblowers either return to their previous work place or change their jobs in response to fear of retaliation. Is anyone strong enough to guarantee whistleblowers that their lives will be safe and their deeds accepted by their fellow workers after revealing the truth of company's misconduct? I doubt. Very often it is a one way road with no return possible. Life will never be the same. Unless whistleblowing is seen as a heroic act, there will be no acceptance or praising. And that might be the saddest part of heroes.

External whistleblowing initially meant informing media. So maybe, that power is strong enough to cover safety shield around the brave when no one else is able to help? Could be, but is not. Media could use their privilege of not revealing the source of information, they can hire lawyers, they even can present a whistleblower as a hero. There is, however, one weak point in engaging media and that is media logic. In order to draw readers', listeners,' or viewers' attention, the case of whistleblowing must be attractive enough to be presented to the wide audience. Not only that, the complexity of a case must, for the purpose of not losing audience attention, be presented in a short digestible form thus omitting some facts.

Business ethics specialists and scientists research such problems theoretically. Those groups, apart from NGOs are believed to be truly and genuinely interested in promoting whistleblowing and taking care of the proper understanding of the idea. Is it enough? Is making people aware of the problem enough to implement it successfully when so many institutions and organizations must be involved? It is but an indispensible step in the long and difficult road towards safe and successful truth revealing. It is difficult or even impossible to point a leader in whose interest whistleblowing should work properly. And that is the problem of organizational structure.

4. The Role of Government

Naturally, one might mention governments as promoters and leaders of propagating a noble idea of truth revealing thanks to which lives, health, or money could be saved. Governments posses all necessary powers and institutions to collect data, process it and draw necessary conclusions and information. The big Yes to that point of view applies only to those institutions that are supervised by governments. That big sector of clerks, officials, delegates. The greatest challenges for governmental owned institutions lie in financial areas with all different forms of financial malpractices. As such, it has been successfully practiced for years in the U.S., huge amounts of money have been saved, lots of whistleblowers granted. Success. The role of a government as a leader is understandable and expected. The private sector is a bigger challenge.

For example, from Polish perspective where courts are believed to be slow and regulations vague, it is hard to expect fruitful cooperation between the mentioned institutions and whistleblowers both from governmental and private sectors. Governments are political powers which path their ways through struggle and convincing opposition. Introducing any kind of political aspect into social life brings endless discussions and debates, majority of which is aimed at weakening the ruling party. When facing opposition from political opponents is whistleblowing worth time and consideration for the ruling party to put it on the agenda of "urgent" matters? If not properly understood by politicians, the need of introducing and protecting the subtle way of revealing the truth through blowing the whistle, might be misinterpreted as a response to improper and inefficient actions of existing institutions aimed at controlling and checking social life and governmental expenditures.

It is difficult to say who should be seen as a leader for promoting and supporting whistleblowing in a country with no whistleblowing recognition. The role of government might be squeezed to implementing proper laws concerning protection and financial rewards both in public and social organizations. The role of NGOs and scientists might be that of implementing proper understanding and acceptance among employees. Lawyers might specialize in qui tam cases and media might present whistleblowers as heroes. Who should start first? Who should invest money in campaigns, lectures, seminars, publishing materials, lobbying groups? Who should convince others that breaking fear and risking life is worth trying for publico bono? In other words, should the sparkle of initiative come from high or down? Government or people? Democracy that guarantees freedom of speech and therefore makes whistleblowing possible in this case is its own enemy. The society must be mature enough to make important decisions, to point leaders and obey their strategy. But that requires time and lengthy education.

5. Moral Dilemma

Americans qualify any case that is believed only to be dangerous as whistleblowing. The British, on the other hand, allow for blowing the whistle only when the crime is absolutely sure and proved. The very core of the problem lies in the moral dilemma. Who decides about absolute certainty and clarity of misconduct? Which motives are correct and acceptable and which are not? Must the motives be of noble standards or is truth itself a sufficient reason regardless of whistleblower's involvement in the case? Tracing down the whole process of blowing the whistle, the most sensitive area lies in *decisions* about deposition of truth. The big question of: why do people want to tell what they know? It is the problem of values, responsibility, loyalty, revenge, beliefs, faith, education, culture.

All of them shape our actions, influence decisions, help to estimate what is and what is not important or urgent, what has the biggest impact on our lives. Despite the fact that whistleblowing belongs to an either/or set of solutions, many factors must be taken into consideration to come to that simple yes-or-no decision. Having so many factors lying at the bottom of decision making it is worth considering each of them in due respect for acting pro publico bono. Institutions that substantially provide for one's paradigm of life are: school, government policy, church, family, work environment. In analyzing each institution I try to discover to what extent they might contribute to shaping brave minds ready to oppose intentional wrongdoing.

Schooling system is probably the most powerful tool in shaping one's mind. It starts at the age of six or seven and lasts, in many cases, for nearly twenty years. Not only knowledge is important but also the way it is conveyed, that is, the system of data transfer. Having different skills and abilities children very often find themselves in a group where certain level of knowledge is required by all regardless of one's talents. Mixed ability group must meet certain standards. How to achieve it? By discipline and single-person evaluation. Depriving children of group work or action learning leads to creating a society of "everyone for himself. With no sense of social responsibility with no chance of developing a positive leader—the very core of democratic society. The Polish "gimanzjum," (high school) for example, is suffering vastly from bullies as the result of unsolved problem of power execution. At present the law gives teachers very limited power over students who demoralize others by swearing, smoking, drinking, using vulgar language, and brutal behavior. School as an institution is very weak in punishing or preventing such behaviors. That certainly influences good students attitude by imprinting sad, subconscious conclusion that nothing can be done. Not only hidden bad behavior cannot be stopped but also open conflicts, with everyone's knowledge, are still unsolved.

Government policy is understood as the efficiency of government in organizing social life. The very concepts of justice, equal chances, supporting good and fighting evil. Those concepts are manifested by society's evaluation of help it can receive in everyday situations. Shall business people expect help or punishment from governmental clerks? Should Police rather help or punish? If, in society's evaluation, the answer to both question is punishment, then it must be understood that there is limited trust. The notion of "everyone for himself" imprinted in school life is enhanced.

Church is a very delicate matter to be judged in respect to whistleblowing since it operates in a very subtle area of spiritual leadership with deep association of human life with a deity. However, regardless of denominations, the Bible in both Old and New Testaments advises people to share their knowledge of wrongdoing. One might expect that the church as an institution can help promoting ethical aspect of business and political life. A decision to take an active part in that promotion lies entirely on church's side.

At the very bottom of the moral dilemma lies the fundamental belief whether or not a single person can change the course of action. The values and beliefs imprinted in mind through work of powerful institutions influence choices whether one should take any steps towards correcting reality or not. The belief in action taken is a sheer manifestation of self esteem and self reliance. At what point of life is that powerful tool developed with positive results within people's minds? A few chosen are strong enough to counteract evil despite environment and external conditions but the majority need help, guidance, and systematic encouragement.

Family seems to be the strongest source of improving self esteem and self reliance. The family wisdom passed from generation to generation is a sum of all experiences, good and bad, aimed at being a life guideline for younger generations. Parents gain their wisdom from grandparents and those from their parents and grandparents. In conclusion, the life wisdom passed within families carry the spirit of times when their ancestors were brought up. That kind of wisdom includes also tackling with truth, attitude towards government and its institutions, the very subtle noticing of people's behavior and its indications. It also provides the pattern of behavior towards workplace, voicing demands and claims, beliefs concerning justice, truth, meaning of life.

The last four generations in Poland were subject to very cruel and inhuman treatment by two totalitarian systems: communism and fascism. Prior to two world wars the country had been partitioned and had not existed at all. The pattern of behavior, which aimed at survival, developed in past generations is still being carried on from generation to generation within families. The memories of wounds inflicted in human minds are still very vivid. The overlook at European historical background leaves no country free from oppressors, ill—treatment, horrors of life. Is this the main reason why whistleblowing could flourish in the USA so strongly? Are bad historical connotations obstacles in proper understanding of whistleblowing? Or maybe the attitude can be changed dramatically?

In order to find the answer it is worth observing functioning of business sector in Poland. Since 1989 the country is fully democratic, with the idea of a free market system, with huge foreign capital investments, and with foreign companies subsidiaries operating in the country. It is understandable and predictable that companies bring their own structures, codes of ethics, philosophy, behavior and all other factors contributing to so called "corporate culture." Is this going to change the fear factor inherited by Polish workers? The newly created post of a hearing officer introduced in some companies is rare and a novelty. Hopefully, the effects will be positive although timely.

6. Financial Reward

One of the most controversial issues concerning whistleblowing is financial reward. Apart from judging motives there are also some logical intricacies. First things first. The basic question is: who is going to judge whistleblower's motives and are they important at all? Should we be in favor of rewarding, on what grounds should the reward be set for protecting environment or human life? It is much easier to set a percentage of money won back but in other cases the value of protected "goods" is much more difficult to be established. But is it morally accepted to reward somebody for warning about catastrophe? Let's suppose that a whistleblower reveals and successfully blocks company's operations that devastate environment. Who personally should be in favor of rewarding that person? Company's CEO who is actually sued? Employees who are "reorganized" and "downsized" in the aftermath of the action? Governmental institution responsible for environmental protection? Apparently no one would be interested in rewarding a heroic action. Certainly it cannot be the whole society that, after all, benefits mostly from that action. Should we be against rewarding then naturally we find ourselves in conflict with the natural law of like cause, like effect. A man is worth his reward for a well-performed job because it is very natural and just. The natural instinct compels to pay back and reward the brave who act for the sake of others. After all each country has its own armor of medals granted to national heroes whose job should be appreciated.

Logical intricacies are even more challenging. If whistleblowing greatest power lies in revealing the truth in order to prevent a catastrophe then, from legal point of view, we reward somebody for preventing *actions that do not happen*. In other words, prevention of crime makes it not take place. How then can anyone evaluate the "loses" that could have occurred but have not? Logically, we reward somebody for something that did not happen. From religious point of view protecting others is a sheer duty of any society member. Law is activated only when an actual crime was committed. If the motive was of pro publico bono, then a public praise is sufficient. There is no justification for financial reward. Reward as a percentage of embezzlement money can be understood as a lifestyle of people whose job might turn into being a permanent governmental spy. That would be the end of whistleblowing as a noble idea. Can anyone be a professional whistleblower?

7. Conclusion

Whistleblowing is a simple but noble mechanism of revealing the truth in order to prevent catastrophe or to stop actions that embezzle money, jeopardize life, health or environment. Being successfully implemented in Anglo-Saxon countries it is expected to be equally successful in others since the only condition is freedom of speech. However, there are many questions of moral, historical, and organizational nature that need clarification. I do hope that seeking good answers will end up in finding them. For the sake of whistleblowing. And thus for the sake of a safer society.

Part Two

Whistleblowing and Ethics

A Business Ethics Theory of Whistleblowing: Responding to the $1 Trillion Question

W. Michael Hoffman and Robert E. McNulty
Center for Business Ethics Bentley University
Waltham, U.S.A.

When is it permissible to blow the whistle and when is it a duty? This is a worthy business ethics question. A good answer will be one that is grounded on sound theory and is able to hold up to scrutiny when applied to the practical affairs of business. The goal of this paper, therefore, is to provide an answer to that question that is both practicable and theoretically cogent. While our theory is intended to be universally applicable, it is grounded in the current conditions in the United States.

1. To be a Whistleblower: The Trillion Dollar Question

To be or not to be a whistleblower is a question of considerable ethical complexity and personal significance. It is not, however, a question of theoretical significance only. According to a recent report by the Association of Certified Fraud Examiners (ACFE), the United States lost almost $1 *trillion* in fraud in 2008. Before Bernie Madoff's epoch-making swindling came to light and before the economic meltdown of 2008-09 was recognized as the worst economic crisis since the Great Depression, ACFE had already estimated that American businesses would lose $994 billion in fraudulent activities in 2008.[1] What makes this pertinent to our essay is how fraud is detected: according to the ACFE report, the number one source of fraud detection came from tips, i.e., from *whistleblowers.* Despite the extensive reporting required of businesses since the promulgation of Sarbanes-Oxley, in the end, it was whistleblowers that served as the primary bulwark against fraud.

Although the social contribution of whistleblowing is gigantic, whistleblowers are often portrayed as disloyal or self-serving bounty hunters. However, whistleblowers frequently put themselves at great risk, and their situation is rendered more perilous by the failings of the U.S. legal system. We would argue that the woeful state of legal affairs may be due in part to a lack of consensus on the parameters of legitimate whistleblowing.

In this chapter, we take a step in responding to a perceived theoretical deficiency by drawing on what we hold to be core principles in business ethics. With this, we suggest when whistleblowing should be considered a duty and when one can be excused from whistleblowing. The position we will propose will serve as a basis to critique the U.S. legal framework, which we claim fails to afford the needed protections to organizations and whistleblowers alike. It is our hope that by advancing a sound theoretical framework, we can contribute to the creation of stronger laws and organizational policies.

Defining "Whistleblowing"

The term "whistleblowing" is thought to have its roots in two different but related activities: first, the term follows from the practice of police or bobbies who blew their whistles when attempting to apprehend a suspected criminal; secondly, it is thought to follow from the practice of referees during sporting events who blow their whistle to stop an action.[2] In this case, the basic justification for whistleblowing is this: the whistleblower perceives something that he or she believes to be unethical or illegal and reports it to authorities so that corrective measures may be taken.

Marcia Miceli and Janet Near provide a good formal definition of whistleblowing as "the disclosure by organization members (former or current) of illegal, immoral, or illegitimate practices under the control of their employees, to persons or organizations that may be able to effect action." They continue by noting that "the whistleblower lacks the power and authority to make the change being sought and therefore must appeal to someone of greater power or authority."[3] The term has come to refer generally to a person who reports on wrongdoings within or by an organization.[4] If an alleged wrongdoing is reported to a person in a position of authority within an organization, it is referred to as "internal" whistleblowing. If the alleged misdeed is reported to outside authorities, such as to regulatory bodies, news media, or public interest groups, it is said to be "external" whistleblowing.[5]

2. Toward a Theory of Whistleblowing

It is our view that to articulate a coherent understanding of whistleblowing a theory is needed in which the nature and parameters of appropriate whistleblowing are specified. Such a theory, we hold, must be situated within the framework of ethics generally, and business ethics in particular. To this end, we seek to provide guidelines to help in assessing when whistleblowing can be thought of as a duty and when it is not. As a way of assisting in this analysis, we will first consider a long established theory on whistleblowing, that of Richard De George. We admire the way in which De George structured his argument and we find his theory relevant as a point of contrast to the view we will advance.

De George's Theory of Whistleblowing and the Problem of Duty

In 1986 Richard De George published the second edition of his textbook, *Business Ethics,* in which appeared his essay entitled "Whistle Blowing."[6] De George's piece has been so frequently cited in articles by other scholars that it is suitable to serve as a point of departure for our theory's development.

De George specifies three positions regarding whistleblowing, i.e., whistleblowing as morally prohibited, as morally permitted, and as morally required. He begins by refuting the position that whistleblowing should be morally prohibited, but notes the cultural resistance to whistleblowing. "There is a strong tradition within American mores against 'ratting' or telling on others," he states. He continues, "The most plausible and most commonly stated rationale for not blowing the whistle is given in terms of loyalty."[7] But even giving the norms of loyalty, De George holds that in some cases whistleblowing should be considered morally permitted or required. Let us look at the five criteria he proposes for determining whether whistleblowing would be morally permissible or required.

According to De George the criteria for *permissible* whistleblowing are as follows.

1. The firm, through its product or policy, will do serious and considerable harm to the public, whether in the person of the user of its product, an innocent bystander, or the general public.
2. Once an employee identifies a serious threat to the user of a product or to the general public, he or she should report it to his immediate supervisor and make his or her moral concern known. Unless he or she does so, the act of whistleblowing is not clearly justifiable.

3. If one's immediate supervisor does nothing effective about the concern or complaint, the employee should exhaust the internal procedures and possibilities within the firm. This usually will involve taking the matter up the managerial ladder, and, if necessary—and possible—to the board of directors.[8]

De George holds that whistleblowing becomes *morally required* when—in addition to the previous three criteria—the following two are also met:

4. The whistleblower must have, or have accessible, documented evidence that would convince a reasonable, impartial observer that one's view of the situation is correct, and that the company's product or practice poses a serious and likely danger to the public or to the user of the products.
5. The employee must have good reason to believe that by going public the necessary changes will be brought about. The chance of being successful must be worth the risk one takes and the danger to which one is exposed.[9]

We are troubled by the basic orientation of De George's analysis, but it is not our intention to provide a thorough critique of his piece as this was done very ably in an article by Gene James.[10] It is worth noting, however, that James aptly points out that De George sets the criteria for whistleblowing so high that many organizational wrongs such as sexual harassment, industrial espionage, insider trading, and many others would go unchallenged.[11]

We admire the way in which De George structured his argument and distinguished between permitted and required whistleblowing. Our purpose in addressing De George is not to have a straw man to knock down, but because the contrast in our respective positions will help to illustrate how our underlying principles of business ethics lead us to a very different—more activist—view of whistleblowing.

To begin, we think De George's main distinction between "morally permitted," and "morally required," is troubling. It seems to render highly tenuous the connection between duty and what is morally right, since if something is permitted but not required, it would carry little moral weight. And yet, the conditions that would be covered by what he terms as "morally permitted," are in fact, very weighty. For example, in his first criterion De George indicates that it is permissible, but not obligatory, to blow the whistle when a firm through its products or policies "will do serious and considerable harm to the public." It is in his fourth and fifth principles that he clarifies that whistleblowing is morally required only with strong documentary evidence and good reasons to believe that the company will change. This suggests that even if someone believes an organization will do serious and considerable harm, that person is not required to blow the whistle.

De George's criteria imply that there is no moral duty for self-sacrifice. Accordingly, whistleblowing is permissible but not required unless conditions 4 and 5 are met—conditions that would go far to minimize the risk of the whistleblowing from potential retaliation. We agree that the safety of the whistleblower is a real concern, but by setting the bar so high, one would be justified in almost never engaging in whistleblowing, even in cases of serious malfeasance. To illustrate the point, in early 2009 there was a peanut processing plant in the state of Georgia that was responsible for a massive salmonella outbreak that led to the deaths of eight people and sickened some 19,000 others. Based on De George's criteria, if I worked at that plant, I would have been fully excused for not blowing the whistle because I might have reasonably believed that so doing would not have resulted in a change in company policy.[12]

The other obvious problem with De George's criteria is his insistence that for whistleblowing to be permissible, the whistleblower must report it first to his or her supervisor and then if remedial actions are not taken, bring the concern up the corporate hierarchy. This principle seems geared toward keeping the problem "in house," perhaps because if the issue were publicly aired, it could cause unnecessary harm to the company.

However, such a concern, while not irrelevant, seems to focus on a secondary issue—the effects of public disclosure—rather than the primary issue, which is identifying the problem and finding a resolution. In some instances, reporting a problem internally might make matters worse by tipping off the perpetrators that their activities have been detected. If one's supervisor or other superiors in the organization were directly or indirectly involved in the offending action or policy, reporting the offence to them would likely exacerbate a bad situation and possibly put the whistleblower at great personal risk.

3. Whistleblowing within the Context of Organizational Reporting

Frequently, whistleblowers are depicted as if they are on opposing sides with the organization. This, however, need not be the case. Let us return to the idea mentioned at the outset of this paper, i.e., the $994 billion in estimated fraud in 2008. According to the report, "almost 50 percent of occupational fraud involved the accounting department or upper management."[13] Conversely, we can infer that about 50 percent does not involve accounting staff or upper management. In at least those cases, we would expect management to welcome whistleblowing—especially in those instances when it is conducted internally—because eliminating such cases of corruption would benefit the organization.

We hold that the appropriateness of whistleblowing depends to a large extent on the circumstances. The criteria used to determine the validity of whistleblowing (irrespective of whether it be considered "permitted" or "required") ought not to depend on the position of the person to whom one reports the misconduct. Instead, the focus should be on how to achieve the most ethical resolution. To put it simply, if there is organizational corruption, there is a victim. A good theory of whistleblowing should provide guidance in how to minimize harm to any of an organization's stakeholders.

4. Establishing Foundational Ethical Principles for Business

It is not enough to indicate that we are unsatisfied with De George's ethical theory of whistleblowing; to take this analysis further, we need to establish some ethical principles based on which we can justify a more robust theory of whistleblowing. To this end, let us first define our basic ideas, such as what do we mean by business ethics? To this, we answer:

Descriptively, business ethics is the discipline that seeks to understand the ethical dimensions of business.
Prescriptively, the purpose of business ethics is to provide guidance in the ethical conduct of business, including practices such as whistle-blowing.

To fulfill the prescriptive objective of business ethics, we propose a central principle from which subsidiary principles can follow, such as guidelines for ethical whistleblowing. As we understand it, the central ethical principle of business ethics is the recognition of the *universal dignity* or worth of all human beings and the necessity for all business actions to reflect respect for that dignity.[14] The following is a more precise expression of that general principle:

> All human beings have intrinsic worth or dignity by virtue of their humanity, and no individual or group has the moral authority to deny others their inherent dignity.[15]

We believe that this principle is strong and rationally defensible. However, for the purpose of this essay, we will take this principle as axiomatic. All other principles of business ethics follow from this axiom, including those of "minimal harm," "just business practices," "stakeholder theory," and "ethical whistleblowing."

5. A Universal Dignity Theory of Whistleblowing

With this foundation, we are now ready to describe what we call the "Universal Dignity Theory of Whistleblowing" (UDTW). The essential principle of UDTW is this:

Whistleblowing is both permissible and a duty to the extent that doing so constitutes the most effective means of supporting the dignity of all relevant stakeholders.

This leads us to propose the following *conditions for ethical whistleblowing:*

1. Compelling evidence of nontrivial illegal or unethical actions done by an organization or its employees that are deemed to violate the dignity of one or more of its stakeholders.
2. A lack of knowledge within the organization of the wrongdoing or failure by the organization to take corrective measures.

If the above justificatory conditions are met, whistleblowing is ethically called for unless the following *exempting conditions* from whistleblo-wing prevailed:

3. One is conditionally exempted from the duty to blow the whistle if one has credible grounds for believing that by doing so one would be putting oneself or others at risk of serious retaliation.

Of these three conditions for ethical whistleblowing, the exempting condition is most difficult to adequately define. The difficulty lies in the fact that as the gravity of an unethical action increases, the justifiability of exemption decreases. Hence, to refer to the previous example of salmonella contamination at a peanut processing facility, there was a risk that people might die as a result of company negligence. In such a case, even if one believed that whistleblowing might put one's livelihood at risk, given the gravity of the misconduct, we would consider such a risk insufficient to exempt one from the whistleblowing duty. If, however, one believed that whistleblowing would put one's life at risk, then this would be a different matter. We leave it for further study to define this exempting condition with greater precision, but we trust that the essential principle is clear.

6. Elaborating on the Theory

The Universal Dignity Theory of Whistleblowing essentially reverses the perspective on whistleblowing from that of De George. In the next few paragraphs we'd like to consider why this is the case, how this affects the interpretation of whistleblowing as a reporting practice, and why we hold this is a better ethical understanding of the place of whistleblowing within organizational reporting.

According to De George unless stringent conditions are met one is *not obliged* to blow the whistle. By contrast, according to UDTW, if an employee has compelling evidence of organizational misconduct, he or she has *a duty to blow the whistle* unless that person has reason to believe that his or her own dignity would be seriously harmed by so doing.

These differences follow from fundamentally different interpretations of the ethics of whistleblowing. De George states, "In all cases, because whistleblowing involves disloyalty or disobedience at some level, we start by requiring that it be justified, rather than assuming it needs no justification."[16] We disagree. As we see it, the charge that whistleblowing is an act of disloyalty follows from a misunderstanding of the nature of loyalty and whistleblowing. Arthur S. Miller, for example, sensibly asserts, "Surely, an employee owes his employer enough loyalty to try to work, first of all, within the organization to attempt to effect change."[17] We concur, but we object to views of disloyalty such as that of James Roche, the former president of General Motors, who stated:

> Some critics are now busy eroding another support of free enterprise-the loyalty of a management team, with its unifying values and cooperative work. Some of the enemies of business now encourage an employee to be disloyal to the enterprise. They want to create suspicion and disharmony, and pry into the proprietary interests of the business. However this is labeled—industrial espionage, whistle blowing, or professional responsibility—it is another tactic for spreading disunity and creating conflict.[18]

We would argue that loyalty is not a moral good in itself. At stake are two forms of competing loyalty, i.e., loyalty to a group and loyalty to the principles of ethical business. Group loyalty is a virtue to the extent that the group is committed to virtuous conduct. Loyalty to unethical principles can lead to ruination.[19] According to the Universal Dignity Theory of Whistleblowing when faced with a choice between loyalty to an organization and loyalty to ethical conduct, ethics should prevail. This is not only due to a commitment to ethical principle, but also because, in fact, it is when organizations act ethically that they act in the interests of all the organization's relevant stakeholders.

Therefore, as we see it, failure to blow the whistle without an exempting justification is disloyal to the company broadly understood; it is an example of remaining impassive in the face of conditions that damage the organization itself. It is worth noting that according to the Association of Certified Fraud Examiners, "In nearly two-thirds of the fraud schemes covered by our study, the perpetrators acted alone..."[20] Such fraudsters violate the organization's dignity and by reporting the malfeasance, the whistleblower acts as the organization's defender.

There is, however, a strong cultural resistance to whistleblowing, which is evidenced in some important research done by the Ethics Resource Center. According to their fifth National Business Ethics Survey, 56 percent of employees indicated that they had personally observed conduct that violated company ethics standards, policy, or the law, and yet 42 percent did *not* report the observed misconduct. Among those who did not report, 54 percent indicated that they failed to report because they didn't believe it would make any difference and 36 percent indicated that they feared retalia-tion.[21] This suggests that there is a widespread belief that companies are unsupportive of whistleblowing. But, referring back to the idea that most fraud is detected through whistleblowing, companies would do well to provide greater support to whistleblowers, particularly by helplines as well as through programs that better train managers how to create ethical cultures that instill responsibility and accountability in all employees to actively protect the integrity of the organization.

Some observers note that whistleblowing is sometimes done out of vengeance or in order to collect a "bounty," and it is naive to see in it a virtuous intent. According to Jeffrey Newman, an expert in the legal aspects of whistleblowing, whistleblower lawsuits are frequently made by "former employees which have been terminated by a company for disclosure of the wrongdoing."[22] Moreover, under the False Claims Act, successful whistle-blowers are eligible for a bounty of up to 30 percent of the government's recovery,[23] which could amount to a considerable sum.

However one interprets facts such as these, the UDTW intends to protect the dignity of all stakeholders. If a vengeful spirit leads someone to trump up false charges, the UDTW would lead to the protection of the offended stakeholder, which might well be the organization itself. And if a whistle-blower is motivated by monetary gain, that is precisely the intent behind any bounty, which does not affect the validity of the allegation. In any case—whether the whistleblowing is motivated by vengeance, greed, or a sense of duty—it is important that the focus on whistleblower motivation does not result in drawing away attention from the alleged misconduct.

7. Blowing the Whistle on the Law

Unfortunately, our ethical analysis of whistleblowing is complicated when we consider the place of the law. From different perspectives, both ethics and the law are concerned with rights as well as with what is right. Laws, as legal statutes, are regulatory conventions established through governing authorities that may or may not be ethical. An important role of ethics is to serve as a basis for critiquing laws. The tension between ethics and the law is particularly stark as it pertains to the problem of whistleblowing, because at least in the United States, the laws governing whistleblowing are in such disarray.[24] This problem was recognized by Vermont senator, Patrick Leahy, who stated:

> Corporate employees who report fraud are subject to the patchwork of vagaries of current state laws, even though most publicly traded companies do business nationwide. Thus, a whistleblowing employee in one state (e.g., Texas) may be far more vulnerable to retaliation than a fellow employee in another state who takes the same action.[25]

The United States has a long history of legislation created to support whistleblowers, stretching back to 1863 and the administration of Abraham Lincoln. At that time, the United States was engaged in the Civil War and in order to provide itself with legal remedies against those who sought to unduly profit by selling substandard goods at premium prices, the government passed the False Claims Act (FCA), which provided whistleblower protections.[26] This was an excellent beginning, but despite the value of the FCA, it is too limited in its scope because it applies only to contractor malfeasance in their dealings with the federal government. In the intervening time since passage of the FCA, many laws have been promulgated, each of which provides protections for various types of whistleblowers, but none of which is comprehensive. For example, the site Whistleblowers.org lists over 120 federal laws pertaining to whistleblowing.[27] There are laws that pertain to illegal acts done by federal agencies and others that pertain to the military.[28] There are laws that pertain to publicly traded companies, but not to privately held companies. Most states have some whistleblowing laws, but they vary greatly from state to state. To further complicate matters, if a person claims to have suffered retaliation for whistleblowing, the federal statutes of limitations for reporting may vary from 30 days to 180 days depending on which law applies to one's particular case.[29] Moreover, states also have their own statutes of limitations.

The Sarbanes-Oxley Act of2002 (SOX) was created in response to high levels of corruption among a number of American firms. SOX has placed onerous reporting requirements on publicly listed companies, but symptomatic of the problem with whistleblower laws generally, the loopholes in SOX greatly undermine its value. For example, the way SOX has been interpreted, the whistleblower protections it affords do not apply to private companies or to the subsidiaries of publicly traded companies.[30]

The upshot of the legal morass is that the laws offer little protection to whistleblowers. For example, according to Richard E. Moberly, one of the leading U.S. experts on whistleblowing, in FY 2006, out of 159 SOX whistleblowing cases that were decided by OSHA, not a single case was won by the whistleblower.[31]

Because there is a considerable gap between the UDTW and the pertinent laws, we suggest that the business ethics of whistleblowing should serve as a basis for legal reform that brings justice and consistency across economic sectors and geographic boundaries.

8. Whistleblowing and Supererogation

Earlier we provided a condition that would exempt someone from the duty of whistleblowing, namely, "One would be conditionally exempted from the duty to blow the whistle if one had credible grounds for believing that by doing so one would be putting oneself or others at risk of serious retaliation." The reason for this exemption is that we cannot expect someone to engage in whistleblowing if doing so would result in putting him or herself or others in harm's way.

It is here that we can see the intersection between business ethics and the law, because if the law does not afford adequate protection, the exemption from the whistleblowing duty could become the norm, and opportunities to rectify injustice will be relatively few. It could be argued that it would be unreasonable to expect a whistleblower to bring harm on him or herself under any circumstances, and that the act of willingly accepting personal harm for the sake of justice is supererogatory and cannot be required. This is where the important but uneasy relation between ethics and the law is relevant. If laws are crafted to provide comprehensive protection to whistleblowers, then the act of whistleblowing would *not* be deemed to be supererogatory, because the whistleblower would typically not be putting him or herself at substantial risk. For this reason we argue that it is imperative that laws be drastically reformed so as to provide comprehensive protections to whistleblowers. In so doing we can minimize the instances of exempting conditions to the whistleblowing duty.

9. Concluding Thoughts: Whistleblowing and the Pursuit of Justice

We began this essay by noting that according to one estimate, in the United States almost $1 trillion is lost to corruption on an annual basis, and that the most important contributor to detecting fraud is whistleblowing. This illustrates in monetary terms the value and importance of whistleblowing. However, we suggest that a good theoretical framework for whistleblowing can contribute to creating more ethical business cultures generally as well as provide a theoretical foundation for legal reform. In so doing, all the organizational stakeholders would be better served, and given the state of international economic interdependence, this would contribute to creating a morally stronger global community.

Notes

1. W. Michael Hoffman, Ph.D., Executive Director, Center for Business Ethics at Bentley University, Waltham MA, USA
Robert E. McNulty, Ph.D., Director of Programs, Center for Business Ethics at Bentley University, Waltham MA, USA
We would like to express our gratitude to Ms. Christina Herron for her valuable research assistance.
Association of Certified Fraud Examiners, "2008 Report to the Nation on Occupational Fraud & Abuse," (Austin, TX, 2008), 4. [Hereafter title abbreviated as "2008 Report".]
2. Marcia P. Miceli and Janet P. Near, *Blowing the Whistle: The Organizational and Legal Implications for Companies and Employees* (New York: Lexington Books, 1992), 15.
3. Roberta Ann Johnson, *Whistleblowing: When It Works—and Why* (Boulder: Lynne Rienner Publishers, 2003), 4.
4. In this paper we will use the general word "organization," to refer to any legally established grouping of people formally brought together to work for a collective purpose. In most cases, however, the kind of organization to which whistleblowing pertains is a "business." Although the origins of our work are in the field of business ethics, the issues with which we are concerned apply to organizations irrespective of their commercial orientation.
5. The idea of internal v. external whistleblowing is standard vernacular. There are some debates regarding whether an "internal whistleblower" engages in whistleblowing at all. For example, Miceli, Near, and Dworkin refer to a 1982 definition of whistleblowing by Norman Bowie, that specifies that the term "whistleblower" applies only to those who "inform the public." See Norman E. Bowie, *Business Ethics* (Englewood Cliffs: Prentice-Hall, 1982), 142. Miceli, Near, and Dworkin conclude, "... from the standpoint of the whistleblower, external whistleblowing is continuing a process—perhaps because internal efforts to get wrongdoing corrected

have failed—rather than doing something radically different." Marcia P. Miceli, Janet P. Near, and Terry Morehead Dworkin, *Whistle-Blowing in Organizations* (New York: Routledge, 2008), 8.

6. Richard T. De George, "Whistle Blowing," in *Business Ethics* (New York: Macmillan Publishing Company, 1986). We will refer to the original version of De Gorge's article, since we will also refer to a critique of his article by Gene James, which also refers to that version of his article. Although De George subsequently revised the article, our comments remain relevant because in subsequent versions, his essential arguments remain intact.
7. Ibid., 226.
8. Ibid., 230-33.
9. Ibid., 234.
10. Gene G. James, "Whistle Blowing: Its Moral Justification," in *Business Ethics: Reading and Cases in Corporate Morality,* ed. W. Michael Hoffman and Jennifer Mills Moore (New York: McGraw-Hill Publishing Company, 1990).
11. Ibid., 336.
12. See Michael Moss, "Peanut Case Shows Holes in Safety Net" *New York Times* 2009. This article reports on another plant with similar circumstances. The article states, "The government finally demanded the records three years later, and verified the whistleblower's claims, after hundreds of people were sickened by salmonella-tainted peanut butter produced at the plant in 2007."
13. Association of Certified Fraud Examiners, "2008 Report," 46.
14. For a fuller investigation of this topic, please see Robert E. McNulty and W. Michael Hoffman, "Business Ethics Perspectives on International Negotiations," in *ABA Guide to International Negotiations,* ed. Jeffery Aresty (Chicago: American Bar Association, 2009).
15. We do not claim originality in this principle. Rather, it is consistent with well established moral principles recognized in cultures everywhere, including the Golden Rule and Kant's categorical imperative. For discussions of each of these, please see Jeffrey Wattles, *The Golden Rule* (Oxford: Oxford University Press, 1996). and Immanuel Kant, *Grounding for the Metaphysics of Morals,* trans. James W. Ellington (Indianapolis: Hackett Publishing Company, 1983).
16. De George, "Whistle Blowing," 237.
17. Arthur S. Miller, "Whistle Blowing and the Law," in *Whistle Blowing,* ed. Ralph Nader, Peter J. Petkas, and Kate Blackwell (New York: Grossman Publishers, 1972), 30.
18. Quoted in Ronald Duska, "Whistleblowing and Employee Loyalty," in *Honest Work: A Business Ethics Reader,* ed. Joanne B. Ciulla, Clancy Martin, and Robert C. Solomon (New York: Oxford University Press, 2007), 409.
19. The obvious example here is Nazism. There are copious examples of how loyalty was exploited by Hitler and the Nazi hierarchy in a way that supported the abdication of other moral norms. See, for example the discussion of this by Hannah Arendt. Hannah Arendt, "Banality and Conscience," in *The Portable Hannah Arendt,* ed. Peter R. Baehr (New York: Penguin Books, 2000), 338.
20. Association of Certified Fraud Examiners, "2008 Report," 46.
21. Ethics Resource Center, "2007 National Business Ethics Survey," (Washington, DC 2008), pp. 1, 3, 6.
22. Jeffrey A. Newman, "The Federal False Claims 'Qui Tam' Actions—Successful Preparation," in *Handling Federal False Claims (Qui Tam) Whistleblower Cases,* ed. Jeffrey A. Newman, et al. (Boston: Massachusetts Continuing Legal Education, Inc., 2000), 8.
23. See the FAQs at http://whistleblowerlaws.com/index.php

24. For an insightful review of whistleblowing laws, see Gerard Sinzdak, "An Analysis of Current Whistleblower Laws: Defending a More Flexible Approach to Reporting Requirements," *California Law Review* 96, no. 6 (2008).
25. Patrick Leahy, "Congressional Record—Senate," (Washington, DC: National Archives, 2002), S7420.
26. Larry D. Lahman, "Bad Mules: A Primer on the Federal False Claims Act," *Oklahoma Bar Journal* 76, no. 12 (2005).
27. See http://www.whistleblowers.org/index.php?option=com_content&task=view&id=816&Itemid=129
28. Moreover, legal protections afforded to whistleblowers have been diminishing. For example, based on the 2006 Garcetti v. Ceballos Supreme Court Decision, public employees may be disciplined, even fired, for blowing the whistle on one's department if the statement is made "in his capacity as an employee and not as a citizen and carries no First Amendment rights." See David A. Drachsler, "Public Employee Whistleblowers after *Garcetti V. Ceballos,*" *Labor Law Journal* 59, no. 2 (2008): 201.
29. OSHA, "Your Rights as a Whistleblower," *OSHA FactSheet (2007),* http://www.osha.gov/OshDoc/data_General_Facts/whistleblower_rights.pdf.
30. See, for example, Jennifer Levitz, "Whistleblowers Are Left Dangling," *Wall Street Journal,* Sept. 4 2008. This article states, "Sen. Patrick Leahy, a Vermont Democrat who helped craft the whistleblower provision—part of the Sarbanes-Oxley corporate governance act—says the law was meant to cover workers in corporate subsidiaries. 'Otherwise, a company that wants to do something shady, could just do it in their subsidiary,' he said."
31. Richard E. Moberly, "Private Sector Whistleblowers: Are There Sufficient Legal Protections?" *Statement Before the Subcommittee on Workforce Protections* (2007).

References

Arendt, H., 2000, Banality and Conscience, *The Portable Hannah Arendt,* edited by Peter R. Baehr, New York: Penguin Books. Association of Certified Fraud Examiners, 2008 Report to the Nation on Occupational Fraud & Abuse, Austin, TX, 2008.

Bowie, N. E., 1982, *Business Ethics,* Englewood Cliffs: Prentice-Hall.

De George, R. T., 1986, Whistle Blowing, *Business Ethics,* 221-38. New York: Macmillan Publishing Company. Drachsler, D. A., 2008, Public Employee Whistleblowers after *Garcetti V. Ceballos, Labor Law Journal* 59, no. 2.

Duska, R., 2007, Whistleblowing and Employee Loyalty, *Honest Work: A Business Ethics Reader,* edited by Joanne B. Ciulla, Clancy Martin and Robert C. Solomon, 408-13, New York: Oxford University Press.

Ethics Resource Center, 2008, 2007 National Business Ethics Survey, Washington, DC.

James, G. G., 1990, Whistle Blowing: Its Moral Justification, *Business Ethics: Reading and Cases in Corporate Morality,* edited by W. Michael Hoffman and Jennifer Mills Moore, 3 32-44, New York: McGraw-Hill Publishing Company.

Johnson, R. A., 2003, *Whistleblowing: When It Works—and Why,* Boulder: Lynne Rienner Publishers.

Kant, I., 1983, *Grounding for the Metaphysics of Morals,* translated by James W. Ellington, Indianapolis: Hackett Publishing Company.

Lahman, L. D., Bad Mules: A Primer on the Federal False Claims Act, *Oklahoma Bar Journal* 76, no. 12 (2005): 901-07.

Leahy, P., 2002, Congressional Record—Senate, S7420, Washington, DC: National Archives.

Levitz, J., 2008, Whistleblowers Are Left Dangling, *Wall Street Journal,* Sept. 4.

McNulty, R. E., and W. M., Hoffman, 2009, Business Ethics Perspectives on International Negotiations" *ABA Guide to International Negotiations,* edited by Jeffery Aresty, Chicago: American Bar Association.

Miceli, M. P., and Janet P. Near, 1992, *Blowing the Whistle: The Organizational and Legal Implications for Companies and Employees,* New York: Lexington Books.

Miceli, M. P., Janet P. Near, and Terry Morehead Dworkin, 2008, *Whistle-Blowing in Organizations,* New York: Routledge.

Miller, A. S., 1972, Whistle Blowing and the Law, *Whistle Blowing,* edited by Ralph Nader, Peter J. Petkas and Kate Blackwell, 25-33, New York: Grossman Publishers.

Moberly, R. E., 2007, Private Sector Whistleblowers: Are There Sufficient Legal Protections?, *Statement Before the Subcommittee on Workforce Protections.*

Moss, M., 2009, Peanut Case Shows Holes in Safety Net, *New York Times.*

Newman, J. A., 2000, The Federal False Claims 'Qui Tam' Actions—Successful Preparation, *Handling Federal False Claims (Qui Tam) Whistleblower Cases,* edited by Jeffrey A. Newman, Roberta T. Brown, Suzanne E. Durrell, David S. Mackey and Nicholas C. Theodorou, 1-157, Boston: Massachusetts Continuing Legal Education, Inc.

OSHA. "Your Rights as a Whistleblower." *OSHA FactSheet* (2007), http://www.osha.gov/OshDoc/data_General_Facts/whistleblower_rights.pdf.

Sinzdak, G., 2008, An Analysis of Current Whistleblower Laws: Defending a More Flexible Approach to Reporting Requirements, *California Law Review* 96, no. 6: 1633-68.

Wattles, J., 1996, *The Golden Rule,* Oxford: Oxford University Press.

The Ethics of Whistleblowing: An Evaluation of a South African Case

Tobias J.G. Louw
University of Fort Hare The Republic of South Africa

South Africa is credited for officially acknowledging the key role of the whistleblower in organizations through advanced legislation contained in the Protected Disclosures Act (hereafter "PDA") of 2000. Notwithstanding this recognition, the image of the whistleblower remains tainted as a "rogue" and "troublemaker." Though protected in theory, the whistleblower often remains unprotected from reprisal practices. This is possible because whistleblowers are singled out for punishment for alleged misdeeds that are presented as unrelated to the whistleblowing issue at hand. This study refers to examples in the South African context, but specifically focuses on the RSA parliamentary "Travelgate" case. Critical questions are raised about the moral dilemmas of the whistleblower, the public and corporate image of the whistleblower, the socio-ethical environment, as well as the further ethical implications of this critique.

1. Introduction

As expected from a situation as culturally diverse in a developing economy such as South Africa, moral awareness among the population is as variable as the social and political environment within which business organizations operate. Specific awareness of rights, e.g., specific rights such as access to information in the workplace, is unacceptably low. This holds true for both the public and private sector.

In the context of pervasive unemployment among the general population in South Africa, this is not unexpected. Similarly, widespread xenophobia-related violence in the country revealed a blatant disregard for the basics of a human rights culture. These events are symptomatic of a society under enormous moral pressure.

Notwithstanding practical problems the RSA in its current stage of socio-political development does have a range of liberal laws that deal with vital human rights issues. These legal facilities provide the platform for a systematic improvement in the ethical reorientation for the civil service. The theme of whistleblowing is one such avenue with the potential to assist the strengthening of a culture of rights awareness, esp. in the public service.

That specific laws exist and are available still begs the question whether they are utilized effectively. Are the relevant legal imperatives sufficient to safeguard the practice of whistleblowing? Do civil service structures make facilities available to support the whistle bowing process? In this regard it is argued that the introduction of trained ethics officers in the civil service is likely to have a positive impact on the morals and morale of employees.

Above considerations beg the question of effective ethics training of all staff, and it is proposed that a systematic integrity training can and will make a qualitative difference, esp. to the overall integrity of the human systems. The problem therefore is to determine how the facilitation of whistleblowing can serve as an opportunity for integrity training in organizations.

In this study a specific issue is taken as leading example to explain the legal framework and socio-economic environment of South Africa. This is the ongoing saga of the so-called parliamentary "Travelgate" scandal. Apart from raising a number of ethical questions, it also provides the opportunity for a critical interpretation of the socio-economic environment as a whole.

In the concluding evaluation, critical remarks are made in regard to the ethical substratum underlying the PDA and other related acts that are seemingly assumed to be universal, the moral dilemmas of the whistleblower, the public and corporate image of the whistleblower, improvement of the socio-ethical environment of places of work, and the potential of and need for Ethics Officers in organizations.

2. Understanding Whistleblowing

Firstly the term whistleblowing needs explaining. Understood correctly, whistleblowing is a practice that raises concerns about malpractice within an organization. These malpractices can take several forms and range from criminal actions such as fraud to questionable ethical practices that are not covered by specific legislation. The PDA contains a general outline thereof.

Whistleblowing is a vital tool for promoting individual responsibility and organizational accountability. Whistleblowers act in good faith and in the public interest to raise concerns about suspected impropriety within their place of employment.

Having said this, it must similarly be acknowledged that all rights have limits. Typically, whistleblowing therefore does not extend to, inter alia, acts motivated by bad faith (e.g. a disgruntled employee who is heel bent on damaging an organization's image), to prematurely uncover matters that should primarily be handled internally and are not matters of public concern to begin with, to involve structures of authority that are not recognized in law, and to engage in whistleblowing on mere suspicion instead of demonstrable evidence.

In trying to tie down a definition of whistleblowing, authors commonly distinguish between internal and external whistleblowing. The former refers to following recognized procedures within an organization with the intention of resolving a problem internally. This is normally required in law as a necessary avenue that needs to be exhausted before steps are taken externally. External whistleblowing is similarly recognized in law, but limited to specific structures of authority.

Finding a single definition of whistleblowing that would be agreeable to all is perhaps too much to ask. The general acceptability of the principle of whistleblowing still needs concrete integration within every organization's unique culture and overarching vision and mission. What matters though rather relates to the degree of protection that is legally allowed for and that needs to be ensured in practice, bearing in mind the purpose of fairness to all concerned stakeholders. The norm is institutionalized internal measures to ensure the anonymity and protection of the whistleblower.

Apart from the legal theory as reflected in the PDA, there exists commonly identifiable structures through which any whistleblower who believes to have been the victimized as a result or relating to an act of whistleblowing can seek relief, e.g., the Commission for Conciliation, Mediation and Arbitration, labor courts and the like. Similarly, several other acts of parliament exist to provide the legal framework for the good governance of labor relations, such as the Basic Conditions of Employment Act, the Labour Relations Act and the Promotion of Access to Information Act.

In order to develop and understanding of the meaning and effect of the PDA, it would be appropriate and necessary to look at concrete cases. Two basic reasons support this next step to be taken: rights, and no less the right of protection against victimization relating to an act of whistleblowing, really obtain meaning within the concrete context of the law "running its course." In any event, the letter of the law doesn't provide a one size fits all solution for all possible scenarios, but is often at best a general framework within which to operate. Let us therefore attend to one such case study.

3. The "Travelgate" Case: A Demonstration of "Ethics" Legislation in Practice

On 13 January 2006 the Chief Financial Officer of the national parliament of the Republic of South Africa, Mr. Harry M. Charlton, was fired. Although his dismissal was the consequence of an internal disciplinary hearing into fifteen charges of misconduct, in which he was found guilty of twelve, he alleges that the disciplinary process was unfair and in reality was conducted with the intention to prevent him from continuing investigations into further alleged fraudulent activities by members of parliament. Subsequently Chalmers started procedures to seek relief from the CCMA (Commission for Conciliation, Mediation and Arbitration), and after failure to reach agreement, the matter went on to the Labour Court.

This case is especially prominent due to the following factors:

a) It has occurred inside the corridors of legislative power, the very body that introduces specific laws to curb instances of fraud and corruption within both the public and private sectors.
b) The internal processes appear to have obviated the need for criminal prosecution, but also appear to have blunted the effect of the "penalties," and therefore sets a morally tainted example.
c) The whistleblower who alleges to be responsible for blowing open the Travelgate case was fired, but on the pretext that his firing had no relation to the whistleblowing case. It thus radically exposes, at the highest level, the internal weakness of the system.
d) The case is multi-faceted as it involves related cases too, and ongoing as only the first phase (exception hearing) has been completed.

For the sake of clarity: the claimant, or plaintiff is Mr. Chalmers, the fired official, and the defendant is the Parliament of the Republic of South Africa. In the exception hearing, these were respectively described as applicant (Chalmers) and respondent (Parliament). [cf. Charlton v Parliament of the Republic of South Africa (C367/06) (2007) ZALC 47 (11 June 2007)].

Parliament as respondent in this case instituted the procedure of submitting a formal exception to the contents and manner of the applicant's claims. Should the exception have succeeded, Chalmers's case would have been over.

Parliament argued, inter alia, that Chalmers was not the whistleblower, that his firing was unrelated to the Travelgate affair, and that the applicant had no cause of action since parliamentary matters fell outside the ambits of the PDA, and that the Labour Court didn't have proper jurisdiction over the matter.

On 23 May 2007 arguments regarding the exception concerns were heard before the Labour Court. The wager was clear: Should the court uphold the exception, the applicant would be prevented from leading evidence to substantiate his claims and his case would come to a standstill, bar the possibility of an appeal against an unfavorable outcome.

To the relief of the whistleblower, the exception matter was adjudged in his favor. This enables him to continue his legal battle to overturn his dismissal, and/or to seek compensation for the unfair dismissal, and also includes plans to sue for defamation of character. Since this second phase is ongoing, it will not form part of this investigation, albeit providing much more substance to further consideration about whistleblowing theory and practice in South Africa.

From the above information it should be clear that ethics in practice does work. Moreover, it works even better if allowed a legal framework within which to operate. Lastly it also sets practical guidelines for further action and consideration, and so provides an effective tool to help convert theoretical values into moral action. This platform is not beyond criticism, but it is far better to have it in place than not have it at all.

What role did the "whistleblowing act" play in the abovementioned court judgment? Our discussion highlights core aspects of this act, and reveals references to other relevant acts of the South African parliament, as well as specific interpretation practices.

4. Revealing the Legal Framework of the Protected Disclosures Act (PDA)

The applicant, Chalmers, based his argument on the PDA and submitted evidence that (a) the internal disciplinary hearing was faulty, (b) the internal hearing was aimed at removing him in order to stop further investigations into wider corruption re. the so-called Travelgate case, and (c) pleading that he should enjoy protection against his employer under the PDA, since his disclosure complied with legal procedures and responsibilities as set out in said act. Furthermore, he alleged that he was, at the time of his dismissal, investigating more widespread fraud of the same instance that involved also senior members of parliament. He argued that the purpose of his firing was to prevent further whistleblowing.

The background to this case is of exceptional interest. The national parliament of the Republic of South Africa, who is also the maker of the relevant legislation, is directly involved in more than one respect. On the one hand, members of parliament were directly involved in fraudulent activities. Internal hearings were held and in most cases admissions of guilt were signed by the twenty-five persons involved. These admissions also included an undertaking to systematically repay the defrauded monies.

(It appears though that parliament has decided to exempt the members involved from any further criminal charges [were to have gone on trial in July 2007!], on the basis of the matter having been concluded through internal disciplinary processes.)

On the other hand, it stands to reason that no body and no individual should deem itself to be above the law. At the very least the national parliament should be above reproach in so far as it concerns matters of legal and ethical conformation. This scenario therefore provides an acid test for the practicability of the PDA, and the moral health of the drive to weed out corrupt practices on all levels of the civil services.

There was therefore no question as to whether the whistleblowing in this case was justified. The plaintiff, however, still needs to prove his case and obtain a favorable verdict, and even that is dependent upon exhausting the further possibility of an appeals process. However in its response to Chalmers's argument, Parliament claimed that Chalmers was not the whistleblower in the Travelgate scandal in the first place, that he showed no clear cause of action, and that the Labour Court had no jurisdiction over the matter. It also claimed that parliament itself was operating outside the ambit of the PDA and that it therefore didn't apply in the Chalmers case to begin with.

For the purpose of this presentation, we shall focus primarily on the way in which the core aspects of the PDA is demonstrated through the exception hearing in the Chalmers vs. Parliament case. It goes without saying that the further development of the case is in process and is therefore an incomplete task. The Supreme Court case of the 17 current and 8 former members of parliament also falls outside the framework of this discussion.

5. Concluding Evaluation

Our concluding argument is threefold: that prominence and priority be granted to the training and appointment of Ethics Officers in public administration departments in SA; that "best practices" re the context and functioning of Ethics Officers be researched for purposes that will be instructive for the SA context; that the role of the Ethics Officer be expanded to include the practice of integrity training.

A qualification needs to be added to the last point: in training, the Ethics Officer needs to be exposed to a more thorough grounding in philosophy as critical and self-critical discipline, both in theory and practice.

References

Alant, N. & Uys, T., 1999, Whistleblowing: Fighting fraud in organizations, Paper presented at the Conference on Fraud and the African Renaissance held at Uganda Martyrs University from 8-10 April 1999.

Crapels, O. & Karssing, E. (eds.), 2002, *Filosoof in depraktijk,* Van Gorcum: Assen.

Delnoij, J., Laurier, J. & Geraedts, F. (eds.), 2006,*Morele oordeelsvorming en de integere organisatie,* Damon: Amsterdam.

Gadamer, H. G., 1977, *Philosophical Hermeneutics,* Transl. D.E. Linge, University of California Press: Berkeley, London. "Government Gazette, Vol. 422, No. 21453," Protected Disclosures Act [No 26 of 2000].

Karssing, E., 2000, *Morele competentie in organisaties,* Van Gorcum: Assen. Kessels, J., Boers, E., Mostert, P., 2002, *Vrije ruimte. Filosoferen in organisaties,* Boom: Amsterdam.

Louw, T. J. G. (ed.), 1992, *G. A. Rauche - Selected philosophical papers,* Fort Hare

University Press: Alice. Murray, D., 1997, *Ethics in organizations,* London, Kogan Page: London. Open Democracy Advice Centre, 2007, Charlton, H. and Parliament of the Republic of

South Africa (2007) (LC). Ottensmeyer, E. J. & McCarthy, G. D., 1996, *Ethics in the workplace,* McGraw-Hill: New York, London, Sydney. "Research Report on Corruption in the South African Private Sector" (commissioned by Business Against Crime South Africa). Ricoeur, P., *Tekst en betekenis.Opstellen over de interpretatie van literatuur,* Transl: M. van Buren, Ambo: Baarn. Rossouw, G. J., *Business ethics.*

Toffler, A., 1999, 1980, *The third wave,* Pan Books: London.

Trompenaars, F., 1996, *Riding the waves of culture. Understanding cultural diversity in business,* Nicholas Brealey Publishing: London.

Van Luijk, H. & Schilder, A., 1997, *Patronen van verantwoordeljikheidEthiek en corporate governance,* Academic Service: Amsterdam.

Whistleblowing as Treated in Jewish Law

Aaron Levine
Yeshiva University
New York, U.S.A.

1. Introduction

This paper explores the ethics of whistleblowing from the perspective of Jewish law. First, we identify the horns of the moral dilemma that the whistleblower (*W*) faces. Specifically, what moral principle tells *W* to disclose what he knows, and what moral principle tells him to remain silent? When *W* is obligated to disclose, what personal and financial sacrifices must *W* make in fulfilling that obligation? Which organizational structures would encourage legitimate whistleblowing but also foster harmony in the workplace? Finally, what role can government assume to encourage legitimate whistleblowing?

2. The Whistleblower and Jewish Law

From the standpoint of Jewish law, the whistleblower is torn between two conflicting ethical duties.

The constraints that Jewish law imposes on freedom of speech argue against permitting whistleblowing.[1] In addition to the prohibition against slander,[2] disclosing a fellow's private information or reporting his misconduct, despite the accuracy of the report, are prohibited. The latter two abuses of free speech fall under the biblical prohibition of "You shall not go about as a talebearer among your people..." [Leviticus 19: 16]. Talebearing comes in two different forms: (1) reporting wrongdoing that someone is planning to do, or has already done, to the listener, and (2) reporting misconduct planned for someone other than the listener.[3]

Arguing for disclosure, however, is the biblical mandate "Do not stand idly by the blood of your neighbor..." [Leviticus 19: 16] (henceforth "Do not stand idly by"). While "Do not stand idly by" requires a bystander to take timely action to save a person from mortal danger, exegetical interpretation of this verse expands the duty to include taking timely action to avert a financial loss for someone.[4]

Does "Do not stand idly by" suspend the tale-bearing interdict completely? Addressing this issue, R. Israel Meir ha-Kohen Kagan [Radin, 1838-1933], in his classical work *HafetzHayyim,* answers in the negative. "Do not stand idly by," in the opinion of *Hafetz Hayyim,* does not suspend the talebearing interdict unless *W* satisfies a number of restrictive conditions. Note that the setting for *Hafetz Hayyim*'s criteria is that all principals are Jewish. His criteria are the following[5]:

1. Disclosing wrongdoing is permissible only if the objective of *W* is to achieve a legitimate benefit. The benefit may consist of making whole a victim, including himself, of some wrong suffered at the hands of an offender, such as theft, fraud or injury.

   Also qualifying as a benefit is a disclosure made to "degrade the evil in the eyes of the public." The benefit here is the deterrent effect that the disclosure will have on potential evildoers.[6]
2. The whistleblower (*W*) must be *certain* that the subject of his report (*S*) has committed the crime or transgression. If *S* is not guilty as accused, *W*'s report to the potential victim (*V*) is slander.
3. Unless *W* is certain that *S*will not accept his complaint, *W* must first ask *S* directly to desist from the conduct and make the necessary amends.
4. *W* must be reasonably certain that *V* will take his report on *S*'s misconduct seriously. Otherwise, the disclosure should not be made. Moreover, without the prospect of credibility, the disclosure could be counterproductive. For example, suppose *V* initially rejects *W*'s report. Subsequently, *V* becomes disenchanted with *S* and regrets that he rejected *W*'s report. When *V* confronts *S* with an accusation of wrongdoing, *V* tells *S* that he (*V*) should have heeded W's report all along. Invoking *W*'s report in his confrontation with *S* violates for *V* the tale-bearing prohibition. *V*'s tale-bearing infraction is indirectly brought on by *W*'s initial report.
5. In informing on *S, W*'s objective should be for *V* to summon *S* to a Jewish court to decide the case.
6. If *W* assesses that his report will cause *S* to suffer more sever penalties than what is due him under Jewish law, the disclosure should not be made.
7. The damaging report must be known to *W* first-hand. If not, *Ha-fetz Hayyim* is unresolved about whether the disclosure should be made. In any event, *W* may not present his report as fact, but may merely disclose what he has heard and advise the concerned party to exercise caution.
8. Since exaggeration is falsehood, *W* must be careful not to exaggerated the reported offense.

9. In reporting against *S*, *W*'s actions should be motivated entirely by a desire to secure what is rightfully his or to show zealousness for truth and justice. If the motivation behind the revelation is, however, a long-standing grudge against the offender or a desire to ridicule or degrade him for his present misdeed, the disclosure should not be made.

   This rule applies only if the sole benefit *W* seeks is to shame the evildoer to effect a deterrent for the future. If, however, the benefit *W* seeks is something tangible, such as the restoration of stolen property, *W* should make his disclosure despite his impure motive.[7]
10. If *W*'s legitimate objectives can be achieved by other means, tale bearing should be avoided. Similarly, in seeking remedy against *S*, *W* must make every effort to minimize *S*'s degradation. Indeed, if minimizing *S*'s offense in his report to *V* does not compromise *W*'s objective, this must be done.

3. Drawing Out the Implications of *Hafetz Hayyim*'s Criteria

Hafetz Hayyim's criteria present several issues for comparison with secular business ethics. One issue relates to the type of wrongdoing *W* observes.

In the opinion of Richard De George, a prominent secular business ethicist, the moral issue for *W* is limited to the instance where the wrongdoing will harm the public. When, however, the wrongdoing harms only the owners of a firm, such as when *W* has evidence that a co-worker is taking kickbacks from a supplier, there is no duty to inform on the wrongdoer. Moreover, if *W* decides to inform on the wrongdoer, *W* has no duty to inform the wrongdoer before reporting on him.[8]

De George's distinction between types of wrongdoers is clearly inconsistent with *Hafetz Hayyim*'s view. In *Hafetz Hayyim*'s view, the moral dilemma is the same regardless of whether the harm affects the public or only a private firm or individual.

Another opportunity for a comparative analysis entails the following moral dilemma. Suppose an auditor working for a pharmaceutical firm discovers that the patent his company obtained for its high blood pressure medicine was based on fraudulent data. In fact, the medication is ineffectual and could even be fatal if taken in combination with other drugs. The company offers to fire the project manager and withdraw the drug on the basis of purported marketing miscalculations. *Hafetz Hayyim*'s tenth condition says, other things being equal, *W* should accept the deal and remain silent about the scandal.

Hafetz Hayyim's insistence that *W*'s complaint, if not resolved, should get aired in a Jewish court, raises the issue of whether his protocol is in basic conflict with American law. It is not. American law imposes no duty for one who happens to have witnessed the commission of a crime or a crime in progress to stop the crime or even report what he knows to the police.[9]

However, the issue of different treatment proceeding from the two legal systems still remains. Assessing how large the difference is begins with the notion that disputes between Jews must be adjudicated according to Jewish law in a Jewish court.[10] But, consider that in monetary matters, the principle is "the law of the kingdom is law."[11] How expansively this dictum is interpreted will have a lot to say about the size of the gap. In this respect, the broad conceptualization R. Moshe Isserles [*Rema,* Poland, 1525 or 1530-1572] proposed for this principle[12] enjoys widespread acceptance.[13] In his view, the ambit of the dictum, with few exceptions, extends to civil matters that either benefit the government or were enacted for the benefit of the people of the land.[14]

Falling within *Rema*'s ambit is the duty of the Jewish court to affirm and enforce government rules and regulations pertaining to commercial activity, such as rent control. When *W*'s disclosure of wrongdoing pertains to violations of government rules for the marketplace, the Jewish court will essentially affirm the secular law in this matter.[15]

Whistleblowing cases often involve the reporting of criminal conduct. Jewish courts, however, other than in the State of Israel, have no standing in criminal matters. Does the concern that the accused will be treated more harshly in the secular criminal system mean that the complaint will just fall through the cracks? Not necessarily. When the perpetrator is a threat to society, as is the case when the wrongdoing is a violent crime[16] or the making of counterfeit money,[17] there is a duty to report the criminal to the secular authorities. Here, the primary concern is that the dangerous individual should be removed from society and the anticipation that the perpetrator will be treated more harshly in secular court is not a consideration.

The ambit of cases where *W*'s complaint may end up with no forum occurs when the wrongdoing is a non-violent crime that does not endanger society as a whole, such as tax evasion and embezzlement. Considerable debate exists among Jewish law authorities whether informing on the culprit to the appropriate government bodies is permissible. One of the sticking points is that these crimes usually carry with them prison sentences, and statistics show that a significant minority of prisoners are criminally assaulted while serving their jail sentences. In these instances, whistleblowing could cause the wrongdoer to be subjected to possibly life-threatening danger and punishment that is much harsher than Jewish law would prescribe.[18]

4. The Personal and Financial Responsibility of the Whistleblower

We now address the issue of to what extent must the prospective *W* sacrifice his own well-being and financial interests in bringing the wrongdoer to justice.

The issue entails a number of scenarios. In one scenario, *W*'s report will extricate an individual from a life-threatening danger. An analogous case occurs when an individual (*R*) can physically rescue someone from a life-threatening situation such as drowning. In that case, authorities rule that *R* is prohibited from attempting the rescue if the rescue operation would endanger *R*'s life in a substantial way.[19] If, however, the rescue operation entails only inconsequential danger, *R* is *required* to undertake the rescue mission and should not be overly concerned with his own safety.[20]

In the above scenarios, authorities dispute the extent of *R*'s financial responsibility. Some limit it to 20 percent of his wealth, while others require *R* to expend his entire wealth, if necessary.[21] In any case, the one who was saved is obligated to reimburse *R* for the necessary expenditures *R* incurred.[22]

A variation of the above case occurs when the threat to life is not to an individual but rather to the public, and the rescue operation endangers *R*'s life. Authorities are here in dispute about whether *R* is required to undertake the rescue operation when more than one person's life is threatened.[23]

Let's apply the above rules to the whistleblower case. Suppose *W*'s disclosure would save someone's life, but *W* assesses that making the disclosure would endanger his own life. Here, *W* is exempt from making the disclosure. Suppose, however, that the disclosure would save many lives, as for example, disclosing a safety design defect in a nuclear plant. Here, some authorities require the disclosure, notwithstanding that doing so puts *W*'s own life in danger. When the disclosure would save one or many lives and involvement would not endanger *W*'s own life, *W* must expend, if necessary, at least 20 percent of his resources to insure that his disclosure gets the attention it requires. *W*'s ability to recover his losses will, however, depend on whether the beneficiaries of his disclosure can be identified. Such identification would be well nigh impossible when the beneficiaries are identified only as the general public. In that instance, it takes government legislation to both set *W*'s reimbursement fee and, when called for, an appropriate reward for his heroic action.

Suppose *W*'s disclosure would not save lives, but only avert a financial loss for someone, but making the disclosure would cause a loss for *W*.

Since making the disclosure would run counter to *W*'s own financial interests, he need not place his fellow's interests before his own financial interests. Under those circumstances, however, it is praiseworthy to make the disclosure and doing so would be regarded as a supererogatory act.[24] The assessment of financial loss is not an exculpating factor for *W*, however, when *W* himself is also guilty of the wrongdoing.

The discussion regarding the limits of the financial duty of *W* is very relevant for whistleblowing cases. Consider that whistleblowers usually fare very poorly at the hands of their company. Most are fired. In some cases, they are shut out of their whole industry. If they are not fired, they are frequently passed over for promotion and are treated as pariahs.[25] It is therefore legitimate for a potential whistleblower to consider that he will lose his job as a result of his disclosure.

5. Organizational Structure to Insure that Disclosure is not Suppressed

Implementing *Hafetz Hayyim*'s protocol within the framework of a corporate culture that treats *W* as a pariah almost guarantees that disclosure of wrongdoing will be suppressed. Consider, if *W* can make a solid case that his company was guilty of fraud in a contract it executed a number of years before, *W* may quickly assess, rightly or wrongly, that disclosing the matter will fall on deaf ears, and the more noise he makes about it, the more likely he will get fired. At the same time, W's supervisor may worry about the reputational harm the company would suffer because of the revelation. Besides, if the defrauded client has not discovered the fraud by now, he may never discover it.

The scenario above illustrates that the moral weakness of the people who could act on the fraud must be overcome by changing their cost-benefit analyses. This objective can be put in Jewish theological terms. It consists of conducting our interpersonal relations in a manner that emulates God's mercy toward humankind (*imitatio Dei,* i.e., "imitation of God").[26]

One aspect of God's mercy is that He weakens of the power of the Evil Inclination for those who strive for moral betterment.[27] Emulating this Divine Attribute translates into a duty for companies to set up a system of "sticks" and "carrots" that tilt members of the firm to virtue and away from wrongdoing.[28]

To assure that complaints of wrongdoing are given a "fair airing" within the company, let's consider the following two ideas. Both relate to organizational structure.

To both encourage employees to come forward and also change the perception that a supervisor will not give serious attention to a complaint, Professor Michael Davis suggests that a firm establish multiple lines of communication. One approach is to implement an "open door" policy, which allows subordinates to approach a senior executive directly. Still another method is to give employees routine access to more than one superior in the organization. Such arrangements give a manager reason to be thankful that he has heard the bad news from a subordinate rather than from a superior and to respond in a way likely to satisfy the subordinate. At the same time, the subordinate has saved the manager from being "blindsided."[29]

Professor Davis' ideas can be expressed in *imitatio Dei* terms. By creating multiple lines of communication, a "stick" is effectively placed in front of an employee's immediate superior. The message is that the superior will jeopardize his own position if he does not give the complaint serious consideration because the subordinate can continue to pursue his objective through other channels.

Recall that *Hafetz Hayyim* proposes that whistleblowing is legitimate only if the objective is to achieve a bona fide benefit. In elaborating on this point, *Hafetz Hayyim* specifically includes *W*'s need to vent his suspicions against someone as meeting the standard.[30]

Including the venting of suspicions as a bona fide benefit requires clarification. Tale bearing is a moral pitfall regardless of its motivation. If *W* does not preface his report by telling his listener (*L*) that his intention is merely to use him as a sounding board, and that *L* should not divulge anything he is about to say, *L* might accept the evil report and be guilty of accepting a tale-bearing report. Moreover, unless a relationship of trust exists between *W* and *L, W* can never be sure that his admonition for confidentiality will be heeded. The above concerns leads to the proposition that *W* may not vent his complaints to *L* to mitigate his disquietude *unless L* is a confidential person and *W* tells him that he desires only to use him as a sounding board and that he should not reveal the information to anyone.

Understanding *Hafetz Hayyim*'s "venting out suspicion" in the above limited manner leads to the proposition, discussed in the secular business ethics literature,[31] that an ethics officer or ombudsman would serve a very useful purpose in reducing illegitimate whistleblowing. The ombudsman would be the person to approach if anyone were concerned that the firm was committing wrongdoing. The ombudsman would then be required to evaluate the information provided to him and determine if further action was warranted. The ombudsman would be required to conduct his investigation while maintaining W's anonymity. If *W* brought his concerns about company policy or the conduct of individuals within the firm to the ombudsman, his report would be protected speech, regardless of the evidence *W* presented to substantiate the report. The position of ombudsman would thus foster *healthy dissent* within the firm.

Once an ombudsman evaluates *W*'s report and determines that the matter should be dropped, *W* may not engage in tale bearing regarding the conduct or the policy. If *W* engages in tale bearing after the ombudsman has determined that *W*'s concerns are baseless, *W*'s speech would no longer be protected speech and the firm would be entitled to discipline *W* and even fire him. One caveat should, however, be noted: If *W* can make a case that will "stick" against the wrongdoer or can show that the firm's policy is dangerous to the public's welfare, *W*'s speech should be treated as protected speech. In fact, *W*'s ability to make the case against the wrongdoing should be taken as *prima facie* evidence that the ombudsman was not doing his job.[32]

While the two ideas just mentioned find support in Jewish theological thought, the *imitatio Dei* principle as a guidepost for government policy has its limitations. This is so because *imitatio Dei* does no more than inform us of various forms of kindness we should engage in based on our traditions of the various ways God manifested His compassion, mercy and kindnesses in his dealing with humankind. But, the general rule for engaging in acts of kindness, as opposed to the charity duty to the needy, is that the duty extends only to exertion of toil and effort, not to a monetary expenditure. The only exception is that when the expenditure is trifling, it is improper for someone to rely on this exemption and take no action.[33]

Applying these principles to organizational structure says that the moral duty of the firm to adopt these measures obtains only if implementing them entails only a trifling cost. In some instances, establishing multiple chains of communication for subordinates might fall into this category. However, hiring an ethics officer would entail a significant expense for all but huge firms. If implementing the ideas entails more than an immaterial expense, doing so is not required, but, rather is praiseworthy on a supererogatory level.

6. Whistleblowing Legislation and Jewish Law

In addressing the role for government here, the most basic point is that *imitatio Dei* is a mandate not only for the private citizen, but also for government.[34]

One application of the government's *imitatio Dei* duty here is straightforward. To encourage legitimate whistleblowing, the law should require that any *W* who follows *Hafetz Hayyim*'s protocol is entitled to job security and protection against discrimination.

In some instances, *W* might be deserving of a monetary award. A case in point is when *W*'s disclosure uncovers a fraud against the government and thereby allows the government to recover a significant amount of money. In that case, the U.S. False Claims Act [1863] views *W* in a *qui tam* (lit., standing in the shoes of the King) capacity and entitles him to a monetary award.[35]

While *W*'s expose is a public service, legislating a monetary award based on the *imitatio Dei* principle runs into the hurdle that this dictum cannot be invoked when the policy that is based on this dictum entails the incurring of a significant expenditure. But, herein lies the difference between what is proposed for government and what is proposed for the private person or business. Specifically, an amount that is substantial for a private entity is immaterial when the cost is shared by the entire federal tax base. Because the U.S. has a progressive income tax, the cost can be spread equitably over approximately 83 million taxpaying households.[36] Consequently, the cost for society for running this program would amount to a trifling per-household cost. Given the above considerations, the proposed legislation is within the parameters of the *imitatio Dei* principle.

A variation of the above case is when *W*'s disclosure averts identifiable loss for a private firm. Here, legislation calling for the identifiable beneficiaries of *W*'s disclosure to compensate him with a percentage of the money his efforts recover will often not amount to only a trifling sum per capita. Legislation taking this form cannot therefore be defended on the basis of *imitatio Dei.* Nonetheless, one could argue that since the beneficiaries are identifiable, a quasi contract exists between *W* and the beneficiaries. The analog in Jewish law is the compensation entitlement for the one who rescues (*R*) lost property and returns it to the owner (*O*). The relevant scenario entails three critical features: (1) to effect the salvage operation, *R* had to abandon his own work; (2) *R* did not stipulate a fee in advance for his service with *O*; and (3) when *R* undertook the salvage operation, *O* or someone who could represent *O* was not available. Under those circumstances, Jewish law presumes that a quasi contract exists between *R* and *O.* Accordingly, *R* has a legitimate claim for both his lost wages and any out-of-pocket expenses.[37]

Applying this analogue to the case at hand supports the view that the law should enforce the quasi contract between *W* and the beneficiaries. In addition, because the entire tax base owes an *imitatio Dei* duty to insure that every business operates with the proper incentives to encourage legitimate whistleblowers to come forward, the government should pay *W* an additional fee consisting of a percentage of the money he recovers.

To minimize the cost to society for compensating *W* with a percentage of the losses recovered, the government could sell its mandated financial obligations to *W* to private insurance companies.

Not all policies emanating from *imitatio Dei,* however, should be given equal weight. The most fundamental policy would be to tax society to finance programs that would foster the moral personality and an environment of trust in society. The success of such programs would translate into a significant reduction in the incidences of wrongdoing, thereby obviating the need for whistleblowing. Elsewhere we have argued that the thrust of this program consists of moral education for youth and continues into the workplace. We show that creating an environment of trust takes on the elements of a pure public good and hence warrants government subsidization.[38]

7. Summary and Conclusion

In Jewish law, the moral dilemma that the whistleblower faces is a conflict between competing ethical duties. On the one hand, the prohibition against standing idly by when one can save a fellow from harm tells *W* to disclose the wrongdoing. On the other hand, the prohibition against talebearing tells *W* to remain silent. *Hafetz Hayyim* resolves the conflict in favor of nondisclosure unless ten restrictive conditions are met. When those conditions are met, disclosure is obligatory. Nonetheless, if the loss *W* is trying to prevent is only monetary, *W* need not sacrifice his own financial interests to advance the financial interests of the potential victim.

Following *Hafetz Hayyim*'s criteria will inevitably result in some wrongdoing going unreported. That result is entirely consistent with American law because American law does not require a person who witnesses a crime to stop the crime or even report what he knows to the police.

To be sure, *Hafetz Hayyim*'s criteria place the wrongdoing within the jurisdiction of the Jewish court system. Several considerations, however, lead to the conclusion that the result would often be consistent with secular law. A case in point is when the wrongdoing is a violent crime or misconduct that otherwise threatens the welfare of society. Here, *W* must turn over his complaint to the appropriate secular authority. In addition, in monetary matters, "the law of the Kingdom is law" requires the Jewish court to affirm and enforce government rules and regulations. The sticking point, however, is when the offense is criminal and does not threaten the welfare of the community as a whole, but carries with it a jail sentence. Since statistics show that a significant percentage of prisoners are assaulted while serving their sentences, the perpetrator would be faced with a penalty far greater than Jewish law would prescribe. In those circumstances, many authorities would require *W* to suppress his disclosure.

To assure that complaints of wrongdoing are given a "fair airing" within the company but also promote harmony in the workplace, Jewish law would recommend a number of policies that relate to organizational structure. One idea is the hiring of an ombudsman. His task would be to let workers vent their complaints, and to facilitate legitimate whistleblowing. A second idea is establishing multiple channels of communication in the workplace. Both ideas proceed from the *imitatio Dei* imperative. That imperative would, however, require only policies that entail "toil and effort" without significant expenditure. If the policy entails significant expenditure, it would praiseworthy, but not mandatory.

Within the framework of the *imitatio Dei* principle and its authority to enforce quasi contracts, the role for government would be to guarantee job security for the legitimate whistleblower and provide financial rewards for heroic action when indicated.

Notes

1. In the secular literature, the desideratum arguing against whistleblowing is the loyalty an employee owes his/her company. Consider that indiscriminate external whistleblowing puts the company and members of the firm at maximum legal exposure for any wrongdoing committed. Keeping the incriminating documents and other evidence within the firm, however, gives the company the opportunity to come up with a strategy that minimizes its potential liability and maximizes its profits. (Leonard M. Baynes, "Just Pucker and Blow?: An Analysis of Corporate Whistleblowers, The Duty of Care, The Duty of Loyalty, and The Sarbanes-Oxley Act," St John Law Review, Fall 2002, Vol. 76, Issue 4, pp.883-888) From the standpoint of Jewish law, the desideratum of loyalty plays no role in deciding the whistleblower's dilemma. What the worker owes his firm is meticulous dedication to the tasks assigned him. However, if the worker knows of wrongdoing, the worker's duty is to remonstrate with the wrongdoer. If the assessment is that doing so would be fruitless, he is duty bound to engage in whistleblowing, provided the restrictive conditions discussed in the text are satisfied. (For details and sources, see Aaron Levine, Moral Issues of the Marketplace in Jewish Law [New York: Yashar Books, 2005, pp. 426—128]).

2. The source for this prohibition is either Leviticus 19:16 or Deuteronomy 23:10. See *Ketubbot* 46a.
3. R. Israel Meir ha-Kohen Kagan (Radin, 1838-1933), *Hafetz Hayyim, Lavin* 1—17, *Essin* 1-14.
4. *Safra* at Leviticus 19:16 *ot* 41; R. Israel Meir ha-Kohen Kagan, *Hafetz Hayyim, Be'er Mayim Hayyim, Hilkhot Issurei Rekhilut* 9:1.
5. *Hafetz Hayyim,* op. cit., *Hilkhot Issurei Lashon Ha-Ra* 10:1-17; *Hilkhot Rekhilut* 9:1-15.
6. R. Binyamin Cohen, *Sefer Hafetz Hayyim im Perush Helkat Binyamin, Hafetz Hayyim,* p. 266 *ot 11.*
7. Ibid, pp. 266-267, 339, 352-353.
8. Richard T. De George, *Business Ethics Concepts and Cases,* 4th edition (Upper Saddle River, NJ: Prentice Hall,1998), pp. 242-246, 257-259.
9. See sources quoted by Michael J. Broyde, *The Pursuit of Justice in Jewish Law, Second Edition* (New York: Yashar Books, Inc. 2007), p. 89.
10. R. Solomon b. Isaac (Troyes, 1040-1105), *Rashi, Exodus* 21:1.
11. Samuel, *Gittin* 10b.
12. R. Moses Isserles (Poland, 1525 or 1530-1572), *Rema, Shulhan Arukh., Hoshen Mishpat* 369:1).
13. R. Moshe Feinstein (New York, 1895-1986), *Iggerot Moshe, Hoshen Mishpat* 2:62;
14. *Rema,* op. cit., 369:11.
15. R. Yosef Eliyahu Henkin (1881-1973), *TeshuvotIvra,* vol. 2, p. 176 and *Teshuvot Ivra,* vol.2, p.176. Historically Jewish communities in European countries were given the authority to operate as autonomous, self-governing entities, even in respect to criminal law. Nowadays, in the absence of self-autonomy, the Jewish community in democratic countries, according to R. Henkin, cedes its duty to legislate in matters of social welfare to the various secular governmental bodies."
16. *Rema,* op. cit., 388:7.
17. *Rema,* op. cit., 388:12.
18. For a comprehensive discussion of the issues of being an informant, see Broyde, op. cit., pp. 79-115.
19. R. Moshe Schick (Hungary, 1807-1879), *Maharam Schick al Taryag Mitzvot, mitzvah* 238; R. Ovadiah Yosef (Israel, 1920), *Yehaveh Da'at* 84; R. Eliezer Yehuda Waldenberg (Israel, 1915-2006), *TzitzEliezer* 9:45.
20. R. Jehiel Michel Epstein (Belarus, 1829-1908), *Ar. ha-Sh.,* op. cit., 426:4.
21. For sources, see Aaron Levine, *Moral Issues of the Marketplace in Jewish Law* (New York: Yashar Books, 2005), pp. 433-437.
22. Ibid, pp. 466-469.
23. Ibid, p. 431.
24. R. Zalman Nehemia Goldberg (Israel, contemporary), *"Ba-Hiyyuvei GemilutHesed"* in *YadREMle-ZehkerEliezerMeirLipschitz,* Jerusalem 1975, pp. 97-111.
25. For sources, see *Moral Issues of the Marketplace in Jewish Law,* op. cit., 437-438.
26. *Sotah* 14a; *Sifrei* on Exodus 34:6-7; Maimonides, *Sefer ha-Mitzvot, Mitzvat Aseh,* no.8, Yad, *De'ot* 1:6.
27. *Resh Lakish, Kiddushin* 30b.
28. For an elaboration on this theme, see Aaron Levine, *Case Studies in Jewish Business Ethics* (Hoboken, New Jersey: Ktav Publishing Company Inc., Yeshiva University Press, 2000), pp. 182-188.
29. Michel Davis, "Avoiding The Tragedy of Whistleblowing," *Business and Professional Ethics Journal,* vol. 8, no. 4, pp. 3-19.

30. *Hafetz Hayyim, Hilkhot Issurei Lashon ha-Ra, k'lal* 10:14.
31. Cf. *Business Ethics Concepts and Cases,* 4th edition, op. cit., 259-261.
32. Ibid.
33. Rav Judah in the name of Rav, *Bava Metzia* 33a and commentary of R. Joseph Hayyim b. Elijah al-Hakham (Baghdad, 1834-1909), *Ban Yehoyada,* ad locum. 26.
34. Maimonides, *Guide of the Perplexed,* trans. S. Pines (Chicago: University of Chicago Press, 1963), chap. 54, pp. 126-127.
35. *Moral Issues of the Marketplace in Jewish Law,* op. cit., pp. 458-459.
36. This statistic is for 2006. See "Fiscal Facts Number of Americans Paying Zero Federal Income Tax Grows to 43.4 Million," Tax Foundation, March 30, 2006, at http://www.taxfoundation.org/research/show/1410.html.
37. Aaron Levine, *"Be-Inyan Sekhar Betailah* (opportunity cost)," *Kol Yaakov,* no.9 (New York: Rabbi Jacob Joseph School, 1976), pp. 39-85.
38. Aaron Levine, "Aspects of the Lemons Problem as Treated in Jewish Law," *Journal of Law and Religion,* vol. xxiii, no.2, 2007-08, pp. 420-423. 26.

On Whistleblowing: From the View of Engineering Ethics

Wang Nan
College of the Humanities and Social Sciences Graduate University of Chinese Academy of Sciences
Beijing, China

1. Introduction

This chapter intends to study the issue of engineers' whistleblowing. The definition and special features of whistleblowing will be given in the first part. The second part will analyze the nature of whistleblowing by reviewing the formative history of engineering briefly. The core of the chapter are the third and fourth parts. They will discuss the restricting factors in whistleblowing from four aspects, and put forward measures for promoting whistleblowing with actual examples at three levels.

Whistleblowing is an issue in all professions with regard to an array of topics (Martin, 2000, p. 138), and is particularly important in the engineering profession. As we know, the products of engineering activities, from food and housing to cars and space shuttles, are all closely related to human well-being and development. Engineers who often act as designer, manager, and executor in engineering activities, compared to other members of engineering community, which is composed of investors, managers and workers, play a greater role in significantly changing the reality of society. Engineers thus have to consider the moral problem of whether their work is producing something that will improve or harm human life. When engineers discover the potential for harm in their work should they point it out to prevent it from happening or keep silent? To choose the former is in fact to take an act of whistleblowing.

2. The Definition of Whistleblowing

It is necessary to examine the definition of whistleblowing before researching it. The word "whistleblowing" is a slang term. It derives from "blow the whistle," which described the practice of English Bobbies, who would blow their whistles when they noticed the commission of a crime. Since the early 1970s, whistleblowing has become a common means of describing dissent in a bureaucracy, particularly when issues of public health, safety, fraud, or abuse of office are involved (Johnson, 2002, p. 4).

In engineering ethics, the classical definition of is that "whistleblowing occurs when an employee or former employee conveys information about a significant moral problem to someone in a position to take action on the problem, and does so outside approved organizational channels (or against strong pressure)" (Martin, 1996, p. 172). What makes this definition unique is that it "does not mention the motives involved in the whistleblowing" (Martin, 1996, p. 173) and even it does not use the affective words of "misconduct," "wrongdoing" which are usually used in other definitions, etc. It implies that this definition avoids assumptions about whether the whistleblowers' motives and the matters they revealed are good or bad, which are the questions where there is no clear-cut answer to a certain extent, and it hence will treat "whistleblowing" on a descriptive level.

According to this definition, "whistleblowing" has the following special features: First, the whistleblower is a (former) employee of an organization, which gives him/her greater opportunities to share the relevant information. Second, when someone meets serious moral problems in which he/she believes, such as criminal, unethical or unjust behavior, or problems threatening the individual or public safety, well-being, he/she will undertake an act of "whistleblowing." Thirdly, there are two channels for the whistleblower to choose from: he/she can transmit the relevant information to a person inside or outside his/her organization. But in either case, the whistleblower will be confronted with great pressures and risks, for example, being transferred to another post, receiving a salary cut, or being dismissed. Finally, the recipient of "whistleblowing" is the person or group in a position to take action on the problem (as opposed, for example, to telling it to a relative or friend who is in no position to do anything) (Martin, 1996, p. 173). It indicated that the whistleblower expects the recipient to resolve or affect the serious moral problem he/she has put forward.

Generally, Whistleblowing can be divided into four different aspects: according to the recipient of whistleblowing, there is internal and external whistleblowing. The former occurs when the recipient of whistleblowing is inside the whistleblower's organization, and the latter occurs conversely. According to the ways of whistleblowing, there will be open and anonymous whistleblowing. The former occurs when someone takes whistleblowing action without revealing his/her identity or asks not to be named openly (a few people to a limited extent know his/her name), and the latter occurs conversely.

3. The Nature of Whistleblowing

The issue of whistleblowing has been central to some classic cases in engineering ethics, such as the Bay Area Rapid Transit case, the DC-10 case, and, above all, the Challenger case (Mitcham, 2005, p. 627). But it has caused much controversy. Some hold that whistleblowing is an act of betrayal on the part of engineers to their employers or organizations, and is an immoral act; others hold that whistleblowing protects public interests and constitutes heroic conduct. The cause lies in the fact that whistleblowing involves a series of moral conflicts, especially conflicts between loyalty to employers, to the profession, and to the public. No topic in engineering ethics is more controversial than whistleblowing (Martin, 1996, p. 172). How and why does this happen? Let us review the formative history of engineer briefly.

Etymologically the word "engineer" and its cognates, which first appeared in the Middle Ages (Latin *ingeniator*) to designate builders and operators of battering rams, catapults, and other "engine of war" (Mitcham, 1994, p. 144). It is clear that the soldier who designed, built, and operated military machines was referred to early on as engineers. Obedience is the first duty of a soldier. Engineers hence should obey commands was the mission of this profession from the birth of it.

In the latter half of eighteenth century, on one hand, under the two industrial revolutions' impetus, the number of engineers increased rapidly; on the other hand, with the popularity of engineering education, the technical knowledge grasped by engineers increased. Engineers began to consider themselves an important force promoting the overall progress of mankind, and they held themselves responsible for everything independently. As a result, engineers began to regard the job they engaged in as an independent profession, equal to that of the traditional professions. They should be loyal to their own profession as well as being loyal to their employers. Consequently, the tension between the engineers and their employers began to appear.

After the Second World War, with the quick development of science and technology, people's multifarious material and cultural needs could be met, while the negative effects of engineering activities were becoming more and more outstanding and serious. The engineering profession was blamed for as a cause of environmental pollution, for design defects in consumer goods and for excessive loyalty in protecting the agreements with employers, etc. (Mitcham, 1999, p. 90). This led to rethinking of engineers' responsibilities: the fact that the good, positive and predictable effects and the bad, negative and unpredictable effects co-existing in engineering demanded that engineers be responsible for public interests, in addition to responsible for their employers and the profession.

However, there are always conflicts among the triple commission of engineers. Profits are the paramount object for enterprises. Entrepreneurs often make their fortune by fair means or foul, even at the expense of public interests. This situation put engineers in an ethical dilemma: they would either be loyal to employers, which meant that they should follow what employers say and keep quite, or be loyal to the profession and public, which meant that they should refuse to practice fraud and ensure the realization of public interests. When engineers choose the latter, they become whistleblowers.

Therefore, the facts above clearly show that whistleblowing is an inherent ethical dilemma of the engineering profession in the context of modern engineering, a necessary result of the complexity of modern engineering technology, and an inevitable phenomenon that arose in certain period in the development of the engineering profession. It seemed that whistleblowing is disloyalty to employers or organizations, but it is not so. On one hand, the purpose of the existence of organizations is providing service for realizing and protecting public interests. On the other hand, whistleblowing subordinates the long-term interests of organizations, and it can solve the problems in organizations as soon as possible to limit the damages. Consequently, whistleblowing is a kind of critical loyalty (Harris, Pritchard, Rabins, 2006, p. 152), namely the loyalty to employers and profession based on loyalty to public interests.

Whistleblowing has negative sides; for example, it is the proof of organizational trouble and management failure, it hurts the persons on whom the whistle is blown and whistleblowers' colleagues, who are innocents in many cases, (Davis, 1998, p. 76) but this should not stop whistleblowing. In its loyalty to employers, the profession, and the public interest, responsible whistleblowing is not bad news all around, it is very good news for the public interests protected by it (Martin, 2000, p. 142). It is necessary to take some measures to lessen the negative sides caused by whistleblowing and improve the protection of public interests to the greatest extent.

4. The Restricting Factors of Whistleblowing in Practice

Accompany with the rapid development of global economy, a plethora of engineering projects having a close bearing on the national economy and the people's livelihood have been put into operation. This hence will undoubtedly provide a golden opportunity to engineering profession. In the course of projects construction, because engineers always have to face with ethical problem about how to deal with the threat to public safety, lives and property coming from certain engineering product or certain aspect of engineering project, their ethical consciousness is closely related to ensuring the progress and quality of engineering projects. However, can whistleblowing take place in a free manner? The engineering practice has proved that it isn't always the case. The characteristics of the engineering profession, the influence of social and cultural matters, and the damage caused by whistleblowing, etc, restrict the act of whistleblowing.

4.1. Complexity of Modern Engineering

On the one hand, modern engineering has become a collective activity, accomplished by cooperation among many individuals and organizations from different countries or regions. For example, there were about 2,000 enterprises, more than 200 colleges, and more than 80 research institutes involved in the Apollo Program, and the total number of people reached 300,000. Consequently, as a member of large collective activities, an individual engineer could not identify his/her role in it. On the other hand, a modern engineering project always integrates many technologies. For instance, the manufacturing of an aerospace vehicle involves a wide range of specialized knowledge, including mechanics, thermodynamics, material science, medicine, electronic technique, automatic control, jet propulsion, computer science, vacuum technique, cryogenic technology, semiconductor technology, and so on. It is often said that differences in the profession make one feel worlds apart. There is even a great deal of difference between different specialties in the same subject. The consequences of one engineering activity are far beyond the imagination of engineers who are good at different specialties. This aspect rendered engineers' sense of duty to public vague and dispersed.

4.2. The Sense of Hierarchy

Engineers are multi-taskers in engineering activities, designers, managers, and executors. But no matter which role they play, they are also employees of a company or organization, so they must be under the supervision of employers. The sense of hierarchy is not only reflected in the relationship between higher and lower, but is also manifested in the relationships among the same ranks.

The younger engineers have less experience and seniority, and may not be entrusted with important tasks and even be uninformed of the whole scheme of an engineering project. This limits the professional self-government of engineers. Hence they come to regard themselves as cogs in the industrial machine or faithful servants of the overseers of organizations to be followed fanatically. Under the circumstances, they may neglect the force or influence they exert in engineering activities.

4. 3. The Influence of Social Elements

Engineering is today captive to society, and it is a social process in which engineers participate rather than simply something that engineers do (Goldman, 1991, p. 121-122). In other words, the engineer's job will be deeply affected by the mixture of economical, political, military, cultural, and environmental elements. The decisions on which engineering projects should be done and how to do them is usually based on a nation's, organization's, or enterprise's economical, political, or military purpose. For example, during the Second World War, for the sake of success in the world-wide anti-fascist war, the United States sponsored and fulfilled the Manhattan Project. In order to prevent the fascists from knowing the true purpose of this project, only a few people were informed about it. Never did the engineers who were left in the dark about the project dream that they involved in the manufacture of weapons of mass destruction. This is just one example; there are a host of similar instances. As a result, it is often difficult for engineers to make ethical judgments accurately and timely in such situations.

In addition, the influence of the cultural environment in whistleblowing should not be neglected. The thinking concept, value system, behavior norms, cultural production, social prevailing in different countries or regions vary. This leads to different opinions of whistleblowers. For example, in Chinese traditional culture, the three cardinal guides (ruler guides subject, father guides son and husband guides wife) and the five constant virtues (benevolence, righteousness, propriety, wisdom and fidelity) demand that people be absolutely loyal to ruler, father, and husband, and not harm others. In a cultural environment like this, the emphasis of engineering ethics is public and enterprises or organizations should obey national interests without question, and the employee should be loyal to enterprises or organizations absolutely. As a result, whistleblowers usually are mistaken for informants, traitors, etc. This misunderstanding puts a lot of stress on whistleblowers' spirit and undermines the act of whistleblowing.

4.4. The Loss of Individual Interests

Whistleblowers are always under the serious threat of salary cuts, loss of the chance of promotion, job loss, and rejection by prospective employers in the same industry, posing particular difficulties for individual development in the workshop. As one of the members of a family, engineers have an obligation to support and assist their parents and rear and educate their children. Having their individual development in workshop blocked by whistleblowing makes them unable to meet their familial obligations. These economic and obligations to family are very important parts in weighing the advantages and disadvantages before making the decision to blow the whistle.

5. Measures on Promoting Whistleblowing

In China we have an old saying: It is better to lead than to block. Whistleblowing is a necessary phenomenon in professional development, and it should be handled well in relation to the protection of the public interest and development of the engineering profession. Thus, avoiding whistleblowing is not a good approach to resolving the problem. Instead, looking for the measures to promote and improve whistleblowing is, to certain extent, the best way. The measures on promoting whistleblowing can be viewed from macroscopic, middle and microcosmic three levels, i.e., national, institutional, and individual levels.

5.1. The Measures at the Macroscopic Level

Macroscopic measures here refer mainly to government behavior. The government can take measures such as the enactment of laws, rules, and regulations, the establishment of specialized divisions, etc., to encourage whistleblowing and protect whistleblowers. The federal government of the United States has done a highly effective job in this regard. The following provide some examples.

The federal government of the United States enacted a series of laws, rules, and regulations to encourage whistleblowing in 1980s, such as the Ethics in Government Act (1978) and a Code of Ethics for Government Service (1980), which set financial disclosure requirements for public officials, and even explicitly required them "put loyalty to the highest moral principals and to country above loyalty to government persons, party, or department."

In order to protect whistleblowers from reprisal, the federal government took measures through administrative legislation. The Whistleblower Protection Act (WPA, 1989) and Sarbanes-Oxley Act (SOX, 2002) were the most prominent ones. The former provided statutory protections for federal employees who engage in whistleblowing, while the latter provided them for corporate whistleblowers "which are left unprotected under current law" (Kohn, Kohn, Colapinto, 2004, p. 3). This has been praised as "earthshaking" in law reform (Kohn, Kohn, Colapinto, 2004, p. xi).

Moreover, the federal government established a specialized division the Office of Special Council (OSC) to deal with whistleblowing. The primary mission of OSC "is to safeguard the merit system by protecting federal employees and applicants from prohibited personnel practices, especially reprisal for whistleblowing." The OSC seeks corrective action remedies (such as back pay and reinstatement), by negotiation or from the Merit Systems Protection Board (MSPB), for injuries suffered by whistleblowers and other complainants.

5.2. The Measures at Middle Level

Middle-level measures may originate from two sources: engineering unions and institutions and nonengineering organizations.

Engineering unions and institutions appeared along with the emergence of modern engineering. They have focused their attentions not only on the advancement of technology, but also on the promulgation and enforcement of ethics codes for members of the profession (Unger, 1994, p. 136). Whistleblowing is also one of their great concerns, for it is inevitably an ethical dilemma. But what measures should engineering unions and institutions take concerning whistleblowing?

First of all, engineering unions and institutions can state explicitly the requirements and responsibilities of whistleblowing in charters or codes of ethics to support and encourage whistleblowing.

At present, few engineering unions and institutions have set the requirements of whistleblowing down in their charters or codes of ethics in many countries. In the United States, the 1990 version of the Institute of Electrical and Electronics Engineers (IEEE) code included the unprecedented mention of a "duty of disclosure" (Frederiksen, et al., 2007, p. 266). In Australia, the Code of Ethics of Institution of Engineers Australia (IEAust) requires engineers to do more than warn their superiors about such life-threatening problems; they are expected to blow the whistle, for example, to inform the relevant government authorities of the situation (Beder, 1998, p. 252-253). Moreover, IEAust set out "practical and common sense guidance" in its code of ethics for members to instruct them when they should take an act of whistleblowing, such as, "make any objections to unethical practices promptly, keep supervisors informed of your actions, consult colleagues for advice, seek legal advice," etc. (Beder, 1998, p. 279).

Engineering unions and institutions can not only establish guidelines for whistleblowing, but also reward whistleblowers or provide funds to help them with emergency expenses or legal costs, especially when they have adhered to the ethical principles in the face of great difficulties. It will help to resolve actual difficulties of whistleblowers. Most importantly, it will represent the supporting and accepting treatment from the profession and even the public.

The Carl Barus Award is one of the most influential and important whistleblower awards. In 1978, the IEEE Society for Social Implications of Technology, chaired by Stephen H. Unger, awarded three whistleblowers involved in the Bay Area Rapid Transit (BART) incident the Award for Outstanding Service in the Public Interest, whose recipients would "demonstrate high ethical standards in protecting or promoting the interests and safety of the public," for having courageously adhered to the letter and the spirit of the IEEE ethics code. In 1991, the award was renamed the Carl Barus Award. It has been awarded ten times for twelve people till now.

In addition, engineering unions and institutions can take measures to promote whistleblowing, for instance, by installing an ethics hot-line, rating employers, legal defense services, support in the job market, making pensions portable, etc (Unger, 1994, 153-156).

As far as nonengineering organizations are concerned, their functions in promoting whistleblowing are just as good as or even better that those of engineering unions and institutions. The reason is that nonengineering organizations, especially the nonprofit and nongovernment organizations will always deal with the matters of whistleblowing as bystanders or onlookers. They try to look at things in an objective and fair-minded attitude. The conclusions drawn by them are receptive. With regard to these characteristics of nonengineering organizations, they can take some measures, such as, providing free legal help to whistleblowers, gathering information from various resources to bring the real facts to light, setting up special reporting hotlines or networks, and offering rewards for whistleblowers, etc.

The Government Accountability Project (GAP) is one such examples. As the United States' leading whistleblower protection organization, GAP (founded in 1977) is a thirty-year-old nonprofit public interest group that promotes government and corporate accountability through counseling, by offering legal expertise, by conducting investigations to help expose cover-ups, by working to strengthen whistleblower laws, and by disseminating information and publishing scholarly articles. Currently, GAP is in the process of educating and training about whistleblowing around the world (Johnson, 2002, p. 14).

5.3. The Measures at Microcosmic Level

As an individual, what should an engineer do about promoting whistleblowing? The most important thing is that engineers should take a prudent and responsible attitude toward whistleblowing. They must understand that the purpose of acting is to protect the public interest not personal interests, such as jealousy or revenge. Only in this way can they try their best to think of the consequences of moral problems sufficiently according to the relevant information, in order to avoid subjective and one-sided guesswork. Calm and objective reflection may ensure that the engineer realize clearly the seriousness and the scale of whistleblowing. It will help the engineer to decide rationally whether to blow the whistle.

Moreover, engineers should improve their ability in dealing with whistleblowing, and using the methods and techniques properly when they undertake an act of whistleblowing. The following is some advice (Martin, 1996, p. 177-178):

1. Except for extremely rare emergencies, always try working first through normal organizational channels. Get to know both the formal and informal (unwritten) rules for making appeals within the organization.

2. Be prompt in expressing objections. Waiting too long may create the appearance of plotting for you advantage and seeking to embarrass a supervisor.
3. Proceed in a tactful, low-key manner. Be considerate of the feelings of others involved. Always keep focused on the issues themselves, avoiding any personal criticisms that might create antagonism and deflect attention from solving those issues.
4. As much as possible, keep supervisors informed of your actions, both through informal discussion and formal memorandums.
5. Be accurate in your observations and claims, and keep formal records documenting relevant events.
6. Consult trusted colleagues for advice-avoid isolation.
7. Before going outside the organization, consult the ethics committee of your professional society.
8. Consult a lawyer concerning potential legal liabilities.

6. Conclusion

The formative history of engineering demonstrates that whistleblowing is an inevitable phenomenon at certain periods of development within the engineering profession. It may appear that whistleblowing constitutes disloyalty to employers. However, it reflects the unification of loyalty to employers, the profession and the public. Whether it will be handled well with regard to the protection of the public interest and the development of the engineering profession. As a result, promoting whistleblowing rather than avoiding it is the best approach to resolve the problem.

Could engineers blow the whistle without a hitch? The answer is no. The characteristics of the engineering profession, the influence of social and cultural matters, and the damage caused by whistleblowing, etc, will restrict engineers in undertaking an act of whistleblowing in practice. In accordance with the restricting factors existing in practice of whistleblowing, the measures on promoting whistleblowing can be viewed from three levels: at macroscopic, middle and microcosmic level, i.e. national, institutional and individual levels.

References

Beder, S., 1998, The New Engineer: Management and Professional Responsibility in a Changing World, South Yarra: Macmillan Education Australia.

Davis, M., 1998, Thinking like an Engineer: Studies in the Ethics of a Profession, New York: Oxford University Press US.

Frederiksen, J. F. et al (eds.), 2007, Philosophy in Engineering, Published by Academica.

Goldman, S. L., 1991, "The Social Captivity of Engineering." In: Durbin, P. T., eds. Critical Perspectives on Nonacademic Science and Engineering. Research in Technology Studies, Vol 4.

Harris, C. E., Pritchard, M. S., Rabins, M. J., Translated by Cong hang-qing, Shen Qi, et al., 2006, Engineering Ethics: Concepts & Cases (In Chinese), Beijing: Beijing Institute of Technology Press.

Johnson, R. A., 2002, Whistleblowing: When It Works-and Why, London: Lynne Rienner Publishers.

Kohn, S. M., Kohn, M. D., Colapinto, D. K., 2004, Whistleblower Law: a Guide to Legal Protections for Corporate Employees, Greenwood Publishing Group.

Martin, M. W., 1996, Ethics in Engineering, New York: McGraw-Hill.

Martin, M. W., 2000, Meaningful Work: Rethinking Professional Ethics, New York, Oxford: University Press.

Mitcham, C., 1994. Thinking through Technology: the Path between Engineering and Philosophy, Chicago: University of Chicago Press.

Mitcham, C., 1999, An Outline of Philosophy of Technology (In Chinese), TianJin: TianJin Science and Technology Press.

Mitcham, C. (eds.), 2005, Encyclopedia of Science, Technology and Ethics, Farmington Hills, MI: Macmillan Reference USA. Unger, S. H., 1994, Controlling Technology: Ethics and the Responsible Engineer, 2nd ED, New York, NY: Wiley. http://www.osc.gov/intro.htm. http://www.whistleblower.org/template/index.cfm.

Part Three

Whistleblowing in Practice

The Perception of Whistleblowing Worldwide

Wim Vandekerckhove
Center for Ethics and Value Inquiry
Ghent University, Belgium

1. Introduction

Legislation protecting whistleblowers is now in place in more than ten countries including the U.S., Australia, the U.K., South Korea, South Africa, New Zealand, Belgium, Japan, the Netherlands, Norway, and Romania. Protecting whistleblowers is on the agenda of international government institutions such as the European Commission and international bodies such as the OECD. This suggests a growing perception by policymakers of whistleblower protection as a necessary mechanism for good governance at organizational level and for setting an equilibrium between organizational secrecy and the interests of communities.

In many respects, this globalization of whistleblowing protection is counter-intuitive. First, originating as a U.S. "invention" in the early 1970s, whistleblowing protection was one of the points on the agenda of Ralph Nader, a consumer advocate. Highly controversial at the time of its origin, its success cannot be explained without referring to the specific cultural context in which it rose (Vandekerckhove 2006). Second, whistleblowing is a social construct. It depends on particular human interactions within an organizational and wider social setting. How one experiences work, the perception of work-floor relationships, and the psychological contract at work between superior and subordinate are crucial elements in telling a whistleblower-story. And we expect these to differ across nations and cultures. Third, Miceli and Near (1992) and recently MacNab and Worthley (2008) have shown that self-efficacy is predictive for individuals to blow the whistle. Self-efficacy relates to a high level of internal locus of control and the belief that individuals can achieve what they intend. We might also expect this general level of self-efficacy to differ across nations and cultures.

Hence, the worldwide surge of whistleblowing legislation raises a lot of questions as to the roles cultural orientation, nationality, and religion have in the likeliness of whistleblowing to occur. This chapter reviews some of the literature on the role of culture and nationality in whistleblowing. Cross-national research shows these factors play a role which is not that straightforward as we might intuitively expect. I subsequently point at a number of "universals" with regard to whistleblowing and try to explain why we are witnessing a globalization of whistleblowing protection despite cultural differences. I conclude with some ideas for future research that might inform practice.

2. What Research Tells Us

Cross-national research started at the end of the 1990s, when it became clear that whistleblowing protection was going to be much more than just a U.S. peculiarity. The work of Sims and Keenan (1999) Brody et al. (1999) and King (1999, 2000) was groundbreaking but is now somehow overhauled. Sims and Keenan (1999) and Brody et al.. (1999) found that in collectivist cultures workers will avoid criticizing a co-worker—which is often the case in whistleblowing—because preserving harmonious working relations takes priority. King (2000) argued that communication styles impact people's preparedness to blow the whistle, as does organizational structure (King 1999), with a highly vertical structure discouraging the use of internal procedures.

As with much cross-national research in management studies, Sims and Keenan (1999) and Brody et al. (1999) used Hofstede's dimensions differentiating cultures: power distance, uncertainty avoidance, individualism-collectivism, masculinity, and Confucian dynamism. King's (2000) research can also be linked with Hofstede's power distance dimension. Further research using Hofstede's model was carried out comparing perception of wrongdoing, personal and organizational propensity, and fear of retaliation among U.S. and Croatian managers (Tavakoli et al. 2003), U.S. and Indian managers (Keenan 2002), and U.S. and Chinese managers (Keenan 2007). In Hofstede's binary scheme, Croatian, Indian, and Chinese cultures are more collectivist compared to U.S. culture, and have a higher power distance as well as uncertainty avoidance. Findings of these studies show Croatian, Indian and Chinese managers have, compared to U.S. managers, a stronger moral perception of minor fraud but an equal moral perception of major fraud, and only Chinese managers seemed to have a lower moral perception of harm to others. Yet, U.S. managers clearly had a higher personal propensity to blow the whistle.

In terms of organizational propensity, U.S. managers scored higher than Croatian managers, equally as Indian managers and lower than Chinese managers. No difference was found with respect to fear of retaliation, with the exception of Croatian managers who reported more fear than their U.S. counterparts. The bottom line for the authors of these studies is that it is more likely that U.S. managers will blow the whistle than their Croatian, Indian, or Chinese counterparts. Of course, research findings cannot carry more sophistication than the research model does, and in the case of Hofstede's model, that isn't much. These findings do little to refute the stereotype of whistleblowing as "just something you do" if you're an American, but something that is totally alien for other countries and cultures.

Other studies do not focus on the individualist-collectivist binary or are simply looking to answer different questions than which nationality makes someone more likely to become a whistleblower.

Tan et al. (2003) studied, within the context of software development projects how individualist (U.S.) compared to collectivist (Singapore) culture mediates the impacts of organizational climate and information asymmetry on the predisposition to report bad news. They found that while an organizational climate where retaliation against whistleblowers is likely, lowers individuals' willingness to blow the whistle in both individualist and collectivist cultures, but that this impact is stronger in individualist cultures. Information asymmetry—the possibility to hide failure or other bad news over time—also results in a lower willingness to blow the whistle in both individualist and collectivist cultures, but here the impact is stronger in collectivist cultures. Lax monitoring increases information asymmetry and hence gives teams more time to turn the project around. In such situations, whistleblowing will only occur if it is good for the team, which implies that self-reporting is better than being discovered.

MacNab et al. (2007) studied the effect of cultural differences between U.S., Canada and Mexico on whistleblowing options, using Hofstede's dimensions. They found that uncertainty avoidance and power difference had an effect on the choice between external and internal whistleblowing, but that Hofstede's individualist-collectivist dimension was not significantly related to either!

MacNab and Worthley (2008) dig deeper into the Miceli and Near (1992) proposition that a person with high self-efficacy is more likely to blow the whistle. Self-efficacy is related to an internal locus of control and can be defined as the conviction that one can engage in behavior that will result in the desired outcome (Bandura 1977). MacNab and Worthley (2008) did their research in the U.S. and Canada testing a set of hypotheses predicting that if higher self-efficacy increases the likeliness of whistleblowing, then factors determining self-efficacy—management experience, age, work experience, gender—will also determine the likeliness to blow the whistle. Although this research found new support for Miceli and Near's (1992) proposition linking self-efficacy and whistleblowing, none of the researched factors determining self-efficacy also determined the likeliness to blow the whistle! This lead MacNab and Worthley (2008) to conclude that organizations with internal whistleblowing procedures should provide training to develop situation specific self-efficacy rather than assume general self-efficacy leading to the use of internal channels will come with the right work force demographics.

Finally, recent research has opened a different perspective on how collectivism relates to whistleblowing intentions. Park et al. (2005) see collectivism and Confucianism as two typical cultural and psychological traits in Asian societies. But whereas previous research sought to find support for the thesis that whistleblowing is against the ideals of Confucianism, Park et al. (2005) show that different teachings of Confucius can lead to both support or non-support for whistleblowing. For their research on whistleblowing intentions of South Korean local government officials, Park et al. (2005) first explored the five basic relationships within Confucianism: sovereign-subject, husband-wife, father-son, old-young, and friends. They argue that individuals' intention to report wrongdoing differ according to which of the five components of Confucian ethics are perceived to apply in different organizational situations of wrongdoing. Sovereign-subject, emphasizing loyalty, favors internal whistleblowing but not external. Husband-wife, emphasizing role distinction, also favors internal whistleblowing. Father-son decreases whistleblowing willingness because the organization is seen as an extension of family. The other relationships also decreased whistleblowing willingness but here one might deal with the wrongdoer in a more direct way than reporting.

Secondly, Park et al. (2005) criticize Hofstede's individualist-collectivist binary and builds a more complex two-by-two matrix using Triandis and Gelfand (1998). This results in four patterns of cultural attitudes:

1. horizontal individualism: one attempts to be distinct from a group;
2. vertical individualism: one competes with others;
3. horizontal collectivism: emphasizes interdependence and common goals;
4. vertical collectivism: sacrifice personal goals and submit to authorities.

Park et al. (2005) found that this matrix allows more complexity in researching whistleblowing intentions: horizontal individualism and horizontal collectivism showed to be positively related to whistleblowing intentions, vertical individualism and vertical collectivism negatively.

Park and Blenkinsopp (forthcoming) used the same two-by-two matrix to compare cultural influence on the kind of whistleblowing routes one would prefer if one was to blow the whistle. It was a comparative study between undergraduate students in South Korea, Turkey, and the U.K. A typology of eight whistleblowing routes was identified using three distinctions: formal vs. informal, anonymous vs. identified, and internal vs. external. What they found was that in all three countries, respondents prefer internal, formal and anonymous whistleblowing routes. However, each country showed other differences within each dimension.

Interesting about this research is that the results per cultural orientation show different preferences. For example: horizontal individualists and horizontal collectivists had clear preferences for internal and both formal and informal routes; vertical individualists disliked internal but favored anonymous and informal routes; vertical collectivists favored anonymous whistleblowing.

Clearly, this kind of research set-up gives a different picture than those suggesting whistleblowing is something only those in the West are prepared to do. The conclusions Park and Blenkinsopp (forthcoming) draw open up a new set of research questions I will be commenting on in later sections, and as I will also point out, it is research that has only recently become possible to carry out. According to Park and Blenkinsopp (forthcoming) there is no straightforward link between country, cultural orientation, and attitudes to whistleblowing. Clearly, attitudes are influenced by nationality and cultural orientation, but not in a predictable way. Park and Blenkinsopp (forthcoming) suggest that it is not cultural orientation but rather nationality which is the more significant factor. They found a poor fit between cultural orientation and country of origin, and the same cultural orientation had different effects in different countries. This leads them to conclude that between-country differences are best explained by non-cultural determinants such as legal system, labor market characteristics, economic peculiarities, etc.

3. Universals in Whistleblowing

In the previous section I have tried to show that cross-national research in whistleblowing gives a very different picture according to the categories used and the assumptions underlying the research set-up. Equating nationality with cultural orientation, and not distinguishing between various whistleblowing routes can no longer generate insights relevant to practitioners and policy makers on whether or not to design and implement whistleblowing protection and procedures. This is a very important point because the pressing question today is not whether or not whistleblowing protection and internal procedures will work in any given country but rather which ones will work best. In order to research this latter question, we need to assume two things: (1) organizational wrongdoing happens in any national context, and (2) people everywhere, of any nationality and with any cultural orientation will notice it, will have concerns about it and some will want to raise those concerns. Only research starting from the acknowledgment of these universalizing assumptions can inform which policies and procedures will work best in particular contexts.

Vandekerckhove (2006) looked for patterns in public debates leading up to whistleblowing legislation in a number of countries around the world. Eight ideal-type rationales for whistleblower protection were developed to compare the different national debates: human rights, network, stakeholders, responsibility, accountability, loyalty, integrity, efficiency. Network, accountability and efficiency showed to be the most successful one. Every country with whistleblowing legislation used at least one of those three as legitimating their legislative initiative. The *accountability construct* is embedded in a discourse of corporate governance . Controlling whether or not individuals carry out their assigned role duties calls for accountability procedures. Whistleblowing policies ensure such accountability is assured in a wide sense. The *network construct* perceives organizations as networks, which are made up of interactions. It is through balanced interactions that trust is built up. Whistleblowing policies ensure power balance within networks. In the *efficiency construct,* whistleblowing policies install an organizational panopticon. This is the way organizational efficiency relating to the human factor can be controlled. Internal whistleblowing ensures organizational transparency for corporate governance, while external whistleblowing serves watchdog accountability (Vandekerckhove 2006: 143). These three constructs are mutually reinforcing thus it is no surprise that they are often used in combination when giving "good reasons" for legislating whistleblower protection. The other rationales are often used at an early stage in the public debate and their meaning within that debate is very specific to the national historical context. For example, the human rights construct was used very differently in the U.S. and South Africa (Vandekerckhove 2006: 286-7). In the U.S., human rights argumentation—basically referring to the First Amendment—dominates the pre-legislative period (1970-1978). The expectations towards whistleblowing legislation developing as First Amendment driven were not realized in the legislation that followed, but it is still present in the discourse of the Government Accountability Project. Both the First Amendment and the employment-at-will doctrine are central to U.S. history, but in the context of whistleblowing they contradict each other. Using human rights arguments in favor of whistleblowing protection points at a power imbalance between society and organization in favor of the latter, and renders employment-at-will illegitimate. In this sense the human rights argumentation is not stabilizing; the concept of human rights cannot be generalized to cover free speech in the workplace. Therefore, whistleblowing policies can only achieve exceptions to the employment-at-will doctrine. Moreover, they can only do so if they are legitimated through constructs that only indirectly allow societal control over organizations, such as the accountability, the network, and the efficiency constructs.

In South Africa, human rights arguments in favor of whistleblowing protection entered the discussion in a totally different way. There, whistleblowing legislation was promoted and enacted as part of a democratization process. Initially, the whistleblowing provisions were part of the Open Democracy Bill, which was later split into the Access to Information Bill and the Protected Disclosure Bill. The preamble of the Protected Disclosure Act (PDA) explicitly places the provisions in a context of democratization, referring to human rights values of human dignity, equality, and freedom. Moreover, the subject element of the act includes "unfair discrimination." Hence, the historical situation of South Africa—dealing with its just ended Apartheid regime—made the human rights construct a necessity for any justification of new government legislation and policy making. Here, the human rights construct was a stabilizing element. But it was not the only "good reason" used. The accountability and the efficiency constructs are also present—the PDA is explicitly aimed at fighting corruption and the King Committee on Corporate Governance advises it to tackle fraud.

A constant pattern in all public debates that were assessed (Vandekerckhove 2006) is that whistleblower protection bills succeed in becoming enacted legislation when they are framed in a rationale of institutional trust (network), good governance (accountability) or combating fraud and corruption (efficiency). This achieves two things: (1) it emphasizes whistleblowing as a source of information and hence makes whistleblowing protection not an option but a necessity for the well-being of private and public institutions, and (2) it thus undercuts any culturally specific reason for not protecting whistleblowers. Let me explain.

The discourse on organizations that became dominant from the 1990s on—and which is based on procedural normative concepts like "decentralization," "flexibility," "network," "corporate governance," "integrity," "trust," "stakeholder"—implicates the necessity of gathering information outside of the hierarchical line about the production process. The parallel evolution is that increasingly internal audits, board-disclosure and internal whistleblowing procedures are put forward as important governance measures. In other words, the globalizing affirmation of understanding organization as networks, of notions such as good governance, and of the norm of efficiency, also globalizes the perceived necessity of whistleblower protection and policies.

This is the reason why many and historically very different countries today have whistleblowing legislation or are debating them. Not because the notion of whistleblowing has been translated to those specific national contexts and cultures, but because the discourse about organizations has seeped through despite cultural and national specificities. In every nation that has whistleblowing legislation, at one point or another the counter argument that "it is not in our culture" has been uttered, including the U.S., where James Roche in 1971 compared whistleblowing to industrial espionage merely "eroding another support of free enterprise" (Roche 1971, quoted in Walters 1975). In Western Europe (e.g., Belgium), the reference is to the Nazis, in Central-Europe (e.g., Romania) to the KGB, the Stasi or the Securitate. In Australia it is against "mateship." In South Korea it supposedly runs counter the teachings of Confucius and in South Africa there was a reference to the *impimpis.* And yet, all these countries today have some form of whistleblowing legislation. That is because only fraud and corporate governance can do the trick. In Australia, while almost all states had legislation protecting public sector whistleblowers, for ten long years private sector protection was debated at federal level through several bills but none got enacted:

> [It seems] a peculiarly Australian thing to not protect private sector whistleblowers.... Every time administrators and drafters of legislation get to this point in Australia, their knees start to shake and they pull back. (De Maria, quoted in Hansard 2002)

When in 2001, HIH, Australia's second largest insurer collapsed causing Australia's largest corporate failure, the Australian Securities and Investment Commission backed a plea to extend whistleblower protection to the private sector. Whistleblower protection was legislated as part of CLERP9, the ninth review of the Corporate Law Economic Reform Program, in 2004.

To sum up, I believe there are three *de facto* "universals" relating to whistleblowing:

1. No society is free from organizational wrongdoing,
2. People everywhere want to raise concern,
3. Every nation has a culturally specific counter-argument to whistle-blowing.

There are also two universalizing trends, namely:

4. Whistleblowing protection becomes a necessity,
5. Countries worldwide legislate forms of whistleblower protection and as a result—or as an anticipating effect—more organizations develop internal whistleblowing procedures.

4. Research for Practice

This last "universal" makes that new field of research possible which I mentioned when commenting on Park and Blenkinsopp (forthcoming). Practice is still in need of cross-national research on whistleblowing but it must be careful not to oversimplify cultural determinants and it must also inquiry into the explanatory potential of non-cultural variables.

Closing this chapter, I specify three research paths that could help to generate insights and knowledge that is relevant for practice. First, research on whistleblowing can now be set up comparing experiences of whistleblowers under different legal protection schemes. There has been some cross-national comparative research on legal provisions (Groeneweg 2001, Vandekerckhove 2006) but very little on how whistleblowers and other stakeholders perceive that legal protection (Lewis 2008, Uys 2008).

Second, we also need more qualitative research into experiences of whistleblowers and other stakeholders with regard to various modes of internal whistleblowing procedures: anonymous/identified/confidential, different types of recipients, in-house or outsourced.

And third, more generally, there is a need to switch from cross-national studies on whistleblowing intentions to studies on the prevalence and nature of whistleblowing, its effects, and the occurrence of retaliation. Such research is currently only available for the U.S. (for example Rothschild and Miethe 1999, Rothschild 2008).

The kind of research suggested here is needed to improve the praxis of whistleblowing policies. We no longer need to wonder or worry whether or not people will want to blow the whistle and raise concern. Neither do we need to argue that in many cases to do so is beneficial for organizations and communities. But we still need to improve the procedural, technical, and human aspects of designing and implementing whistleblowing mechanisms in different countries, regions, sectors and organizations, and across different cultures.

References

Bandura, A., 1977, Self-Efficacy: Toward a Unifying Theory of Behavioral Change, *Psychological Review,* 84(2), 191-215.

Brody R. G., Coulter J. M. & Lin S., 1999, The Effect of National Culture on Whistle-Blowing Perceptions, *Teaching Business Ethics,* 3(4), 383-398.

Groeneweg, S., 2001, *Three Whistleblower Protection Models: A Comparative Analysis of Whistleblower Legislation in Australia, the United States and the United Kingdom,* Available at: http://www.psc-cfp.gc.ca/research/.

Hansard, 2002, Reference: Public Interest Disclosure Bill 2001 (2002), *Official Committee Hansard, Finance and Public Administration Committee,* Thursday, 16 May 2002 (Canberra: Senate).

Keenan, J. P., 2002, Comparing Indian and American Managers on Whistleblowing, *Employee Responsibilities and Rights Journal,* 14(2), 79-89.

Keenan, J. P., 2007, Comparing Chinese and American Managers on Whistleblowing, *Employee Responsibilities and Rights Journal,* 19(2), 85-94.

King, G., 1999, The Implications of an Organization's Structure on Whistleblowing, *Journal of Business Ethics,* 20(4), 315-326.

King, G., 2000, The implications of differences in cultural attitudes and styles of communication on peer reporting behaviour, *Cross Cultural Management: An International Journal,* 7(2), 11-17.

Lewis, D., 2008, Ten Years of Public Interest Disclosure Legislation in the UK: Are Whistleblowers Adequately Protected? *Journal of Business Ethics,* 82(2), 497-507.

MacNab, B. & Worthley, R., 2008, Self-Efficacy as an Intrapersonal Predictor for Internal Whistleblowing: A U.S. and Canada Examination, *Journal of Business Ethics,* 79(4), 407-421.

MacNab, B. e.a., 2007, Culture and Ethics Management: Whistle-blowing and Internal Reporting within a NAFTA Country Context, *International Journal of Cross Cultural Management,* 7(1), 5-28.

Miceli, M. P. & Near, J. P., 1992, *Blowing the Whistle,* Lexington Books. Park, H. & Blenkinsopp, J., forthcoming, Whistleblowing as Planned Behavior - A Survey of South Korean Police Officers, *Journal of Business Ethics,* Available at: http://dx.doi.org/10.1007/s10551-008-9788-y

Park, H., Rehg, M. T. & Lee, D., 2005, The Influence of Confucian Ethics and Collectivism on Whistleblowing Intentions: A Study of South Korean Public Employees, *Journal of Business Ethics,* 58(4), 387-103.

Rothschild, J. & Miethe, T. D., 1999, Whistle-Blower Disclosures and Management Retaliation: The Battle to Control Information about Organization Corruption, *Work and Occupations,* 26(1), 107-128.

Rothschild, J., 2008, Freedom of Speech Denied, Dignity Assaulted: What the Whistleblowers Experience in the U.S., *Current Sociology,* 56(6), 884-903.

Sims R. L. & Keenan J. P., 1999, A Cross-Cultural Comparison of Managers' Whistleblowing Tendencies, *International Journal of Value-Based Management,* 12(2), 137-151.

Tan, B. C. Y. e. a., 2003, Reporting Bad News About Software Projects: Impact of Organizational Climate and Information Asymmetry in an Individualistic and a Collectivistic Culture, *IEEE Transactions on Engineerig Management,* 50(1), 64-77.

Tavakoli, A. A., Keenan, J. P. & Cranjak-Karanovic, B., 2003, Culture and Whistleblowing An Empirical Study of Croatian and United States Managers Utilizing Hofstede's Cultural Dimensions, *Journal of Business Ethics,* 43(1), 49-64.

Triandis, H. C. & M. J. Gelfand, 1998, Converging Measurement of Horizontal and Vertical Individualism and Collectivism, *Journal of Personality and Social Psychology,* 74(1), 118-128.

Uys, T., 2008, Rational Loyalty and Whistleblowing: The South African Context, *Current Sociology,* 56(6), 904-921.

Vandekerckhove, W., 2006, *Whistleblowing And Organizational Social Responsibility,* Ashgate.

Walters, K. D., 1975, Your Employees' Right to Blow the Whistle, *Harvard Business Review* 534, 26-34 cont. 161-62.

Whistleblowing in Germany

Guido Strack
Whistleblower-Netzwerk e.V.
Cologne, Germany

1. Whistleblowing Unwanted

"The greatest rogue in the whole land is, and will remain, the informer." This is a quote attributed to Hoffmann von Fallersleben (1798-1874), author of the lyrics of the German national anthem. It is frequently used by those who want to block any discussion on the necessity to support whistleblowers and the concept of whistleblowing in Germany. After two dictatorships using denunciations as a tool, after Gestapo and Stasi,[1] the Germans are fed up with informers.[2] Whistleblowers, just another English term most people know nothing about, often are immediately measured by the same yardstick as those informers—without further discussion.

Normally there is no reflection that Hoffmann made his statement against police spies in the mid-19th Century and that today he could certainly be described as a whistleblower himself. In 1842, he had lost his professorship at the University of Wroclaw because he had, based on his national liberal convictions, criticized the prevailing conditions in his poems which had the ironic title "non-political songs" (1840/1841).[3]

Those who exert criticism in Germany must still often fear losing their jobs. It is true that, especially in comparison to the Anglo-Saxon countries, there is a sophisticated labor and employee protection legislation. However, when dealing with the issue of whistleblowing it often fails—as will be shown later. And the situation is aggravated by the fact that, under the pressure of globalization and mass unemployment, the German employee protection is noticeably on the decline.

2. Case Examples

The history of whistleblowing in Germany has not yet been written and this can not be done on this occasion. If whistleblowers are defined as people who no longer silently tolerate illegal activities, maladministration or danger to humans, the environment and the economy, but reveal those abuses within or outside their business, their company, their organization or their bureaucracy, they have always been around, also in Germany. But as elsewhere, they are the exception, not the rule, or to use a quote of Reich-Chancellor Otto von Bismarck: "courage on the battle field is our common good, but it is not infrequently you will find that very honorable people lack civil courage."[4]

Perhaps even Martin Luther, one of the world's most famous Germans, could be classified as an early whistleblower.[5] In the organization to which he belonged he had pointed out maladministration and this led to reprisals against him, just like this led to reprisals for so many others later. At the same time, his case shows the consequences that incorrect handling of whistleblowers may have for the organization itself.

While there is hardly any knowledge about early whistleblowers in the private sector there are at least a few cases in the public service in German history that can be categorized as whistleblowing or closely related as performance refusal for ethical reasons:

> Regiment commander Johann Friedrich Adolf von der Marwitz (1723-1781), who later served the resistors of the 20 July 1944 as a role model, refused during the Seven Years' War to follow the command of Frederick II of Prussia ordering him to plunder a Saxon castle. Instead, he quit the service. The inscription on his grave stone reads: "Chose disgrace where obedience did not bring honor."[6] Frederick II also faced resistance by Chamber Court President Christian Ludwig von Rebeur, who in the case of the miller Arnold invoked his judicial independence: "We have decided like that and this must be sufficient."[7]

In addition to individual officers, soldiers and judges from the nineteenth century, especially professors are still remembered for expressing criticism and facing the consequences: men like Ludwig Uhland, Friedrich List, and the Gottingen Seven (the professors F.C. Dahlmann, E. Albrecht, Jacob and Wilhelm Grimm, G. Gervinius, H. Ewald and William Weber).[8] Safeguarding their own rights against the access of authority often went along with highly political statements.

For the period at the beginning of the twentieth century one could point to chemist Clara Immerwahr (1870-1915). As the wife of Fritz Haber, she intensively opposed her husband's activities in exploration and use of poison gas.[9]

Whistleblowing and resistance mingled as this was the case during the periods of the German dictatorships. This is not the place to analyze the resistance during the Nazi-era nor that in the German Democratic Republic (GDR), but one could point to the dunning words on the pamphlets of the White Rose: "We *must* attack the evil, where it is most powerful." [...] "Everyone wants to excuse himself from his blame, everyone does it and afterwards sleeps with quiet and best conscience. But he can not absolve. Everyone is *guilty, guilty, guilty...*" and the words of Sophie Scholl: "All of you think what we have written and said, but you lack the courage to speak it out."[10]

Referring to the example of the "Goettingen Seven" and based on their responsibility as scientists, on 12 April 1957, eighteen nuclear scientists spoke up against the plans to equip the West German army with nuclear weapons. Their "Goettingen Declaration"[11] was supported by fourteen important nuclear scientists of the GDR on 3 Mai 1957. In 1959, the Goettingen Eighteen also became the nucleus of the Association of German Scientists (VDW).[12]

In the Federal Republic of the postwar period, in the upsurge of the economy, the issue of criticism at the workplace initially did not play a big role. In some ways it is also significant that in the German language until today there is no equivalent word for the meaning which the term whistleblower acquired in the English speaking countries throughout the last decades. In the search for concrete cases from the period after 1945 only a few names get into the focus, largely unknown to the general public in Germany even though some of those cases were of significant importance.

One example is the case of Klaus Forster, a tax investigator who in the middle of the 1970s revealed the Flick-Scandal during which political parties handed out excess donations receipts in a 1:5 ratio and used charity organizations for money laundering. The scandal involved highest political circles, but Chancellor Dr. Helmut Kohl later on could not remember any details due to a "blackout." Forster who persisted and only wanted to do his duty was first impeded from the top and finally assigned to another job against his will. In 1983 he finally resigned from the tax administration.[13]

The pattern of obstruction from above and unwanted employee transfers can also be found with other tax investigators that blew the whistle. While Werner Borcharding in the 1990s in Munster protested against alleged tax gifts for a local industrialist,[14] Rudolf Schmenger and his colleagues suffered from obstruction from above at the beginning of the new century in Frankfurt as they did not want to follow the order of the state government of Hesse to withdraw during investigations against banks and big illegal tax evaders. When Schmenger even after his transfer still did not rest, he was medically classified as having a querulant personality and forced to take early retirement. Meanwhile the Medical Association is investigating against the doctor who made the wrong diagnosis and Schmenger, now holding a positive medical certificate, is working as a private tax consultant.[15]

Taxes and a lot of money are also involved with whistleblowers from the banking sector. Werner Demant,[16] clerk at Commerzbank Frankfurt, had suspicions about illegal transfers of securities to Luxembourg and Switzerland in the bank. His internal message was unsuccessful, so he finally turned to the authorities and thus a major banking scandal was triggered, which revealed how some banks systematically offered help for tax evasion. Demant was terminated and his career came to an end. DG Bank employee Andrea Fuchs[17] is having a similar experience. She also—first internally—pointed to possible illegal insider trading, meanwhile, however, she is in legal disputes with DZ Bank for already twelve years, which has just issued another termination.

But also in the German health care system, there are some whistleblowers. One example is the Berlin doctor Cora Jakobi,[18] whose public criticism of a practice of premature dismissal on grounds of cost savings led to labor court disputes. Veterinary Margrit Herbst[19] lost her job at the slaughterhouse Bad Bramstedt and was sued for damages when she—after unsuccessful internal approaches—made the public aware of BSE risks. While those cases already happened in the 1990s, in the recent years some other can be found in the care taking business. These courageous whistleblowers pointed to the incredibly cynical abuses in nursing homes. It is thanks to women such as Brigitte Heinisch,[20] Heike Hengl[21] and Petra Richers[22] that meanwhile there is a public debate on greater quality control and quality assurance in the care sector and that also politics cannot ignore this issue any longer. However, these women paid a price for their civil courage and encountered considerable pressure and the loss of their jobs, some of them still suffering the economic and health consequences even today.

Even more serious are the consequences in those cases where no one blew the whistle. There are some examples of dramatic disasters in Germany of the post-war period where there were prior risk indications clearly visible for insiders. Had there been more courageous whistleblowers and responsible persons listening to them the Thalidomid scandal and the ICE train crash in Eschede probably could have been avoided, just like the collapse of the ice rink roof in Bad Reichenhall.[23] While the analysis of the causes of the sinking of the Harold of Free Enterprise led to a public awareness of the need to protect whistleblowers in Britain, thus enhancing early risk detection,[24] in Germany, this awareness is still lacking.

3. Whistleblowers and Employers' Interest

While whistleblowing in the last century, above all, was an issue of a critical-alternative milieu and whistleblowers were seen as persons acting altruistic for public interests, the concept of whistleblowing in Germany has become popular for very different reasons since several years now. This was triggered by the Enron and Worldcom scandals in the U.S. and the impact of the U.S. Sarbanes-Oxley Act.[25] Another trigger was the increased discussion about the fight against corruption and economic crime, not least because of the development of appropriate provisions in U.S. and International law.

The Sarbanes-Oxley Act (SOX) obliges companies listed at U.S. stock exchanges to establish independent internal audit committees and to provide opportunities for employees to make protected and, if desired, also anonymous internal whistleblowing disclosures in relation to accounting or financially relevant issues (Sec. 301). At the same time, SOX (Sec. 806) foresees penal sanctions and a duty to repair damages for those disadvantaging whistleblowers. The primary background of this statute is the protection of the interest of the shareholders and not that of the general public. SOX applies directly only to some large German corporations listed in the U.S., but also to German subsidiaries of U.S. companies. However, due to the paramount role of the United States for the international financial markets, SOX meanwhile spreads as a global de facto standard.

Point of reference in the German stock corporation law is Section 91 Paragraph II of the AktG ("Aktiengesetz").[26] According to the currently prevailing opinion this paragraph does not necessarily mean that a whistle-blower system needs to be established, however it stipulates certain measures, especially the creation of a monitoring system for the early detection of developments threatening the continuation of the company. This, as well as the further developments of jurisdiction concerning personal liability of directors and supervisory council members, has for sure enhanced reflections on whistleblowing systems within the German economy.[27]

Other enhancements came from the UN Convention against Corruption (UNCAC Article 33[28]), the Council of Europe conventions against corruption (Article 22 of the Criminal Law Convention[29] and Article 9 of the Civil Law Convention[30]) and the OECD Guidelines for Multinational Enterprises (Section II.9),[31] which also stress the importance of whistleblowing in the fight against corruption and demand to enable repression-free whistleblowing.

In addition to and beyond these legal obligations meanwhile more and more companies have recognized that non-compliance with regulatory rules and internal economic crime can lead to major damages to the company and that the management often learns about these abuses only thanks to whistleblower information. Finally, there is a growing recognition that the promotion and channeling of internal whistleblowing is a means to prevent or at least limit the occurrence of external whistleblowing and its risks for the company's reputation.

Some companies even go as far as to oblige their employees to blow the whistle. The most blatant example was the U.S. group Wal-Mart, which, during its attempt to get into the German market (which had meanwhile been stopped), issued internal ethics and conduct guidelines ordering all employees to report any violations of these guidelines by fellow employees to the management. The regional Labor Court in Duesseldorf[32] found these guidelines to be invalid, as they included the prohibition of love relationships in the workplace and thus violated human rights. Another reason for the cancellation was that the clause about whistleblowing would have required the approval of the workers' council. This need for the consent of the internal workers' representatives when establishing whistleblowing systems has meanwhile been confirmed in other high-court jurisdiction.[33]

Another legal problem in introducing and arranging internal whistleblower systems is data privacy. However, this initial obstacle for SOX compliance can be considered as a solvable problem thanks to the decision of the Article 29 group of European Data Protection Supervisors on 1 February 2006.[34] Thus, when certain preconditions are met, whistleblower systems can be designed in such a way that they are compatible with European and also with German data protection laws. Main points are the protection of the rights of concerned persons/suspects by means of early information and data erasure and the restrained use of anonymous reporting. The latter, at least according to the non-legally binding statement of the Article 29 group, is possible, but should not be propagated. Preferable shall rather be the establishment of confidential communications, where the whistleblower is know by a person acting as intermediary—like an ombudsman—but where his identity is not disclosed to the employer and third parties.

Starting with the companies bound to comply with SOX, whistleblower systems have meanwhile found their way via large enterprises down to the medium sized. The practical implementations that can be found within German companies today vary a lot and a "best practice standard" is not yet established. As basic forms one can distinguish facilities for (anonymous) message reception (mostly via telephone or email boxes), systems with a back channel (such as anonymous internet reporting with the opportunity to establish a mailbox) and ombudsman systems (mostly with an outside lawyer who is bound to secrecy, but also with some in-house lawyers or journalists).[35] These basic forms stand alone or are offered in parallel or in different combinations. The circle of possible messengers also varies. Often, all employees are addressed, but sometimes only individual employee groups. Sometimes in addition to all employees also suppliers, business partners and customers are possible messengers. Differences can also be found concerning the issues to which messages can relate, ranging from a narrow area of financial manipulations or corruption and economic crime in general to all types of breaches of internal and/or external rules. More differences lie in the degree of involvement of the workforce in the formation and implementation of these systems as well as in the advertising and training efforts undertaken to make the systems known. Finally, it is also crucial who the person or entity who ultimately receives the messages is (such as a specific—compliance—department, the Chairman, or the Supervisory Board) and to what extent this person or entity possesses the willingness, competence and necessary independence to investigate and clarify the facts even if allegations are directed against the members of upper management. Common to most systems is that they promise whistleblowers protection against discrimination in case of not deliberately false declarations by means of non-identification (be it through anonymity or confidentiality).

The establishment of such an internal whistleblower system constitutes a positive first step towards addressing the issue of whistleblowing. The current implementations that can be found in Germany, however, fall short of what is needed. The most obvious reason for this shortcoming is that they, by dealing with the fear of reprisals that shall be taken away through anonymity or confidentiality guarantees, address only one of the three main obstacles for whistleblowing. Where whistleblowers are currently pushed into anonymity, they can not be positively rewarded for their activities, although it actually is a cultural change towards the acceptance of the reporting of errors and failures and a repression-free communications culture that would be needed. This is especially required to effectively overcome the second obstacle, namely that of the psychological hurdles and the culture of silence, non-interference and misunderstood loyalty. Also in relation to the third obstacle there has not been done enough yet, for a further reason for which whistleblowing often does not take place is that the potential whistleblower believes that the flaw would not really be eliminated even if he sends the message.

What therefore seems to be needed is orientation to internationally recognized "best practice standards" as they are for example set out in the relevant code of practice of the British Standards Institution (BSI).[36] The following should be demanded: that the workforce has a say in the design, introduction and implementation of such a system; that the system is available to all employees and also to business partners of all kinds; that it covers all types of business-related abuses and risks; that a variety of confidential and anonymous reporting channels are available and accessible and that, apart from these channels, also low-level and non-binding information and counselling services for potential whistleblowers are offered.

Lastly, there have to be guarantees that the messages lead to thorough investigations and that abuses and risks are really addressed even when this leads to conflicts with the interests of the management. This requires transparency and external control, or at least an escalation possibility to the outside. Therefore within the company it should in any case be possible to involve the Supervisory Board or owner level. Ultimately, however, also a possibility of reporting to government agencies is necessary as this is the only way to ensure compliance with long-term public interests that go beyond short-term business interests.

4. The Legal Situation of Whistleblowers

At constitutional level, the German *Grundgesetz* (Basic Law) guarantees, apart from the general freedom of action (Article 2, Paragraph 1 GG), the freedom of conscience (Article 4 GG) and the freedom of information and expression (Article 5, Paragraph 1 GG), also the right to petition (Article 17 GG), which, in addition to the classic petitions to the parliament, also includes the right to address requests or complaints to the relevant government agencies. This concerns also the reporting of offences to the public prosecutor, which in Germany is a right but normally no obligation. According to Criminal Law (Sec. 138 of the German Criminal Code StGB), such an obligation exists only in exceptional cases namely knowledge of the planning of extremely serious offences.

Whistleblowing to authorities should therefore not be problematic at all and thanks to a section in the Labor Law (Section 612 a of the German Civil Code BGB), which forbids any discrimination caused by a permitted exercise of rights, should not lead to sanctions. In reality, however, it is problematic as the jurisprudence up to now more or less ignores these norms. One justification put forward for this is that the fundamental rights shall directly apply only in the relation between the citizens and the state, so that only the state is prohibited to sanction a petitioner. In other cases, it is reasoned that an anonymous exercise of fundamental rights would not be possible. So while the economy is pushing for anonymity, the state simply denies protection.

In addition, case law repeatedly refers to the fundamental liberties of the employer, namely the occupational liberty (Article 12 GG) and the right to property (Article 14 GG) which shall guarantee him protection of his trade secrets and shall, in conjunction with the basic principles of labor law, also allow him to immediately lay off workers for launching criminal complaints against their superiors or the employer as this is seen as a breach of loyalty. Only thanks to a decision by the Federal Constitutional Court in 2001[37] a certain process of rethinking started. According to this judgment, a dismissal violates the fundamental general freedom of action and the rule of law principle when it is carried out because someone served as a witness for the public prosecutor and thus did nothing else but follow his civic obligations. The Federal Constitutional Court also stated that "normally" the same would be applicable in case of a voluntary notification to the law enforcement agencies, at least if the whistleblower acted in good faith, assuming the existence of a criminal offence, perpetrated for example by his employer.

In two decisions from the years 2003 and 2006,[38] the highest non-constitutional court, the Federal Labor Court, virtually turned this positive case law of the Federal Constitutional Court upside down. According to it, the worker may only report the crime if this is proportionate. The principle of proportionality, which normally only comes into play if the government interferes with the fundamental rights of the citizens, is used here to put additional burdens on the employee. Now, he must therefore examine in particular whether there are any less incriminatory means compared to launching a criminal complaint, which according to the second step of the reasoning of the Federal Labor Court usually means that the employee has a duty to first seek in-house clarification. Where he has failed to do this, his dismissal would therefore be legal, unless exceptionally an internal clarification would have been unreasonable, i.e., because this could have only been done by contacting the suspect himself and may have given him an opportunity to cover up the crime.

In addition, the potential whistleblower also has to keep in mind that informing the authorities must be appropriate, i.e. that clarification interests of society must outweigh his loyalty obligation. This often leads to the court undertaking its own appreciation of values after the event, not taking sufficiently into account how the situation presented itself to the whistleblower at the moment when he took his decision. As a result, the currently prevailing case law leads to one advice for potential whistleblowers who do not want to risk their jobs: Don't become a whistleblower!

Even a whistleblower, who thanks to good legal advice in advance manages to meet all the criteria of the case law is far from being protected against retaliation. To qualify for the protection of Section 612a BGB (Civil Code), he must not only demonstrate that his whistleblowing was legally permissible but also prove that discrimination actually took place and that this happened because of his whistleblowing. As long as an employer has not explicitly mentioned this as the reasons for termination this proof is practically almost impossible. But even where this obstacle is overcome there is finally Section 10 Paragraph 2 of the Termination-Protection Employment Law (KSchG), which foresees that an employment contract can come to an end by a decision of a judge even if the termination as such was illegal in cases where a continuation of the employment contract would be unacceptable for the employer. In this case, the employer must pay a lump sum, but against the background of an increased poverty risk due to "social reforms" like Hartz IV, high unemployment rates, low wages and often only a small chance to find another job in the same industry, especially as a known whistleblower, this is often a very weak compensation.

Even besides official warnings and termination of employment there are effective sanction mechanisms against criticism at the workplace: bullying. A large-scale study funded by the German Federal Government in 2002[39] concluded that over 60 percent of bullying victims stated as the cause of bullying against them: "I have practiced criticism in the company." This is also the most common cause of bullying. Yet in Germany authorities hardly do anything against bullying and nothing for whistleblowers.

This finding is also likely to remain unchanged by the proposal issued in the summer of 2008[40] from three federal ministries of a new whistleblowing section in the Civil Code (Section 612a new Civil Code), as this proposal is concentrating on codification of established case law. While thanks to requirements of the European legislation we nowadays have explicit bans of retaliation combined with special onus of proof rules providing a certain relief for victims of such discriminations, even in this respect no modifications are proposed for whistleblowers. Also the obligation to try to resolve matters in-house first will in principle be held up. In addition, the proposal contains a collection of vague legal terms, so that even the lack of predictability of subsequent court decisions would hardly be improved.[41]

The really good idea of codifying whistleblower protection therefore is likely to lead to nothing. There is even a danger that more workers believe to be protected, become whistleblowers and afterward learn that there was no effective protection. Currently, however, it is still unclear whether the proposal will have a chance to make it anyhow into the law books. The lobby of the employers' associations and the economic wing of the largest government party still try to prevent this.

Until now, the principle of official secrecy forbids government officials any job-related statements without explicit permission of the administration. This also applies to criminal complaints and whistleblowing. From April 2009, the new Civil Service Status Law (Section 37, Paragraph 2, No. 3 BeamtSG) will lead to a slight relaxation since, thanks to the implementation of international anti-corruption conventions, officials from then on will explicitly have the right to directly bring corruption offences (Section 331-337 of the Criminal Law StGB) to the attention of the public prosecutor. For all other offences even then the official secrecy requirements will continue to apply.

5. Poorly Organized Support

Also organized support for whistleblowers in Germany is quite limited. Founded in 1994, the ethics protection initiative (Ethikschutzinitiative) of the International Network for Engineers and Scientists for Social Responsibility (INESPE) had attempted through continuous work to make whistleblowing more popular in Germany and had asked for a legal protection for whistleblowers. The aim was to enable the public interest to be heard in the business sector and especially in the field of scientific research wherever there are threats to humans and to the environment. Added to this was the desire to help whistleblowers also in their particular case and to assist them i.e. in disputes concerning their workplace and in their fight against deficiencies. Despite initial successes such as cinematic portraits of three whistleblowers,[42] a major International Congress,[43] its own website[44] and some publications,[45] the momentum of many contributors decreased and finally was limited mainly to the tireless work of the Managing Director and journalist Antje Bultmann. She attempts to help individual whistleblowers and to keep the issue in the media and in 2006 became one of the initiators of the association Whistleblower-Netzwerk e.V.

Since 1999, the Ethikschutzinitiative together with two scientists' organizations, the German section of the International Association of Lawyers Against Nuclear Arms (IALANA) and the Federation of German Scientists (VDW), sponsors the German Whistleblower Award which is awarded every two years.[46] A characteristic feature of the state of whistleblowing in Germany is that so far all award winners, except for Margrit Herbst in 2001 and Liv Bode and Brigitte Heinisch in 2007, came from abroad.

VDW and IALANA focused their whistlebower work on the awards and accompanying publications[47] primarily by Antje Falter and Dr. Dieter Deiseroth. The latter is Judge at the Federal Administrative Court and made with the exact description and analysis of the case of Margrit Herbst[48] a significant contribution to the discussion of whistleblowing in Germany. In numerous publications, they pointed out both the problems of individual cases as well as the lack of legal protection of whistleblowers in Germany in general.

Originally on the initiative of the lawyer and former TI board member Bjorn Rohde Liebenau, also the German Chapter of Transparency International[49] repeatedly addressed the issue of whistleblowing. However, it deliberately excluded individual cases and referred these cases to the Fairness Foundation in Frankfurt,[50] which focuses on the promotion of fair structures in enterprises and organizations and provides—in addition to fairness training—for some years now a telephone hotline which offers advice for whistleblowers. Mr Rohde-Liebenau meanwhile became with several publications and an analysis for the EU Parliament[51] an expert in the field and with his company RCC now offers services to companies as Ombudsman and in implementing good risk management.[52]

Finally there is media researcher Professor Johannes Ludwig who focuses on whistleblowing and media. On his websites,[53] he documents well-researched stories of whistleblowers and their treatment in the media and provides tips for whistleblowers on how to deal with journalists. In addition to the author, who himself as a whistleblower at the EU Commission became aware of the whistleblowing issue just a few years ago, Johannes Ludwig now belongs to the Executive Board of the Whistleblower-Netzwerk e.V.[54]

This association, founded in the autumn of 2006, tries, in a certain continuity of the work of the Ethikschutzinitative to help whistleblowers, to raise awareness about whistleblowing in Germany and to lobby for effective whistleblower protection rules both on corporate and on governmental level. In 2007, the association together with the whistleblower NGOs "Explisit" from Norway and "Freedom to Care" from the UK issued an opinion paper on the EU green paper on labor law[55] which, in Brussels, however, got little attention. In addition, a conference of journalists was co-organized. In 2008, the whistleblower network issued opinions on legislative procedures and was also involved in the parliamentary hearings on the currently planned introduction of a whistleblower section in the Civil Code.[56] For 2009, a major project is planned which will cover the preparation of case documentations, lobbying for legislation and the analysis and influencing of the currently existing whistleblower systems in German corporations. Further information on the work of the association as well as news reports and interesting facts can be found under www.whistleblower-netzwerk.de and in the blog section of that website.

Notes

1. Judith Rauhofer, Blowing the whistle on Sarbanes-Oxley: Anonymous hotlines and the historical stigma of denunciation in modern Germany, International Review of Law Computers and Technology (2007), volume 21, issue 3, pp. 363-376.
2. On the research on informers in Germany: e.g. I. MarBolek; O. Stieglitz (Hg.): Denunziation im 20. Jahrhundert, Sonderheft der Zeitschrift Historische Sozialforschung 96/97 (ISSN: 0172-6404), Koln 2001, and M. Schroter (Hrsg.), Der willkommene Verrat-Beitrage zur Denunziationsforschung, Weilerswist 2007, ISBN 978-3-938808-38-2.
3. http://www. fallersleben-bildungswerk.de/hoffmann.html.
4. Martin Knobbe, *Die Tugend der Wachter,* in: Stern 31/2005, Hamburg 2005, p.113.
5. http://findarticles.com/p/articles/mi_m4339/is_n2_v19/ai_20823856; http://pwp.lincs.net/sanjour/Fraud%20Magazine%209-07.htm; http://www.erudit.org/revue/ri/2001/v56/n1/000156ar.html.
6. Alfons Wenzel, Zivilcourage im offentlichen Dienst, Munchen 1965, (p. 34).
7. Karl Dickel, Friedrich der GroBe und die Prozesse des Mullers Arnold, Marburg 1891, p. 15.
8. Hunger, Bohme/Vierhaus, Stadtgeschichte, p. 197ff.; Lampe, Jorg H.: Politische Entwicklungen in Gottingen vom Beginn des 19. Jahrhunderts bis zum Vormarz, in: Bohme/Vierhaus, Stadtgeschichte, pp. 45-137, here: 91ff. (http://www.uni-goettingen.de/de/30770.html).

9. http://www.ippnw.de/soziale_verantwortung/claraimmerwahr_auszeichnung/ index.html?expand=828&cHash=0b81139b16; http://www.uni-muenster.de/PeaCon/wuf/wf-92/9210501m.htm.
10. Alfons Wenzel, Zivilcourage im offentlichen Dienst, Munchen 1965. (p. 61), http://www.bpb.de/themen/EG49IN,0,0,Wir_sind_Euer_b%F6ses_Gewissen%21.html.
11. http://www.dhm.de/lemo/html/dokumente/JahreDesAufbausInOstUndWest_erklaerungGoettingerErklaerung/index.html; Bohme, Ernst: Zwischen Restauration und Rebellion. Die Georgia Augusta und die politische Kultur Gottingens in den funfziger Jahren, demnachst in: Gottinger Jahrbuch 2005; Friedensinitiative Garchinger Naturwissenschaftler (Bearb.): 30 Jahre Gottinger Erklarung. Nachdenken uber die Rolle des Wissenschaftlers in der Gesellschaft (Schriftenreihe Wissenschaft und Frieden 11), Munchen 1987; http://www.uni-goettingen.de/de/54319.html.
12. http://www.vdw-ev.de/ueber-vdw/geschichte-und-ziele.html.
13. https://www.berlinonline.de/berliner-zeitung/archiv/.bin/dump.fcgi/2000/0125/none/0002/index.html; Mira Gajevic, Jochen Arntz, Forsters Fall, Berliner Zeitung dated 25 January 2000.
14. Werner Borcharding, wegen Gesetzestreue strafversetzt, Business-Crime-Magazin, 1-2004, pp. 22-26. http://business-crime-control.de/doc/bcmag/bc012004/Gesetzestreue%20aus%20 BC1-2004.pdf
15. http://www.hr-online.de/website/rubriken/nachrichten/indexjsp?rubrik=5712&key=standard_document_12776660; http://www.heise.de/tp/r4/artikel/25/25520/Lhtml.
16. http://www.bpb.de/files/7NTX8Y.pdf; *Ich verpfeife meine Firma—Zivilcourage im Beruf,* Germany, documentary, 1997, 45 min., film by V. Thurn, content.
17. http://www.bpb.de/files/7NTX8Y.pdf; *Ich verpfeife meine Firma—Zivilcourage im Beruf,* Germany, documentary, 1997, 45 min., film by V. Thurn, content.
18. http://www.bpb.de/files/7NTX8Y.pdf; *Ich verpfeife meine Firma—Zivilcourage im Beruf,* Germany, documentary, 1997, 45 min., film by V. Thurn, content.
19. Deiseroth, Dieter: Whistleblowing in Zeiten von BSE—Der Fall der Tierarztin Dr. Margrit Herbst; ISBN: 3-8305-0258-3; 2001.
20. Deiseroth, Dieter; Falter, Annegret (Hg.): Whistleblower in Altenpflege und Infektionsforschung—Whistleblowerpreis 2007 an Brigitte Heinisch und Dr. Liv Bode; ISBN: 978-3-8305-1455-8; 2007.
21. http://www.verdi.de/gesundheit-soziales/branchenpolitik/pflegeeinrichtungen/data/seite_7_drei_20.pdf.
22. http://www.message-online.com/82/krueger.htm.
23. http: //anstageslicht.de/index.php?UP_ID=14&NAV_ID=55.
24. http://www.guardian.co.uk/Archive/Article/0,4273,4036250,00.html.
25. http://frwebgate.access.gpo.gov/cgi-bin/getdoc.cgi?dbname=107_cong_public_laws&docid=f:publ204.107.
26. http://www.gesetze-im-internet.de/aktg/ 91.html.
27. Keun, Iris-Carola: Interne Whistleblowing-Stelle fordert Praventionskultur -Hohere Chancen zur Aufklarung doloser Handlungen; in: Borsenzeitung; ISSN: 0343-7728; 2007; Nr. 221, Verlagsbeilage v. 16.11.2007, p. 10.
28. http://www.pcaw.co.uk/news_attachments/whistleblowing_uncac.pdf.
29. http://conventions.coe.int/Treaty/Commun/QueVoulezVous.asp?NT=173&CM=8&DF=9/9/2008&CL=ENG.
30. http://conventions.coe.int/Treaty/Commun/QueVoulezVous.asp?NT=174&CM=8&DF=9/9/2008&CL=ENG.
31. http://www.olis.oecd.org/olis/2000doc.nsf/LinkTo/NT00002BE6/SFILE/00085743.PDF.

32. LAG-Duesseldorf-Beschluss vom 14.11.2005, Aktenzeichen: 10 TaBV 46/05, http://www.juraforum.de/urteile/urteil/lag-duesseldorf-beschluss-vom-14-11-2005-az-10-tabv-4605.html.
33. Bundesarbeitsgericht, Beschluss vom 22. Juli 2008—1 ABR 40/07; http://juris.bundesarbeitsgericht.de/cgi-bin/rechtsprechung/document.py?Gerich t=bag&Art=pm&Datum=2008&nr=12892&pos=0&anz=58.
34. http://ec.europa.eu/justice_home/fsj/privacy/docs/wpdocs/2006/wp117_en.pdf.
35. Further information and links leading to examples can be found under http://www.whistleblower-net.de/content/view/60/57/lang,de/.
36. PAS 1998/2008, which was established with support of the UK charity "public concern at work" and is available on their website: http://www.pcaw.co.uk/bsi/.
37. Bundesverfassungsgericht vom 2.7.2001—1 BvR 2049/00; http://www.bundesverfassungsgericht.de/entscheidungen/rk20010702_1bvr204900.html.
38. Bundesarbeitsgericht vom 3.7.2003—2 AZR 235/02 und vom 7.12.2006, 2 AZR400/05.
39. http://www.baua.de/nn_28474/de/Publikationen/Forschungsberichte/2002/Fb951,xv=vt.pdf. 39.
40. http://www.bundestag.de/ausschuesse/a10/anhoerungen/a10_81/16_10_849.pdf.
41. The documents relating to the hearing on § 612a n.F. BGB are available under: http://www.bundestag.de/ausschuesse/a10/anhoerungen/a10_81/index.html. These include the expertise by the author. The statement of the Whistleblower-Netzwerk is available under: http://www.whistleblower-net.de/content/view/87/80/lang,de/.
42. *Ich verpfeife meine Firma—Zivilcourage im Beruf,* Deutschland, documentary, 1997, 45 min., a film by V. Thurn, content.
43. http://www.buergerwelle.de/pdf/whistleblower_kongressbericht.pdf.
44. http://web.archive.org/web/*/http://ethikschutz.de.
45. Ethikschutz-Initiative INESPE: Wenn das Gewissen NEIN sagt—Ethisch handeln in der abhangigen Arbeit—Ein Ratgeber in Konflikfallen; ISBN: 3-923637-49-7; 1995. Cf. also: Bultmann, Antje (Hg.): Auf der AbschuBliste—Wie kritische Wissenschaftler mundtot gemacht werden sollen; ISBN: 3-426-77265-5; 1997.
46. http://www.vdw-ev.de/whistleblower/whistleblower-Preis.html.
47. Deiseroth, Dieter; Falter, Annegret (Hg.): Zivilcourage im BSE-Skandal—und die Folgen—Whistleblower-Preis 2001 fur die Tierarztin Dr. Margrit Herbst Dokumentation und kleine Wirkungsgeschichte—VDW-Materialien Nr. 2; 2002. # Deiseroth, Dieter; Falter, Annegret (Hg.): Whistleblowerpreis 2003—Daniel Ellsberg; ISBN: 3-8305-0973-1; 2005. # Deiseroth, Dieter; Falter, Annegret (Hg.): Whistleblower in Gentechnik und Rustungsforschung—Whistleblower-Preis 2005 an Theodore A. Postol und Arpad Pusztai; ISBN: 978-3-8305-1262-2; 2006. # Deiseroth, Dieter; Falter, Annegret (Hg.): Whistleblower in Altenpflege und Infektionsforschung—Whistleblowerpreis 2007 an Brigitte Heinisch und Dr. Liv Bode; ISBN: 978-3-8305-1455-8; 2007. # Deiseroth, Dieter; Gottling, Dietmar (Hg.): Der Fall Nikitin—eine Dokumentation zur Verleihung des Whistleblowerpreises 1999; ISBN: 3-923637-56-X; 2000.
48. Deiseroth, Dieter: Whistleblowing in Zeiten von BSE—Der Fall der Tierarztin Dr. Margrit Herbst; ISBN: 3-8305-0258-3; 2001.
49. http://www.transparency.de/.
50. http://www.fairness-stiftung.de/.
51. http://www.risk-communication.de/Whistleblowing-Rules-In-EU-Institutions.pdf.
52. http://www.risk-communication.de/.
53. http://www.whistleblowerinfo.de/; http://www.anstageslicht.de/index.php?UP_ID=14.

54. http://www.whistleblower-net.de/.
55. http://www.whistleblower-net.de/content/view/41/43/lang,en/.
56. http://www.whistleblower-net.de/content/view/87/80/lang,en/.

The Law and Practice of Whistleblowing in the United Kingdom

David Lewis
Middlesex University, U.K.

1. Introduction

The purpose of the U.K.'s Public Interest Disclosure Act 1998 is "to protect individuals who make certain disclosures of information in the public interest." It does so, primarily, by inserting a new Part IVA into the Employment Rights Act 1996 (henceforward ERA 1996).[1] PIDA 1998 was the model for South Africa's Protected Disclosures Act 2000 and has been regarded as an exemplary piece of legislation in debates in other countries, for example, the Netherlands, New Zealand and some Australian states.[2] This chapter will outline the U.K. statutory provisions and will then consider recent research on how whistleblowing procedures operate in practice.

2. What Types of Wrongdoing Can be Disclosed and by Whom?

Section 43B(1) of ERA 1996 defines a "qualifying disclosure" as one which a worker reasonably believes tends to show a matter falling into one or more of the following: (1) a criminal offense; (2) a failure to comply with any legal obligation; (3) a miscarriage of justice; (4) danger to the health and safety of any individual (i.e., not necessarily a worker); (5) damage to the environment; (6) the deliberate concealment of information tending to show any of the matters listed above. Apart from disclosures made to legal advisers, the U.K. provisions only apply to whistleblowers who act in good faith.

Turning to specific exclusions, the U.K. legislation applies to Crown employment (but not the security services) in the same way as it applies to other workers, save where a certificate of exemption has been issued on grounds of national security.[3] Workers are allowed to make disclosures about a matter which occurs outside the U.K. or which is not covered by U.K. law. The matter disclosed may have occurred in the past, be currently occurring or likely to occur and the statute does not require any link between the matter disclosed and the worker's employment. However, a disclosure will not be protected if the person "commits an offence by making it." An additional problem is that Sections 43G & H ERA 1996 (see below) provide that whistleblowers must not be acting for personal gain. Section 43D ERA 1996 ensures that disclosures made to a legal adviser are protected but such advisers are not authorized to reveal information protected by professional privilege. Section 43J ERA 1996 prevents employers from contracting out of the provisions in Part IVA by invalidating a worker's agreement (whether contained in a contract or settlement of legal proceedings) not to make a protected disclosure.

As regards who can disclose, protection is afforded to workers rather than just employees. For these purposes the definition of "worker" in Section 230 ERA 1996 is extended to include certain agency workers; certain workers who would not otherwise be covered because they are not obliged to carry out all of their duties personally; NHS practitioners such as GPs, certain dentists, pharmacists and opticians; and certain trainees. In addition, Section 43K(1) ERA 1996 ensures that former workers are covered.

3. How Should Disclosures be Made and Whom?

Section 43C(l) ERA 1996 protects workers who make qualifying disclosures in good faith to their employer or to another person who is responsible for the matter disclosed. According to Section 43C(2) ERA 1996, workers are to be treated as having made disclosures to their employer if they follow a procedure which the employer has authorized, even if the disclosure is actually made to someone else (for example, an independent person or organization). Section 43E ERA 1996 protects workers in appointed organizations if they make a disclosure in good faith to a Minister of the Crown rather than their legal employer. Section 43F(1) ERA 1996 protects workers who make disclosures in good faith to a person (or class of persons) prescribed for the purpose by the Secretary of State. However, the worker must reasonably believe that (1) the matter falls within the remit of the prescribed person, and (2) that the information and any allegation contained in it are substantially true.

Section 43G ERA 1996 enables workers to make a protected disclosure in other limited circumstances. In order to be protected workers must: (1) act in good faith; (2) reasonably believe that the information and any allegation contained in it are substantially true; (3) not act for personal gain; (4) have already disclosed substantially the same information to the employer or to a person prescribed under Section 43F ERA 1996, unless they reasonably believe that they would be subject to a detriment for doing so, or that the employer would conceal or destroy the evidence if alerted; and (5) act reasonably. For these purposes regard shall be had, in particular, to: (a) the identity of the person to whom the disclosure is made; (b) the seriousness of the matter; (c) whether there is a continuing failure or one likely to recur; (d) whether the disclosure is made in breach of a duty of confidentiality owed by the employer to another person; (e) any action the employer (or prescribed person) has taken or might have been expected to take in relation to a previous disclosure; (f) whether the worker has complied with any procedure authorized by the employer for making a disclosure.

Section 43H ERA 1996 deals with disclosures about exceptionally serious wrongdoing. Again, in order to be protected: (1) workers must act in good faith; (2) they must reasonably believe that the information and any allegation contained in it are substantially true; (3) they must not act for personal gain; (4) the relevant failure must be of an exceptionally serious nature; and (5) in all the circumstances it must be reasonable to make the disclosure. In this respect particular regard will be had to the identity of the person to whom the disclosure is made.

4. Protection Against Victimisation

Section 47B(1) ERA 1996 gives workers the right not to be subjected to any detriment for making a protected disclosure and it is made clear that detriment covers both actions and a deliberate failure to act. This section fails to deal with a detriment imposed by someone who has no direct relationship with the worker. Nevertheless workers may complain that their employer has subjected them to a detriment by failing to protect them from the actions of third parties, for example, another employer. In addition, workers who have been dismissed for making a protected disclosure and are not qualified to claim under the general unfair dismissal provisions, can bring a claim under Section 47B ERA 1996. Section 103A ERA 1996 makes it automatically unfair to dismiss employees on the grounds that they have made a protected disclosure and no qualifying period of service is required. Similarly, Section 105(6A) ERA 1996 makes it unfair to select employees for redundancy if the reason for doing so is that they have made a protected disclosure. Section 128 ERA 1996 makes interim relief available and there is no limit on the amount of compensation that can be awarded to those who have been penalized for making a protected disclosure.

5. How Prevalent are Whistleblowing Procedures and Why were They Introduced?

A survey of 600 colleges and universities conducted by researchers at Middlesex University in 2000 (henceforward the further and higher education survey), revealed that 91 percent of respondents had a whistleblowing procedure (Lewis, Ellis & Kyprianou, 2001).[4] 43 percent of these procedures had been in operation for more than twelve months. When asked why their procedure had been introduced, 260 institutions indicated that it was a result of good practice, 193 suggested compliance with the law, 114 stated that it was a management initiative, 6 said that it was prompted by an incident and two mentioned that it was introduced as a result of a trade union initiative. In 2001 the same researchers carried out a survey of the 414 English and Welsh local authorities (henceforward the local authority survey) on behalf of the Employers Organisation for Local Government (Lewis, Ellis & Kyprianou, 2002).[5] 93 percent of respondents stated that they had a whistleblowing procedure and 86 percent of procedures had been in existence for more than a year. The most frequently cited reasons for introducing a procedure were good practice (89 percent), compliance with the law (44 percent) and management initiative (43 percent). A Middlesex University survey in 2002 (Lewis, Ruff, Ellis and Kyprianou, 2003a) found that 19 percent of maintained schools, 17 percent of Dioceses and 71 percent of local education authorities (LEAs) had whistleblowing/confidential reporting procedures (henceforward referred to as the schools survey).[6] A majority of school procedures had been in place for less than two years. Good practice and compliance with the law were the main reasons for having a confidential reporting procedure. A 2003 survey of NHS trusts (Lewis, Ellis & Kyprianou, 2003b)[7] found that 99 percent stated had a confidential reporting /whistleblowing procedure and 78 percent of procedures had been in operation for more than two years. The main reasons given for introducing a procedure were: good practice; compliance with the law; national advice to employers and management initiative. The latest research is a survey of 262 organizations who had been in the FTSE top 250 between

July 2006 and February 2007 (Lewis 2008). 86 percent of those supplying information stated that their whistleblowing procedure had existed for more than 2 years. The reasons given for introducing the procedure were: good practice (93 percent); compliance with the law (42 percent); and management initiative (28 percent).

5.1 Trade Union Involvement

In the further and higher education survey, 78 percent of respondents indicated that a trade union was consulted about the introduction of a whistleblowing procedure. 97 percent of local authorities who had a procedure and 99 percent of NHS trusts stated that a trade union was consulted about its introduction. In the schools survey, all types of respondent were highly likely to have consulted trade unions about the introduction of their confidential reporting procedure. Only 14 percent of respondents in the FTSE survey said that trade unions were consulted about the introduction of their procedure.

5.2 Who Can Use the Whistleblowing Procedure?

The respondents to the further and higher education survey indicated that their whistleblowing procedures were open to a wide range of people. 319 institutions made their procedure available to employees, 130 to students, 81 to contractors, 67 to self-employed people, 66 to members of the public, 57 to sub-contractors and 52 to suppliers. In the local authority survey, 100 percent of respondents stated that employees could use the procedure, 48 percent indicated that the procedure was open to contractors, 42 percent to councillors, 34 percent to sub-contractors, 30 percent to suppliers, 27 percent to the self-employed and 26 percent to members of the public. In the schools survey, virtually all confidential reporting procedures were available to both teaching and non-teaching staff and a significant number of respondents opened their procedure to people who do not work for them. In addition to clinical and non-clinical staff, NHS trusts stated that their procedures could be used by a range of people including: agency workers; contractors; sub-contractors; suppliers; patients and members of the public. In the FTSE survey, 38 percent of respondents allowed contractors to invoke their procedure, 28 percent permitted sub-contractors to use it, 20 percent said that it could be used by self-employed people and 10 percent stated that members of the public could invoke it.

5.3 What Issues Should be Covered?

In the further and higher education survey, 89 percent of respondents who had a procedure indicated that it had never been used and the remainder stated that it had been invoked on less than 5 occasions. The following types of issue had been reported: 33 mentioned malpractice, 21 stated fraud, 12 indicated health and safety concerns, 11 pointed to harassment and 6 to discrimination. By way of contrast, 57 percent of respondents in the local authority survey had some experience of their procedure being invoked. However, the main types of issue reported were similar: fraud, malpractice and harassment.

The 2002 survey showed that confidential reporting procedures had seldom been used by schools but LEAs had considerable experience of them. The issues most likely to be handled by schools under this procedure were bullying by students and health and safety. 77 percent of NHS respondents indicated that they had some experience of the procedure being used and 19 percent stated that it had been used on more than 5 occasions. The types of issue most frequently reported were: clinical matters; harassment/ bullying by staff; financial irregularities; discrimination and health and safety. In the FTSE survey, 76 percent of respondents stated that their procedure had been invoked, 38 percent said that it had been used up to five times and 28 percent indicated that it had been used on 20 or more occasions. In relation to the types of issue reported, 63 percent cited financial irregularities, 55 percent identified health and safety, 52 percent mentioned harassment and bullying, 50 percent indicated malpractice, 34 percent stated discrimination, 25 percent computer misuse and 16 percent alcohol or drug abuse.

5.4 Is Confidentiality and Anonymity Guaranteed?

In the further and higher education survey, 95 percent indicated that confidentiality was maintained but only 54 percent of respondents permitted anonymous reporting. In the local authority survey, 94 percent had procedures which specified that confidentiality would be maintained and 89 percent of respondents allowed concerns to be reported anonymously. The schools survey also revealed that the vast majority of procedures specified that both anonymity and confidentiality will be maintained if a concern is raised. 71 percent of NHS respondents allowed concerns to be reported anonymously while 97 percent specified that confidentiality would be maintained. In the FTSE survey, 78 percent of respondents stated that their procedure allowed a concern to be reported anonymously whereas 94 percent said that their procedure specified that confidentiality would be maintained.

5.5 Dealing with Reprisals and Malicious Allegations

In the further and higher education survey, 72 percent of respondents indicated that their procedure provided for disciplinary action to be taken against those who victimize anyone reporting a concern. The equivalent figure in the local authority survey was 85 percent of respondents. In both the further and higher education and local authority surveys 90 percent of respondents stated that their procedure provided for disciplinary action to be taken against those who maliciously reported a concern. In the schools survey, respondents were highly likely to provide for disciplinary action to be taken against both malicious disclosers and people who victimize. Eighty percent of NHS respondents stated that disciplinary action could be taken against those who maliciously report a concern and 76 percent claimed that such action could be taken against those who victimized a person using the procedure. In the FTSE survey, 62 percent of respondents provided for disciplinary action to be taken against those who maliciously report and 70 percent stipulated that such action could be taken against those who victimize a person raising a concern.

5.6 The Availability of Advice and Assistance

In the further and higher education survey, 83 percent of respondents stated that people could bring a representative to a meeting to discuss a concern and 51 percent indicated that independent advice was available. 97 percent of respondents in the local authority survey indicated that a person reporting a concern could bring a representative of their choice to a meeting and 62 percent stated that independent advice was available. Representatives were also allowed in the overwhelming majority of procedures identified in the schools survey and, with the exception of Dioceses, the majority of respondents stated that independent advice was available. 97 percent of NHS respondents indicated that people could bring a representative of their choice to a meeting and 78 percent stated that independent advice was available to a person reporting a concern. In the FTSE survey, 24 percent of respondents stated that independent advice was available to a person reporting a concern and 65 percent indicated that such a person could bring a representative of their choice to a meeting.

5.7 With Whom Should a Concern be Raised?

In the further and higher education survey, 93 institutions stated that concerns should be reported to a line manager, 70 to the Principal/Vice-Chancellor, 57 (colleges) to the clerk/secretary to the Corporation and 48 to the Head of Human Resources. As alternative recipients of concerns, 127 indicated the clerk to the Governors/the Governors themselves, 99 respondents mentioned the Principal/Vice-Chancellor and 46 suggested the Head of Human Resources. 65 percent of respondents in the local authority survey said that concerns should normally be reported to the line manager. However, a range of people were regarded as alternative recipients of a concern. Both in schools and under LEA procedures concerns should normally be reported to the head teacher. Governors were most frequently specified by school respondents as alternative recipients of a concern and the Head of Human Resources by LEAs. 72 percent of NHS respondents stated that concerns should normally be reported to the line manager. The most frequently cited alternative recipients of a concern were: the Head of Human Resources; the chief executive and the Head of Department. In the FTSE survey, 68 percent of respondents indicated that line managers were the initial point of contact. As regards alternative recipients, human resources was identified by 33 percent, the Head of Department by 29 percent, the Head of Legal Services by 28 percent and the Chief Executive by 27 percent.

5.8 Who Has Overall Responsibility for the Procedure?

In the further and higher education survey, 58 percent of colleges indicated that the Governing Body had overall responsibility for the whistleblowing procedure, 21 percent pointed to the Principal and 10 percent to the Human Resources Department. In universities, 45 percent stated that the Governing Body had overall responsibility, 40 percent mentioned the Vice-Chancellor and 11 percent pointed to the Human Resources Department.

In local authorities, the monitoring officer (39 percent) and the chief executive (34 percent) were most likely to have overall responsibility for the procedure. The Head of Human Resources was mentioned by only 8 percent of respondents. The governors were most likely to have overall responsibility in schools but in LEAs the responsibility was more evenly divided—the Head of Human Resources being mentioned by 20 percent of respondents. The Chief Executive (69 percent) and the Director of Human Resources/Personnel (21 percent) were the people most likely to have overall responsibility for the procedures in NHS trusts. In the FTSE survey, the people most likely to have overall responsibility were the company secretary or auditors (21 percent).

5.9 Who Investigates Concerns?

The further and higher education survey reveals that the person most likely to be responsible for investigating concerns at colleges was the clerk/secretary to the corporation. At universities, auditors were most likely to have this responsibility. In the local authority survey, respondents indicated that the following investigated concerns: internal audit (64 percent); monitoring officer (51 percent); line manager (41 percent); Head of Department (37 percent); chief executive (30 percent) and Head of Human Resources (29 percent). The head teacher is most likely to investigate under both school and LEA procedures. In NHS trusts, the person most likely to have responsibility for investigating concerns was the line manager (44 percent). In the FTSE survey, 31 percent of respondents pointed to Human Resources and the following were each mentioned by 28 percent: the Head of Legal Services, auditors and the line manager.

5.10 Feedback

In the further and higher education survey, 90 percent of respondents stated that people were kept informed about the progress of an investigation. The equivalent figure in both the local authority survey and NHS trust surveys was 91 percent. In schools, almost all respondents stated that their procedures ensure that people reporting a concern are kept informed about the progress of any investigation. Eighty-five percent of respondents in the FTSE survey stated that their procedure ensured that people reporting concerns are kept informed about the progress of any investigation

5.11 Taking the Matter Further

In the further and higher education survey, 88 percent of respondents had a procedure which specified another person who could be approached if the whistleblower was dissatisfied with the outcome of an investigation. The equivalent figure was 79 percent in the local authority survey and 89 percent in NHS trusts. In schools, the vast majority of procedures also specify who can be approached if such a person was dissatisfied and 67 percent of respondents in the FTSE survey so indicated.

5.12 Communicating the Procedure

In all bar one of the surveys referred to in this chapter, the method most commonly used was the staff handbook. The other methods most frequently used in the further and higher education, local authority, school and FTSE surveys were the induction program and printed policy statements. In NHS trusts the most frequently cited methods were the induction program, Internet web pages[8] and printed policy statements/ manual.

5.13 Training

In the further and higher education survey, 14 percent of respondents indicated that training in the whistleblowing procedure was provided. By and large this was designed for people who might have to handle concerns rather than those who might wish to raise them. 33 percent of respondents in the local authority survey indicated that training was provided for managers in how to handle concerns. Coincidentally, the same percentage stated that training was provided for employees in how to use the procedure. In both cases, the induction process and written instructions were the forms of training most frequently mentioned. The schools survey indicated that only in LEAs did a majority of respondents provide training for managers in how to handle concerns. Schools who did offer training were most likely to use general staff training and induction. LEAs were more likely to use an initial seminar or briefing session and written instructions. Less training was provided for potential users of the procedure. The most frequently used methods in schools were the induction process and oral instructions. LEAs were most likely to use the school induction process and written instructions. 59 percent of NHS respondents stated that training was provided for managers in how to handle concerns and general staff training was the most frequently cited method. Only 30 percent indicated that training was provided for employees in how to use the procedure and there was very heavy reliance on the induction process. In the FTSE survey, 39 percent of respondents provided training for managers in how to handle concerns and 23 percent offered training for potential users of the procedure.

5.14 Monitoring and Reviewing the Procedure

In the further and higher education survey, 77 percent of institutions claimed that their whistleblowing procedure was monitored and, of these, 77 percent stated that this occurred annually. 55 percent of respondents in the local authority survey stated that the effectiveness of their procedure was monitored and, of these, 73 percent stated that this occurred annually or more frequently. The schools survey showed that most confidential reporting procedures were monitored and this was likely to be done annually. LEA procedures were most likely to be scrutinized by the council's Monitoring Officer and monitoring in schools was likely to be carried out by Governors and the head teacher. 73 percent of NHS respondents claimed that the effectiveness of their procedure was monitored and in the majority of cases this was regarded as a function of the human resources/personnel department. 51 percent of those who monitored did so annually. In the FTSE survey, 69 percent of respondents stated that their procedure was monitored and 48 percent claimed to monitor more frequently than annually.

6. Conclusion

If the public interest in protecting whistleblowers was never clearly articulated prior to the PIDA 1998, this legislation attempts to do so, albeit in a restrictive fashion. For these purposes the public interest manifests itself in the form of facilitating protected disclosures. Although Lord Nolan commended the PIDA 1998 "for so skilfully achieving the essential but delicate balance... between the public interest and the interests of employers," it could be argued that in reality employers' interests have been given prominence. Indeed, some would argue that internal whistleblowing/confidential reporting procedures can work against the public interest in that they facilitate cover-ups and deprive the public of information about wrongdoing. Nevertheless the research conducted to date suggests that public sector organisations and the FTSE top 250 have responded positively to the pressures to introduce whistleblowing procedures.

Notes

1. The references below are to the ERA 1996 as amended.
2. See generally: Vandekerckhove(2006).

3. Sections 191 (2) and 193 ERA 1996.
4. There were 349 respondents, giving a response rate of 58 percent. The survey covered more than 0.25 million staff.
5. There were 281 respondents, giving a response rate of 68 percent. The survey covered at least 1.5 million staff.
6. Replies were received from 30 percent of the 717 English community, voluntary -aided and foundation schools contacted, 40 percent of the 65 Dioceses and 47 percent of the 151 LEAs. The overall response rate was 33 percent. The total number of staff covered was 15,358 in schools, 27,212 by Dioceses and 415,939 by LEAs.
7. A postal questionnaire was sent to 278 English and Welsh NHS Trusts in the summer of 2003. 154 completed questionnaires were returned, giving a response rate of 55 percent. The total number of staff covered by the survey was 497,388.
8. This was mentioned by 59 percent of respondents in the FTSE survey.

References

Lewis, D., Ellis, C., & Kyprianou, A., 2001, Whistleblowing at work: the results of a survey of procedures in further and higher education, Education & the Law, Vol.13 No. 3 pages 215-225.

Lewis, D., Ellis, C., & Kyprianou, A., 2002, A survey of confidential reporting procedures in English and Welsh local authorities, Employers Organisation for Local Government, London.

Lewis, D., Ruff, A., Ellis, C. & Kyprianou, A., 2003a, A survey of confidential reporting procedures in maintained schools, dioceses and local education authorities, Centre for Legal Research, Middlesex University, London.

Lewis, D., Ellis, C. & Kyprianou, A., 2003b, A survey of confidential reporting/whistleblowing procedures in National Health Service Trusts, Centre for Legal Research, Middlesex University, London.

Lewis, D., 2008, A survey of whistleblowing/confidential reporting procedures used by the FTSE top 250 firms, Centre for Legal Research, Middlesex University, London.

Vandekerckhove, W., 2006, Whistleblowing and organisational social responsibility: a global assessment, Ashgate, Aldershot.

Whistleblower Legislation in Australia—Analysis and Reform

A. J. Brown
Law School, Griffith University,
Brisbane, Australia

Paul Latimer
Department of Business Law and Taxation,
Monash University,
Melbourne, Australia

In recent years, every Australian public law jurisdiction has passed legislation in the public interest to protect whistleblowers. Whistleblower protection has also been passed in corporate law, workplace relations law, consumer law and financial regulation. This chapter identifies important issues for consideration in whistleblower regulation—issues which are clearly well-intentioned and increasingly comprehensive, but which often remain undeveloped, uncoordinated and at times confusing. We work in some of the research findings from a recent Australian research report (2008) and some of the recommendations in a report to parliament (2009) in identifying a strong case for greater consistency in the key legal thresholds and operational requirements imposed by Australian whistleblower protection regimes, including useful potential for common tests and processes covering both the public and private sectors.

1. Introduction

In a democracy, power is held by the people (the citizens) through their right to vote in free elections. All citizens have equal access to power.

All citizens have universally recognized freedoms and civil liberties. One of the foundations of a democracy is the accountability for the actions of those who have been elected. There is no accountability without transparency and the disclosure of what is happening.

An informed society underpins a democratic society, which must encourage, support and protect whistleblowers. Whistleblowers promote an informed society and provide an essential and valuable service to the public by making known and exposing wrongdoing.

Disclosure—which may take the form of leaks of wrongdoing—raises the question of the need for public interest disclosure protection as an important part of transparency and accountability, which are in turn critical to both effective and responsible public administration. Good policies to protect those who make public interest disclosures, and to make sure that the issues they raise are dealt with appropriately, support public accountability and good government.[1]

Consensus has emerged across Australian public policy since the 1990s that internal witnesses to suspected wrongdoing—corruption, misconduct and maladministration—are a crucial resource in the pursuit of public integrity. It is also well established that reprisals, harassment and poor management of internal witnesses can seriously compromise integrity efforts, with damaging results for individuals, public agencies and governments.[2]

Whistleblower research

There is much anecdotal evidence from around the world, including Australia[3], on whistleblowing. Earlier Australian whistleblower research of, for example, De Maria found "nothing to celebrate" on his "tour through the entrails of our society, except perhaps the valor of the whistleblowers who guide us into the netherworld of corruption, incompetence, cover-ups and organizational vendettas" with "the non-suffering" whistleblower as "a contradiction in terms."[4] Others point to empirical indications that a whistleblower's fate need not necessarily be grim.[5]

There is new evidence of global significance from the recently completed three-year Australian Research Council Project Whistling While They Work (WWTW),[6] led by the first co-author and including the second co-author of this chapter.

Surveys in the project indicated that 71 percent of all respondents had direct evidence of at least one example of wrongdoing. Sixty-one percent found at least one form of perceived wrongdoing at least "somewhat serious," while 28 percent said they had formally reported the wrongdoing which they considered was the most serious. Twenty percent of respondents were estimated as having reported the most serious wrongdoing outside their organizational role (they were potential whistleblowers). In the case of 12 percent of respondents, the reported (most serious) wrongdoing involved "public interest" wrongdoing such as corruption, defective administration or waste, as opposed to personnel and workplace grievances. Using this conservative estimate, if 12 percent of all public servants had also reported some form of public interest wrongdoing outside their role in the two years, this estimate would equate to 197,000 public servants Australia-wide.[7]

There are many questions arising from the diversity of current laws,[8] with lingering fears that reprisals remain the norm, that legal protection can only ever be symbolic and that a whistleblower or witness protection scheme remains a poor substitute for effective disclosure laws.

2. How do Public Sector Whistleblower Protection Laws Function in Australia?

Australia has three levels of government—the Commonwealth government based in the national capital of Canberra, six states[9] and two federal territories[10] and local (city, municipal, shire) government. The six states developed from the original six British colonies in Australia, three of which (New South Wales, Queensland and Tasmania) were established as places of exile (gulags) for criminals deported from England in the 18th and 19th centuries. The states became largely self-governing in the second half of the nineteenth century.

The *Commonwealth of Australia Constitution Act 1900* (UK), which contains the Australian Constitution, was drafted in Australia by the "fathers of federation" in the 1890s but enacted as a statute of the British parliament. The Constitution transferred a number of areas of national and international importance such as the power over inter-State "trade and commerce" and the power over corporations to the new Commonwealth of Australia Parliament. These Commonwealth powers have been the basis for the expansion of the Commonwealth government into areas previously considered to be matters of State and territory law. Australia became "independent" from the UK when the colonies became States in the Commonwealth of Australia in 1901.

In practical terms, Australian law is now dominated by "Commonwealth," "federal," "national" or "Australian" legislation of the Commonwealth Parliament in Canberra passed for Australia-wide application.

Australia has moved on from its British origins two centuries ago, and has been enriched with immigration from many countries, resulting in Australia being one of the world's most multi-cultural countries.

Whistleblower laws in Australia have been passed since the early 1990s by all Australian state and territory jurisdictions to provide some legislative protection for public sector "whistleblowers" and/or employees making public interest disclosures.

2.1. Aims of Whistleblower Legislation

Ideally the formal objectives of most whistleblower legislation should include at least three main objects, whether in the short title, the long title or in an objectives section of the legislation:[11]

"The stated objectives of public interest disclosure legislation should be:

- to support public interest whistleblowing by facilitating disclosure of wrongdoing
- to ensure that public interest disclosures are properly assessed and, where necessary, investigated and actioned
- to ensure that a person making a public interest disclosure is protected against detriment and reprisal."

The preferred title is the Public Interest Disclosure Act instead of the "Whistleblower Protection Act" or "Protected Disclosures Act":

2.2. Consistent Legal Threshold—Objective or Subjective Coverage for Whistleblower Laws?

When, how and in what manner should "whistleblower protection" be invoked, and what objectives should guide them? Despite many laws, answers to these questions currently remain fragmented.

Confusion on these issues limits the ability of organizations to encourage disclosures and proactively manage outcomes, and creates uncertainty about when external legal protections are triggered, whether disclosure management is a routine governance issue or a rare and avoidable crisis risk, and even how many cases are involved. Reported disclosures may only be a subset of the total disclosures actually being handled, and a smaller set again of total internal witnesses managed.

Name	**Long title**[12]
Public Service Act 1999 (Commonwealth of Australia), s16[13]	An Act to provide for the establishment and management of the Australian Public Service, and for other purposes
Public Interest Disclosure Act 1994 (Australian Capital Territory)[14]	An Act to encourage the disclosure of conduct adverse to the public interest in the public sector, and for related purposes
Protected Disclosures Act 1994 (New South Wales), currently under review	An Act to provide protection for public officials disclosing corrupt conduct, maladministration and waste in the public sector; and for related purposes
Public Interest Disclosure Act 2008 (Northern Territory)	An Act to provide for the disclosure and investigation of improper conduct of public officers and public bodies, to protect persons making disclosures and others from reprisal, and for related purposes
Whistleblowers Protection Act 1994 (Queensland), reviewed in 2006	An Act to protect whistleblowers and for other purposes
Whistleblowers Protection Act 1993 (South Australia)	An Act to protect persons disclosing illegal, dangerous or improper conduct; and for other purposes.
Public Interest Disclosures Act 2002 (Tasmania), currently under review	An Act to encourage and facilitate disclosures of improper conduct by public officers and public bodies, to protect persons making those disclosures and others from reprisals, to provide for the matters disclosed to be properly investigated and dealt with and for other purposes
Whistleblowers Protection Act 2001 (Victoria), currently under review	No long title
Public Interest Disclosure Act 2003 (Western Australia)	An Act to facilitate the disclosure of public interest information, to provide protection for those who make disclosures and for those the subject of disclosures, and, in consequence, to amend various Acts, and for related purposes

3. What are the Main Whistleblower Problems in Australia?

3.1. Public-Private Coverage of Whistleblower Regulation

Australian whistleblower laws reflect their origins in the public sector and focus on public sector whistleblower, yet some of the best-known whistleblowing involves disclosure by private sector employees.[15] We submit that private sector whistleblowing laws also deserve protection by legislation.

There have been calls in Australia to ensure that whistleblower protection should occur in a "sector blind" fashion.[16] Australia's first two whistleblower laws were sector blind, and this continues in some jurisdictions with protection of disclosure by "anybody" or "any person," whether public sector or private sector.[17]

However, these models are not the norm, and private sector whistleblower protection has also been pursued in:

1. An Australian Standard on "Whistleblower Protection Programs for Entities" (AS 8004-2003)[18]—which sets out systems for all medium-to-large organizations, and
2. Statutory protection in the Corporations Act 2001 (Cth) and in the Workplace Relations Act 1996 (Cth) in 2004.

Public and private sector whistleblowing regulation is currently following separate tracks:

1. Australia's public sector laws have evolved with the threefold objectives set out above with consequences that do not always apply in the private sector. These public sector laws deal with the making and investigation of disclosures including procedures for how public sector agencies and investigative authorities should handle disclosures. Even if these principles were extended to the private sector, they would vary between different types of regulatory regime (such as corporate regulation, consumer protection, environmental protection and financial services/investor protection), and their complexity would mitigate against combining all public and private sector wrongdoing under one law.
2. There are differences between public and private sectors in how "public interest" disclosures are defined, and how agencies are expected to respond to them. Some types of misconduct in the public sector may give rise to a private cause of action in the private sector. Public sector legislation can impose more rigorous requirements for public agencies than might be reasonably expected of all private sector entities.
3. A third reason for parallel whistleblower legislation is Australia's federal system. Much private regulation is now covered by federal regulation (as

> mentioned above), while the public sector is regulated under nine separate Commonwealth, state/territory and dozens of local government jurisdictions. Under the continuing trend towards uniform national business regulation, there is little interest in state laws trying to regulate private sector whistle-blowing. Similarly, even if there was national "sector-blind" legislation, it would not replace the need for state public sector laws.

It is therefore important to clarify the confusion caused by the private coverage inadequately attempted in two State jurisdictions of Queensland and South Australia. Both jurisdictions would be better served by a comprehensive law focused simply on the public sector, with anti-reprisal mechanisms for other complainants placed in other legislation. Such reform would help clarify the purpose and nature of these schemes.

3.2. Who is a Whistleblower?

While whistleblowing legislation is intended to protect "whistle-blowers," none of Australia's current legislation defines the term "whistleblower" or "whistleblowing."[19] Whistleblowing is taken to mean disclosures by organization members of matters of "public interest"—that is, suspected or alleged wrongdoing that affects more than the personal or private interests of the person making the disclosure.

This chapter recommends the following definition of whistleblowing: "Whistleblowing is disclosure by organization members (former or current) of illegal, immoral or illegitimate practices under the control of their employers to people or organizations that might be able to effect action."[20]

The WWTW survey found that there were no personality traits which would identify a whistleblower. Respondents who reported wrongdoing outside their role (non-role reporters—that is, potential whistleblowers) shared most of the same attitudes to their organization, job and management as non-reporters. Non-role reporters were slightly more likely to be female and have spent longer in their organizations than others. There was little evidence that employees who report wrongdoing are predisposed to conflict or are likely to be disgruntled or embittered employees, driven to report by perverse personal characteristics.[21]

3.3. The Whistleblower's State of Mind

Australian whistleblower legislation has no standard to determine the whistleblower's state of mind and whether an honest and reasonable belief will suffice for whistleblower protection.

None of the jurisdictions requires evidence of a "genuine" belief by the whistleblower. For example, South Australia and Western Australia require that the whistleblower "believes on reasonable grounds that the information is true."[22] Some jurisdictions apply the "believes on reasonable grounds" test to the whistleblower's state of mind.[23]

While whistleblowing can involve these elements, we question whether all whistleblowers fulfill these heroic stereotypes, how many want to be heroes, and whether a major goal of organizational responses is not specifically to lessen the amount of heroic suffering that must be endured. In reality, people also blow the whistle for different reasons, and valid disclosures have to be managed for their "prosocial" (socially positive) benefits even when made for purely self-serving reasons.[24]

Whistleblower protection is not intended to be given only for evidence of "genuine" belief, and there are many and different conditions under which a "genuine" whistleblower would not be protected by whistleblower laws. Regardless of the intention of the whistleblower, disclosure is only protected if it falls within the Act,[25] and the legislation does not generally apply if the discloser fails to assist with investigation,[26] or if the disclosure:

- breaches legal professional privilege,[27]
- is anonymous,[28] or false or misleading,[29]
- questions government policy[30]
- is only made to avoid disciplinary action,[31] or
- is made on frivolous or other grounds.[32]

In the words of the WWTW Report,[33] a disclosure should qualify as a "public interest disclosure" if the person making the disclosure holds an honest and reasonable belief that the disclosure shows proscribed wrongdoing (the subjective test) and the disclosure does show, or tends to show, proscribed wrongdoing, irrespective of the person's belief (the objective test).

The motivation or intention of the person making the disclosure should not be relevant. Nor should a person be required to use a special form or declare that it is a public interest disclosure.

3.4. What is "Wrongdoing"?

All Australian jurisdictions encourage the disclosure of wrongdoing, but there is no standard for the wrongdoing to be disclosed and protected. No doubt they are all aware of the perceived problem of whistleblower legislation opening the disclosure floodgates, so only some jurisdictions protect anonymous disclosures and only some protect disclosure by reprisal targets. There is no consistency on whistleblower protections, which varies from the weak to the strong, and different jurisdictions protect different disclosures.

Different public interest disclosure is protected in different ways, depending on whether the disclosure is in the public sector or in the private sector (above, topic III[1]). Depending on the legislation, disclosure usually includes for example disclosure of corruption, danger to the environment or to public health, illegal activity, maladministration, official misconduct, and serious and substantial waste. Therefore whether a person can disclose the following under whistleblower laws will have different answers in different jurisdictions.

The WWTW report adopted a wide definitional approach of wrongdoing (including public and private interest) consistent with the need to encourage an "if in doubt, report" approach to workplace problems.[34] In the words of the report, legislation should specify the types of proscribed wrongdoing for a public interest disclosure.[35] These should include crime, a breach of the law, official corruption (including abuse of power, breach of trust and conflict of interest), official misconduct, and defective administration (including negligence or incompetence, improper financial management, and any failure to perform a duty that could result in injury to the public, such as an unacceptable risk to public health, public safety or the environment).

The WWTW survey found that what is considered wrongdoing to be disclosed appears to be influenced by the public employee's organizational context, their perceptions of the seriousness of the wrongdoing and their beliefs about whether reporting the wrongdoing will serve any good purpose. The likelihood of reporting increases when employees assess wrongdoing to be more serious and frequent, when they have direct evidence of the wrongdoing (as opposed to simply observing it) and when it affects them personally. The likelihood of reporting decreases when these features are not present, when employees assess that the wrongdoing involves multiple participants or when the participants are at a higher organizational level than the observer.[36]

The most important reasons stated by employees for reporting wrongdoing, when they were motivated to do so, were that they had confidence that action would be taken if they did report and that they had knowledge and confidence in the whistleblowing process.

Confidence that they would be supported or protected after their report was a lesser consideration for most employees who reported, and was a less important consideration than generally believed by respondents to the case-handler and manager surveys in the case study agencies.

In the case of respondents who did not report wrongdoing, the main reasons were:

- the belief that no action would be taken, or
- a fear of reprisal, or a fear that management would not protect them from reprisal (especially when the perceived wrongdoers included managers).[37]

3.5. Existing Legislation Does Not Reflect Whistleblowing of Wrongdoing

Most Australian whistleblower legislation focuses on the making and handling of "public interest disclosures,"[38] or "protected disclosures,"[39] or both "protected disclosures" and "public interest disclosures."[40]

The minimalist nature of these laws comes as a stark reminder of the wide gap between the basic nature of these laws, and the larger, more ambitious goals of facilitating disclosures and protecting those who make them. The rhetorical symbolism of whistleblower protection—for example when these laws are discussed publicly by the governments that introduce them—naturally focuses on these larger goals. The reality is that these Australian laws have never been capable of delivering these goals. They have been designed to remove specific legal barriers or to create specific legal obligations so as to at least make disclosures and reprisal remediation possible.

Indeed, the substance of the existing laws is so basic that one can legitimately wonder why they were needed at all—surely, existing legislation would both permit and protect public employees who report, say, defective administration as defined by the Ombudsman legislation of each jurisdiction,[41] financial mismanagement that would breach financial administration and audit legislation,[42] or criminal conduct such as theft, fraud or bribe-taking. The existing laws often already provide a legal framework in which the role of whistleblowers could or should have been recognized, leaving conceptual and practical questions which still remain for resolution today, as discussed later in this chapter.

The fact that governments conclude that separate, stand-alone legislation was needed—with or without associated amendments to other legislation—indicates the very great practical difficulties that confront the realities, as opposed to the mere legal possibility, of disclosure facilitation and management. For disclosures to come to light, and for those who make them not to suffer unnecessarily, organizational cultures need to transform from closed hierarchies (in which risks of mistakes or wrongdoing are not openly acknowledged) to more open environments (with more sophisticated systems for ensuring that individuals and organizations take responsibility for problems and can deal with them in an open, constructive and efficient manner). The symbolism of stand-alone whistleblower protection laws is a direct reflection of the importance of this challenge, even if the laws themselves are a very blunt instrument.

This chapter provides a comparative analysis of the scope of Australia's whistleblower laws across the Commonwealth, six states and two federal territories. This analysis demonstrates inconsistencies in definition and coverage, and narrow versus wide approaches, with the result that an employee of the same organization operating Australia-wide may be permitted to blow the whistle for the same wrongdoing in one jurisdiction but not in another jurisdiction. This situation is not sensible in Australia's national economy.

3.6. Who to Report To?

There are differences in the Australian legislation on who a whistleblower can report to (the disclosure channels).[43] Disclosure options include disclosure to an "appropriate authority," a "proper authority" or a body authorised. Examples include anti-corruption authorities, the Auditor-General, the media, members of parliament, the Ombudsman and the police. Because of the differences in the different jurisdictions, a whistleblower in a company operating in one Australian jurisdiction (Commonwealth, state, territory) may not be able to disclose conduct occurring in that jurisdiction but may be able to disclose the same conduct in the adjoining jurisdiction.

The WWTW research demonstrated that most whistleblowing begins and ends within the organization.[44] Of the majority of whistleblowers who reported internally in the first instance, most also did so up the management chain (84 percent of all whistleblowers) rather than through specialist internal units or processes (less than 10 percent).[45]

The WWTW Report recommended that whistleblower legislation should allow a public interest disclosure to be made to a variety of different people or agencies.[46] This would include the whistleblower's supervisor, the CEO of the agency, any designated unit, person or hotline in an agency, and any external agency with jurisdiction.

A common external reporting agency may be the solution, but it would have to overcome the fact that whistleblowing obligations are sourced in so many different statutes at Commonwealth, state and territory levels. The WWTW Report recommended an oversight agency with responsibility for public interest disclosures to administer the legislation. It should have clearing house responsibilities, including being notified by agencies of all disclosures, recording them and how they were dealt with and resolved, and advisory and management roles.[47]

There is an important role for private sector organizations to facilitate disclosure, such as the Project on Government Oversight in the U.S.—an independent non profit organization which investigates and exposes corruption and other misconduct to achieve more open, accountable and hones federal government.[48]

3.7. Agency Procedures

Reporting by a whistleblower is only part of the story. The WWTW research evaluated agency responses—the comprehensiveness and effectiveness of agency procedures—and found that employees must be aware of and have confidence in whistleblower legislation. In agencies where they do, employees have more positive attitudes to whistleblowing, higher likelihood of reporting, higher trust in the anticipated management response and there is a higher likelihood that serious wrongdoing will be exposed or "flushed out" (ie, there are lower inaction rates).[49]

The WWTW survey found that there were systemic weaknesses in the internal disclosure procedures in the 175 agencies that responded to the survey regarding whistleblowing—especially regarding support and protection of whistleblowers. Only five of the 175 agencies had developed reasonably strong procedures for the management of whistleblowing, measured against the current Australian Standard.[50]

The survey found that more senior staff members in most agencies did not have a good understanding of their own whistleblower procedures. This indicates a need for the development of new best-practice or model procedures, clearer statutory requirements and better oversight of the quality of procedures and the adequacy of their implementation.

The research found that there was some follow-up of whistleblower reports including organizational changes. Sixty-three percent of public interest whistleblowers reported that their disclosure was investigated,

56 percent of whom indicated that the investigation resulted in improved organizational outcomes.[51] Whistleblowers were most likely to be satisfied with the handling of their disclosure if they were kept informed and the investigation resulted in positive, substantive outcomes.[52]

3.8. Whistleblowing to Media and Parliament

Disclosure to the media and parliament should be encouraged and protected as one of the foundations of a democratic society to bring evidence of wrongdoing to the attention of the public and to promote official action on disclosures. The WWTW survey indicated that less than one percent of all whistleblowers went outside official channels to the media at any stage—usually as a last resort.[53] Australian whistleblower legislation is not consistent on whether or not to protect whistleblowing outside official channels.

Disclosure to the media is only protected in New South Wales.[54] Preconditions include prior disclosure to the relevant authority, and that the authority has decided not to proceed, or has investigated but not completed within six months. "Journalist" includes print and electronic media, but would it include a freelance analyst such as a stockbroker commentator in the media? In the views of the WWTW Report and the House of Representatives Report,[55] a disclosure made to a person or body that is not designated by the legislation to receive disclosures (for example, the media) should be protected in exceptional circumstances as defined in the legislation.

The democratic process should promote disclosure and debate under parliamentary privilege. Several but lamentably not all Australian jurisdictions provide for a whistleblower to make a protected disclose to a member of parliament. There should be protected whistleblower disclosure to the media and members of parliament as one of the foundations of any democratic society.

3.9. Internal Disclosure Procedures/Internal Witness Management Systems

Practical protection for whistleblowers is as important as legal protection, yet not all jurisdictions require agencies to develop procedures for whistleblower protection.

Reliance on internal disclosure procedures is important because total reliance on ex post facto criminal and civil sanctions will only provide limited deterrence against reprisals, and will only rectify damage after it has already been done. As a complement, the internal focus demands capacity for sensitive case-handling, risk management, reprisal prevention and early intervention in conflict at numerous organizational levels.

There is evidence of private initiatives to promote whistleblowing on the basis that encouraging whistleblowing may reduce impropriety and increase productivity. However despite their importance, the existing positive efforts in more proactive, positive internal witness management have been subject to very little research, particularly in the case of the crucial intra-organizational strategies.

A person who has made a disclosure to which the legislation applies should be protected against criminal or civil liability, or other detriment, for making the disclosure.[56]

3.10. Public Reporting and Coordination

Public information and coordination is an important part of any whistleblower program. Whistleblowers must be aware of the procedures, and whistleblower awareness can be—and must be—enhanced by public education, training and support. For example, some jurisdictions provide that the Ombudsman must prepare and publish guidelines under the Act.[57]

There must be clear procedures on how a public body is to determine that a disclosure is a public interest disclosure, when the whistleblower must be notified, and whether and when the disclosure will go further (for example, to the Ombudsman).[58]

In the words of the WWTW Report, all public interest disclosures to an organization should be formally recorded.[59] This includes data collection in Annual Reports, and follow-through by the agency such as prompt and appropriate action, and/or investigation or referring the disclosure to an external agency. It is important to keep the whistleblower informed of action proposed to be taken, the progress of any action and the outcomes of any action.[60]

3.11. Anti-Reprisal Provisions

There is the risk that instead of earning respect for their courage (hero), the names of whistleblowers do become known and that they suffer reprisal, bullying and victimization (traitor).

The whistleblower legislation does provide for many different forms of anti-reprisal provisions. Most whistleblower legislation prohibits victimization and reprisal, and imposes civil and/or criminal penalties for breach, injunctions, remedies in tort for victimization and civil remedies for reprisals.[61]

The WWTW research found that the overall treatment of whistleblowers was better than expected. There was no evidence that the "non-suffering" whistleblower was "a contradiction in terms,"[62] and it was not inevitable that a whistleblower would suffer mistreatment from co-workers or management, even if reporting is frequently a difficult and stressful experience.[63]

3.12. Reprisal by Management

Contrary to common assumptions, mistreatment of whistleblowers is more likely to come from management than from colleagues or co-workers.[64] While 90 percent of all whistleblowers said they were at least "somewhat" likely to report again, only 59 percent of reporters who said they were treated badly said that they would report again.[65]

The WWTW survey confirmed that mistreatment or harm suffered by whistleblowers was most likely to be intimidation, harassment, heavy scrutiny of work, ostracism, unsafe or humiliating work or other workplace-based negative behavior—not by co-workers or colleagues but by managers. Even successful whistleblowers often report adverse psychological experiences (for example, increased stress) from whistleblowing, though not as adverse as those treated badly.

Based on relationships between the internal witness and employee surveys, approximately 62 percent of all whistleblower respondents might be estimated as having suffered increased stress as a result of reporting wrongdoing (the most common form of adverse impact), with about 43 percent of all whistleblowers estimated as suffering extreme stress.[66]

3.13. Whistleblower Protection

Agencies should establish proper internal procedures for receiving, recording and investigating disclosures, for protecting people who make disclosures and for safeguarding the privacy of those who make disclosu-res.[67] They should ensure that staff are made aware of their responsibilities under the legislation, including the responsibility to support and protect any person making a disclosure. Agencies should assess whether the person who made the disclosure—or any other person—faces any risk of detriment or requires special protection, and if so, they should take all reasonable measures to protect a whistleblower from direct or indirect detriment, actual or foreseeable. There should be remedial action if a person suffers detriment as a result of making a disclosure such as compensation (pecuniary and/ or non-pecuniary), disciplinary or criminal action.[68]

There could be a low-cost tribunal to deal with compensation applications with expertise in determining the rights and responsibilities of employers and employees.[69]

As recommended by the WWTW report, there should be ongoing concern for the whistleblower and assessment of the impact the disclosure into the future.[70]

4. Whistleblower Conclusions from Australia

This chapter has tested common criticisms of the efficacy of Australian public law whistleblower laws, and has included some findings of the new research published in 2008 in the WWTW report.

We identify a strong case for greater consistency in the key legal thresholds and operational requirements imposed by Australian whistleblower protection regimes, including common tests and processes covering both the public and private sectors. In large part, the prospect for accelerating the transition towards more effective, less "symbolic" regimes depends on a clearer consensus regarding the public importance of employee disclosures and the organizational advantages of open, proactive approaches to disclosure management.

Notes

1. Senator John Faulkner, 'Launch of Whistling While They Work', Parliament House, Canberra, 9 September 2009, at < http://www.smos.gov.au/speeches/2008/sp_20080909.html>.
2. See, eg A. J. Brown (ed), *Whistleblowing in the Australian Public Sector -Enhancing the theory and practice of internal witness management in public sector organisations,* ANU E Press, Australian National University, Canberra, 2008, at <http://epress.anu.edu.au/anzsog/whistleblowing/html/frames.php>. Earlier Australian research includes Electoral and Administrative Review Commission, Queensland, *Report on protection of whistleblowers,* Brisbane, Queensland, 1991; Senate Select Committee on Public Interest, *Whistleblowing* (1994); John McMillan, 'Whistleblowing', in Noel Preston (ed), *Ethics for the Public Sector: Education and Training,* Federation Press, Sydney, 1994.
3. William De Maria, 'Queensland Whistleblowing: Sterilising the Lone Crusader' (1992) 27 *Australian Journal of Social Issues* 248; William De Maria, *Unshielding the shadow culture: Queensland whistleblower study, Result Release One,* Univer-

sity of Queensland, 1994; William De Maria and Cyrelle Jan, *Wounded Workers: Queensland Whistleblower study, Result Release Two,* University of Queensland, 1994; William De Maria, 'Whistleblowing' (1995) 20 *Alternative Law Journal* 270; Quentin Dempster, *Whistleblowers,* Sydney, ABC Books, 1997; Brian Martin, *Suppression Stories,* Fund for Intellectual Dissent, Wollongong, 1997; William De Maria, *Deadly Disclosures: Whistleblowing and the Ethical Meltdown of Australia,* Wakefield Press, 1999.

4. In Queensland: De Maria (1999), above n 3, xiii, 25.
5. Lisa Zipparo, 'Factors which deter public officials from reporting corruption' (1999) 30 *Crime, Law and Social Change* 274.
6. Hereafter WWTW. The research was jointly funded by the Australian Research Council, the five participating universities and 14 industry partners including integrity agencies such as the Commonwealth Ombudsman and public sector agencies from six Australian governments: <www.griffith.edu.au/centre/slrc/ whistleblowing>. The project's research involved a survey of 7,600 public officers from 118 public agencies in the Commonwealth and state governments. The study was the largest of its kind ever undertaken in Australia, and one of the largest per capita ever undertaken in the world. The authors thank their colleagues on the Whistling While They Work Project Team as well as the industry partners and the participants for their assistance with this research. Some of this paper has drawn on and further details can be found in AJ Brown, *Public Interest Disclosure Legislation in Australia: Towards the Next Generation—An Issues Paper* (Commonwealth Ombudsman, NSW Ombudsman, Queensland Ombudsman, 2006); <http://www.ombudsman.gov.au/commonwealth/publish.nsf/AttachmentsByTitle/ whistling_issues_summary/$FILE/issues_papar_whistleblower_summary.pdf.>. A. J. Brown (ed), *Whistleblowing in the Australian Public Sector* (2008), above n 2. The findings and views expressed in this chapter are those of the authors and do not necessarily represent the views of the Australian Research Council or the project industry partners.
7. Brown (2008), above n 2, xxiii, Ch 2.
8. See, eg, NSW Ombudsman, *The Adequacy of the Protected Disclosure Act to Achieve its Objectives,* Issues Paper, April 2004. <http://www.nswombudsman.nsw.gov.au/publication/PDF/discussion/Adequacy%20off%20Protected%20Disclosures%20Act.pdf?id=125>.
9. New South Wales (state capital, Sydney), Victoria (Melbourne), Queensland (Brisbane), Western Australia (Perth), South Australia (Adelaide) and Tasmania (Hobart).
10. Australian Capital Territory (Canberra), Northern Territory (Darwin).
11. A. J. Brown, Paul Latimer, John McMillan and Chris Wheeler, 'Best-practice whistleblowing legislation for the public sector: the key principles', Ch 11 of A. J. Brown (ed), *Whistleblowing in the Australian Public Sector* (2008), above n 2, 283 (WWTW Principle 1—Objectives and title).
12. Discussed, eg, Elletta Callaghan, Terry Dworkin and David Lewis, 'Whistleblowing; Australian, U.K., and U.S. approaches to disclosure in the public interest', 44 *Virginia Journal of International Law* 879, 886-887 (2003/2004).
13. eg, Senate Select Committee on Public Interest Whistleblowing, *In the Public Interest,* Commonwealth Parliamentary Paper 140, 1990, at < http://www.aph. gov.au/SENATE/committee/history/uwb_ctte/pi/index.htm>. The "piecemeal" regulation of private sector whistleblowers was recognised by the House of Representatives Report (2009), above n 13, as a matter to be "reviewed in the future"; p 178.
14. The *Whistleblowers Protection Act 1993* (SA) s 4 protects 'public interest information' by any ' adult person' about any ' illegal activity' whether within public

agencies or private companies. The *Whistleblowers Protection Act 1994* (Qld) ss 18 and 19 allows public officials to disclose dangers to public health or safety arising in any sector, and any person (including private sector whistleblowers) may disclose any dangers to the environment or the health or safety of persons with disabilities, in any sector. See also, eg, *Public Interest Disclosure Act* 1994 (ACT) s 15 ('any person'); *Whistleblowers Protection Act 2001* (Vic) s 5 ('natural person'); *Public Interest Disclosure Act* 2003 (WA) s 5 ('any person').

15. Available at <http://www.saiglobal.com/PDFTemp/Previews/OSH/as/as8000/8000/8004-2003(+A1).pdf>.
16. 'Whistleblower' or 'whistleblowing' is defined in the four Acts which use 'whistleblower protection' in their title or the relevant provision: *Public Service Act* 1999 (Cth) s16 (Protection for whistleblowers); *Public Interest Disclosure (Protection of Whistleblowers) Bill 2002* (Cth); *Corporations Act 2001* (Cth) Part 9.4AAA (Protection for whistleblowers); *Workplace Relations Act 1996* (Cth) Part 4A (ss 337A-337D) ('Protection for whistleblowers') was added to Schedule 1, Chapter 11 of the *Workplace Relations Act 1996* (Cth) in 2004; *Whistleblowers Protection Act 1994* (Qld); *Whistleblowers Protection Act 1993* (SA); *Whistleblowers Protection Act 2001* (Vic).
17. Brown (2008), above n 2, xxi., 8, based on Janet Near and Marcia Miceli, 'Organisational Dissidence: the case of whistleblowing' (1985) 4 *Journal of Business Ethics* 1, 1-4. Whistleblower laws should protect both the contractor carrying out government functions and the outsider who contracts with government who may, for example, have experience of corruption on the part of purchasing officers eg *Corporations Act 2001* (Cth) s 1317AA(1)(a)(iii) 'person who has contracted for the supply of services or goods to a company'. The House of Representatives Report (2009), above n 13, recommended that whistleblower protection cover public sector insiders as broadly defined, which would include public contractors. If in doubt, every person who works directly—and often indirectly—in Australian government programs should be covered: recommendation 3.
18. Brown (2008), above n 2, xxiv, Ch 3.
19. *Whistleblowers Protection Act 1993* (SA) s 5(2)(a); *Public Interest Disclosure Act 2003* (WA) s 5(2)(a). The notion of 'reasonable grounds' (which has replaced 'bona fide') presumably requires that the disclosure is made in good faith—ie that the person has a legitimate complaint and is not making an unfounded disclosure for ulterior motives.
20. *Public Interest Disclosure Act 1994* (ACT) s 3 'public interest disclosure'; *Whistleblowers Protection Act 1993* (SA) 5(2)(a)(ii); *Public Interest Disclosures Act 2002* (Tas) s 6(1); *Whistleblowers Protection Act 2001* (Vic) s 5(a); *Public Interest Disclosure Act 2003* (WA) s 5(2)(b) ('the information may be true'). The House of Representatives Report (2009), above n 13, recommended whistleblower protection only for a disclosure made with an honest and reasonable belief that the matter is disclosable: recommendation 10.
21. Janelle Dozier and Marcia Miceli, 'Potential predictors of whistle-blowing: a prosocial behavior perspective' (1985) 10 *Academy of Management Review* 823; Richard Fox, 'Protecting the whistleblower' (1993) 15 *Adelaide Law Review* 137.
22. *Protected Disclosures Act 1994* (NSW) Part 2 s 7 provides that 'A disclosure is protected by this Act if it satisfies the applicable requirements of this Part'.
23. Eg *Whistleblowers Protection Act 1993* (SA) s 6(3).
24. Eg *Public Interest Disclosure Act 1994* (ACT) s 8.
25. *Public Interest Disclosure Act 1994* (ACT) s 16.
26. Eg *Whistleblowers Protection Act 1994* (Qld) s 56 makes it an offence to intentionally give information that is false or misleading in a material particular; *Whistle-*

blowers Protection Act 1993 (SA) s 10 makes it an offence to make a disclosure of false public interest information where the disclosing person knows it to be false or is being reckless about whether it is false. The House of Representatives Report (2009), above n 13, recommended no whistleblower protection for a disclosure found to be false: recommendation 12.

27. *Protected Disclosures Act 1994* (NSW) s 17; *Whistleblowers Protection Act 1994* (Qld) s 17(2).
28. *Protected Disclosures Act 1994* (NSW) s 18.
29. Implied in all Acts, and explicit in, eg, *Public Interest Disclosure Act 1994* (ACT) s 17; *Protected Disclosures Act 1994* (NSW) s 16; *Public Interest Disclosure Act 2003* (WA) s 8(2)(b).
30. Brown (2008), above n 2, Principle 3 (Person making disclosure), 283.
31. Ibid, xxi.
32. Ibid, Principle 2 (Subject matter of disclosure), above n 2, 283.
33. Ibid, xxiv, Ch 3.
34. Loc cit.
35. *Public Interest Disclosure Act* 1994 (ACT); *Public Interest Disclosure Act 2008* (NT); *Whistleblowers Protection Act 1994* (Qld); *Whistleblowers Protection Act 1993* (SA); *Public Interest Disclosure Act 2003* (WA). The House of Representatives Report (2009), above n 13, has recommended whistleblower protection for serious matters as widely defined: recommendation 7.
36. *Protected Disclosures Act 1994* (NSW).
37. *Public Interest Disclosures Act 2002* (Tas); *Whistleblowers Protection Act 2001* (Vic).
38. See, e.g., *Ombudsman Act 1976* (Cth); *Ombudsman Act 1989* (ACT); *Ombudsman Act 1974* (NSW); *Ombudsman (Northern Territory) Act* 1978 (NT); *Ombudsman Act 2001* (Qld); *Ombudsman Act 1972* (SA); *Ombudsman Act* 1978 (Tas); *Ombudsman Act 1973* (Vic); *Parliamentary Commissioner Act 1971* (WA).
39. Such as tendering irregularities, contract management, procedures for invoicing and reconciliations, outstanding deliverables and ownership rights to contract materials.
40. E.g., Paul Latimer and AJ Brown, 'In whose interest? The need for consistency in to whom, and about whom, Australian public interest whistleblowers can make protected disclosures' (2007) 12 *Deakin Law Review* 1. The House of Representatives Report (2009), above n 13, recommended the Commonwealth Ombudsman and the Workplace Ombudsman as the lead external agencies for whistleblower reports to ensure that internal disclosure systems are of good standard and that whistleblowers are not being left as collateral damage: recommendations 17-20. Under the recommendations, it will be clear for the first time in the Commonwealth public sector that public servants can and should go straight to the Ombudsman and other integrity agencies if they do not have confidence in their own agency's response. Instead of feeling that they are breaking the rules, a whistleblower going outside will be recognized as an act of loyalty to the true mission of their own department, and the broader public interest.
41. Ninety-seven percent of the whistleblowers identified in the WWTW survey reported internally in their agency in the first instance; ninety percent of the whistleblowing ended internally within the agency. Only 2.9 percent of whistleblowers had reported to an external agency or body in the first instance, and only 9.7 percent of whistleblowing involved an external agency or body at any stage: Brown (2008), above, n 2, xxv, Ch 4.
42. Of the 138 whistleblowers surveyed in more depth in the case study agencies (internal witness survey), 80 percent still chose to report internally in the first instance

and, for 70 percent, their whistleblowing remained internal: Brown (2008), op cit, xxv, Ch 4.

43. Ibid, Principle 4 (Receipt of disclosure), 284.
44. Ibid, Principle 7 (Oversight agency), 284.
45. <http://www.pogo.org>.
46. Brown (2008), above n 2, xxxv, Ch 10.
47. Loc cit.
48. Ibid, xxvi, Ch 5.
49. Ibid, xxvi, Ch 5. The House of Representatives Report (2009), above n 13, has recommended new obligations on senior public sector managers to act on internal disclosures and to better support the officials who make them—including explicit requirements to assess the risks of adverse action that could befall whistleblowers—and manage those risks rather than leaving their welfare to chance: recommendation 15.
50. Ibid, xxv, Ch 4.
51. *Protected Disclosures Act 1994* (NSW) s 19.
52. Brown (2008), op cit, Principle 10 (Disclosure outside an agency), 286; the House of Representatives Report (2009), above n 13, has recommended whistleblower protection for disclosures to the media and members of parliament: recommendations 21, 22.
53. Ibid, Principle 9 (Protection of person making a disclosure), 285.
54. *Public Interest Disclosures Act 2002* (Tas) s 38; *Whistleblowers Protection Act 2001* (Vic) s 69.
55. *Public Interest Disclosures Act 2002* (Tas) s 34(1); *Whistleblowers Protection Act 2001* (Vic) ss 28-31; WA s 23(1)(f). The *Public Interest Disclosure Regulations 2003* (WA) provide coordination if disclosure has been made to more than one proper authority.
56. Brown (2008), above n 2, Principle 5 (Recording and reporting), 284.
57. Ibid, Principle 6 (Acting on a disclosure), 284.
58. Eg *Public Interest Disclosure Act 2008* (NT), Part 2 Div 3 (Protection from reprisal).
59. De Maria, above, n 4.
60. Seventy-eight 78 percent of public interest whistleblowers said they were treated either well or the same by management and co-workers. Twenty-two percent of whistleblowers said they were treated badly by management and/or co-workers: Brown, above n 2, xxvii, Ch 5.
61. Eighteen percent of whistleblowers indicated that they were treated badly by management, compared with 9 percent of whistleblowers who indicated they were treated badly by co-workers (with 5 percent indicating they were treated badly by both): Brown (2008), op cit, xxvii, Ch 5.
62. Ibid, xxvii.
63. Ibid, xxviii.
64. Ibid, Principle 11 (Agency responsibility to ensure protection), 286.
65. Ibid, Principle 12 (Remedial action), 286.
66. Ibid, 287.
67. Ibid, Principle 13 (Continuing assessment and protection), 286.
68. The long title sets out the purpose of the legislation, and may be referred to as an aid in the interpretation of the legislation so long as it does not contradict clear and unambiguous language in the legislation.
69. Two Private members whistleblower bills introduced by Senator Murray (Australian Democrats) have lapsed: *Public Interest Disclosure (Protection of Whistleblowers) Bill* 2002 (Cth) and the *Public Interest Disclosures Bill* 2007 (Cth). The current

Commonwealth promised before the 2008 election which it won that it will 'implement public interest disclosure reform for whistleblowers': Australian Labor, *Government Information—Restoring trust and integrity,* Election 2007 Policy Document, October 2007: <http://www.alp.org.au/download/now/071026_government_information_policy.pdf>. This has been advanced in the report of the Standing Committee on Legal and Constitutional Affairs, *Whistleblower Protection: a comprehensive scheme for the Commonwealth public sector,* Report of the Inquiry into whistleblowing protection within the Australian Government public sector, House of Representatives, Canberra, February 2009, available at http://www.aph.gov.au/HOUSE/committee/laca/whistleblowing/report.htm. The Committee has recommended repeal of s 16: recommendation 8.

70. The proposed *Public Interest Disclosure Bill 2006* (ACT) lapsed on election day, 18 October 2008.

Whistleblowing: The South African Experience

Tina Uys
Department of Sociology University of Johannesburg
The Republic of South Africa

1. Introduction

According to the World Democracy Audit [2007] eleven of the 25 most corrupt countries in the world are in Africa (Kenya, Republic of Congo, Liberia, Sierra Leone, Ivory Coast, Central African Republic, Congo Guinee, Sudan, Chad and Somalia). South Africa's is ranked 43rd. Although the merits of the methodology used by this perceptions index are constantly debated, one is probably justified in arguing that the African continent is currently plagued by a culture of corruption that Lala Camerer [1996: 48] describes as "more damaging to the nation's psyche than visible, violent street crimes." As a result of this perception of widespread corruption, international organizations such as the World Bank and the International Monetary Fund require evidence of active attempts by applicant countries to curb fraud and corruption in order to qualify for financial assistance.

In some African countries such as South Africa, Zimbabwe and Nigeria attempts have been made to reduce the levels of fraud and corruption by promoting whistleblowing by employees. In South Africa legislation was introduced in 2000 to protect whistleblowers in the public and the private sector. This legislation followed the example of the British Public Interest Disclosure Act 1998 [PIDA 1998].[1] These attempts at protecting whistleblowers for having the courage to speak out, provide evidence that whistleblowing is considered an important tool in fighting organisational wrongdoing and the ethical apathy that accompanies it.

Some researchers on whistleblowing such as William de Maria [2005] have raised serious concerns about the possible negative consequences of the importation of western-based whistleblower protection legislation into developing countries. It is therefore important to take into account the social context in which whistleblower protection legislation is created and implemented. This chapter deals with whistleblowing in the South African context. It focuses in particular on how cultural perceptions in South Africa impact on the effective implementation of the legislation to protect whistleblowers.

2. The History of Whistleblowing in South Africa

The first documented case of whistleblowing in South Africa is that of Adam Klein, a young prosecutor who approached the editor of Noseweek, Martin Welz [2004: 7] in the early 1980s. He complained about abuses taking place at the Bantu Commissioners "courts" which were set up by the apartheid government to enforce the pass laws. These laws controlled the movements of black people who were required to carry a pass if they wanted to visit so-called "white" areas. Welz tells the story:

> The resulting *Sunday Times* expose helped ensure the closure of that iniquitous institution [the Bantu Commissioners courts] - a compliment to the value of Klein's speaking out. But Klein paid a steep price for his bravery: the security police continued to hound him and anyone who dared employ him, for years, effectively destroying his career. Today, more than 20 years later, he lives unacknowledged and in poverty. That haunts me.

Another early case of whistleblowing is that of Nico Alant, an exchange control investigator employed by the South African Reserve Bank. During the late eighties and early nineties he expressed his concerns about what he perceived to be a lack of "due diligence" (reasonable care) at the Reserve Bank, through internal memoranda and discussions with his superiors. The negative response from his superiors compelled him to take the matter up with authorities outside the Reserve Bank, which eventually resulted in his employment being terminated [Uys 2000; 2008].

A third case is that of Mark Hess who resigned from his job in November 1998. He was an attorney at a Cape Town law firm specialising in claims against the Road Accident Fund. In early 1999 he took evidence of large-scale defrauding of mostly poor and often illiterate clients to Noseweek, who instituted a class action on behalf of the victims of the scheme [Welz 1999: 4, 12-14].

It is probably not a coincidence that the phenomenon of whistleblowing started to achieve prominence in South Africa during the early nineties at about the time of South Africa's transition to democracy. It began to receive serious attention from the South African press [Beresford & Van Niekerk 1996, Calland 1999, Welz 1999, Sunday Independent 1999] from the middle nineties. The timing is hardly surprising, as similar to other countries undergoing rapid transformation, South Africa's young democracy is experiencing high levels of crime, including fraud and corruption. In an attempt to address these problems and promote accountability, the Protected Disclosures Act no 26 of 2000 (PDA 2000) was passed in June 2000 and came into operation the following year.

3. The Protected Disclosures Act, No 26 of 2000[2]

The aim of PDA 2000 is: "to make provision for procedures in terms of which employees in both the private and the public sector may disclose information regarding unlawful or irregular conduct by their employers or other employees in the employ of their employers; to provide for the protection of employees who make a disclosure which is protected in terms of this Act; and to provide for matters connected therewith".

The Act says that an employer may not cause occupational detriment (disciplinary action, dismissal, transfer, harassment etc.) to an employee who has made a Protected Disclosure in good faith. A Protected Disclosure is a disclosure about the employer's criminal conduct, failure to comply with any legal obligation, a disclosure about danger to health, safety or the environment made to certain specified persons. These persons are a legal adviser, the employer itself, a member of cabinet or the executive council of a province, the Public Protector, Auditor-General or other prescribed bodies. No other bodies, to which Protected Disclosures may be made, have as yet been prescribed. In certain special circumstances a disclosure is protected even if it is made to the press.

The strategy of the PDA is the creation of procedures that, if followed by employees who wish to disclose irregularity in the workplace, should prevent retaliation by their employers. The PDA applies only to employees. This means that an employee's protection under the Act ends on the termination of the employee's employment. This implies that if whistleblowers succumb to pressure by the employer to resign or to accept retrenchment packages they not only lose their jobs, but also protection under the Act.

The general aim of the Act is clearly to encourage employees to blow the whistle internally first and to encourage employers to implement internal mechanisms for dealing with disclosures. It is also apparent that the focus is largely on the messenger and the procedure that he or she followed rather than on the content of the message. Consequently there is no assurance that the allegations made by the whistleblower will be investigated.

The dismissal of a whistleblower is deemed to be automatically unfair under the Labour Relations Act ("LRA"). Other forms of occupational detriment, short of dismissal are deemed an unfair labour practice under the LRA. Where a whistleblower suffers occupational detriment, PDA 2000 allows the whistleblower to go to the High Court or the Labour Court to enforce his/her rights. The Act applies to both the public and private sectors. The Labour Court under section 194(3) of the LRA may award compensation of up to 24 months remuneration if a dismissal is automatically unfair. This compensation is unsatisfactory if one takes into account that whistleblowers have usually placed not just their job but their whole career on the line.

It is also important to note that the PDA does not make it an *offence* for an employer to cause occupational detriment to a whistleblower employee, nor does the Act make provision for punitive damages where the employee has suffered such detriment.

Practice has taught us that it is very difficult to prove that an employer has caused the whistleblower occupational detriment. Few employers will admit that action taken by them against the employee had anything to do with the employee's disclosure of alleged irregularity. It is to be expected that, as the whistleblower becomes more and more isolated in the workplace and the tension between the whistleblower and colleagues increases, the whistleblower's work performance and personal relations will be negatively affected. If disciplinary charges relating to alleged incompatibility with colleagues and poor work performance are then brought against the whistleblower, the whistleblower will have the onerous task of proving that this situation was the direct result of him/her having made a disclosure about alleged irregularity. Considering that the employer controls the disciplinary process and that most disciplinary codes do not allow external legal representation, the whistleblower has little chance of successfully presenting his/her case.

As far as could be determined, only five cases brought under PDA 2000 in the Labour Court have been reported so far and the applicants were successful in three of them. The extent of the protection provided by PDA 2000 in these cases merits further discussion. In the case of Grieve v Denel (Pty) Ltd, 2003, 4 BLLR 366, Keith Grieve was employed as a

Safety and Security Manager at a company that manufactures explosives. Together with others he submitted a report to his employer's board of directors alleging misconduct on the part of a senior employee. He was then suspended and a disciplinary hearing was convened, ostensibly to deal with charges of racism and downloading of pornography on his office computer. Keith applied to the Labour Court for an order preventing the employer from continuing with the disciplinary action until a determination had been made about whether the employer had committed an unfair labour practice in suspending him. He based his application on the protection afforded to whistleblowers in terms of PDA 2000. The interdict was granted and Keith was re-instated. His employer then called in consultants to investigate all of Keith's work. As a result of this investigation a disciplinary hearing was held and he was found guilty of insolence and insubordination. The Chairman of the hearing concluded that there was an irretrievable breakdown of trust and Keith was dismissed.

Allison Pedzinsky was a compliance manager at Andisa (formerly SCMB) Securities responsible for monitoring the statutory, regulatory and supervisory compliance of her employer with regard to its financial trading business. When she discovered that certain members of staff, some of them senior managers, were involved in irregular trading of shares she reported the matter to her immediate supervisor as well as to other persons in the SCMB Group Compliance Structures. A little over a month later she was informed that her position would become redundant due to operational requirements. After the Commission for Conciliation, Mediation and Arbitration process had been exhausted, the Labour Court found that the dismissal was automatically unfair in terms of section 187(1)(h) of the LRA as she had made a protected disclosure in terms of the PDA. Andisa Securities were ordered to pay two years' salary as well as her legal costs (Pedzinsky v Andisa Securities (Pty) Ltd formerly SCMB Securities (Pty) Ltd, Case no JS396/2004).

In the third successful case, as Managing Director of the Masters' office business unit in the Department of Justice, Mike Tshishonga resisted pressure from the Minister of Justice to appoint a friend of his as a liquidator in one of the largest liquidations to be conducted in South

Africa. After being removed from his position on instruction of the Minister, and unsuccessfully raising his concerns with various designated entities, Tshishonga turned to the media. He was then suspended and charged with misconduct, where the disciplinary hearing ruled in his favour. When the Director-General refused to reinstate him, arguing irretrievable breakdown of trust, he was forced into negotiating a settlement which culminated in the termination of his employment. The Labour Court awarded him one year's salary as well as his legal costs (Tshishonga vs The Minister of Justice and Constitutional Development and the Director-General of the Department of Justice and Constitutional Development, Case no JS898/2004).

In all three cases the whistleblowers were apparently successful in their action under PDA 2000. Their success lies mainly in the fact that they were vindicated and their reputations restored, at least in the eyes of the law. In all other respects they seem to have lost: in terms of finances, emotional stress, strained relationships and attempts to get their careers back on track. Although Grieve was initially reinstated, he lost his job five months later. This resulted in him having to sell his house and accumulating debts in order to start a business in a completely new field. Pedzinsky's judgement came at a stage when she had been without a job for two years and two months. The reimbursement with regard to her legal costs was on a party to party basis as prescribed by the court rules, but this does not cover the attorney and client costs for which she was still liable. Although Tshishonga seems to have suffered least financially, he still has a long way to go to re-establish his career.

As is demonstrated by the three cases as well as numerous others that never reached the Labour Court [Auriacombe 2005; Uys 2000, 2006, 2008] the track record of PDA 2000 with regard to the protection of South African whistleblowers is poor. In their analysis of the protection provided to whistleblowers in terms of PDA 2000 Lewis and Uys [2007: 85-88] identify three main shortcomings of this legislation. In the first place it does not act as a sufficient deterrent to prevent employers from victimising whistleblowers. Second, the protection it provides is not wide enough and thirdly, it does not require independent investigation of the whistleblower's claims. A fourth shortcoming related to the implementation of the legislation is that the cultural context within which the protection is provided is not taken into account sufficiently. In particular, the South African tendency not to make a clear distinction between whistleblowing and informing is problematic.

4. Whistleblowing, Informing and Anonymous Reporting

Whistleblowing is a contested concept, both in the eyes of academics and the general public. It is often sensationalised by the media and used in various popularised forms with different connotations depending on the attitudes and experiences of the user. Academic authors also define whistleblowing in various ways. Peter Drucker [in Orr 1981: 4], a highly regarded management expert, stated for example:

> "Whistle-blowing," after all, is simply another word for "informing." And perhaps it is not quite irrelevant that the only societies in Western history that encouraged informers were bloody and infamous tyrannies - Tiberius and Nero in Rome, the Inquisition in the Spain of Philip II, the French Terror, and Stalin. ... For under "whistleblowing," under the regime of the "informer," no mutual trust, no interdependencies, and no ethics are possible.

This statement compelled Leonard Orr, then managing editor of *Business and Society Review* to request comments from "leading businessmen and thinkers" [Orr 1981]. Orr's article consisting of responses to this request raises a number of issues that are of particular interest to an understanding of whistleblowing in the South African context.

In the first instance most responses collected by Orr make a clear distinction between informers and whistleblowers. While informers usually focus on promoting the ideology or interests of a power holder, often receiving a reward of some kind, whistleblowers disclose information about practices which they perceive to be illegal, unethical or dangerous. Rather than promoting tyranny, whistleblowers therefore place limits on the abuse of power by power holders. Abbotts [in Orth 1981: 6] expresses it well:

> A common thread among tyrannies is suppression of critical information and a demand that the individual's highest loyalty is to the ruling establishment. A society that discourages whistle-blowing demands that a citizen's highest loyalty must be to an employer - either the state or the corporation. Such a society fosters a tyranny of its own.

Equating whistleblowing with informing is particularly problematic in the South African context. During apartheid informers to the police and security structures were called *"impimpis"* and their betrayal of the struggle against apartheid were viewed in a very negative light [Camerer 2001: 1]. Charles van Onselen [2008: 265] attributes this term to Joseph Silver, a human trafficker, pimp and informant to corrupt police during the time he spent in South Africa at the turn of the twentieth century. An editorial opinion in the *Daily Dispatch* [1999] expresses the abhorrence of *impimpis* in stark terms:

> TO BE called an *impimpi,* a security police informer, during the apartheid struggle was about the most odious label one could get in the anti-apartheid fraternity.

As punishment for their betrayal, *impimpis* were often *"necklaced"* (a tyre filled with fuel was placed around their necks and set alight). The promotion of whistleblowing in South Africa therefore requires a clear distinction between whistleblowing and the activities of an *impimpi.*

PDA 2000 attempts to institutionalise whistleblowing by encouraging organisations to implement internal procedures by means of which internal disclosures can be made. Unfortunately companies often believe that implementing anonymous hotlines is sufficient to comply with the requirements of PDA 2000. This practice tends to blur the distinction between whistleblowing and informing in the eyes of the employees. Martin Welz [2004: 7], editor of *Noseweek* puts it strongly:

> I suspect that these facilities [anonymous hotlines] are aimed at stopping theft from corporations, rather than at ensuring they behave ethically. While most major corporations and state institutions pay lip-service to the principle of transparency and the protection of whistleblowers, experience has taught me that they can be as determined and vindictive as the criminal fraternity when it comes to hunting down those they see as squealers.

A second concern is related to the issue of competing loyalties. Alan Westin [in Orr 1981: 9] identifies the corporate dilemma of whistleblowing as

> [H]ow to balance competing loyalties - faithfulness to the employer and acceptance of management's right to manage versus a duty to society or to one's own ethical and professional standards.

Whistleblowers are often under the impression that they are acting in the best interests of the organisation. They believe that as loyal employees the organisation expects of them to disclose suspicions of wrongdoing so that the allegations can be investigated before they escalate and result in major harm to the organisation's reputation. In contrast, the employer often views the revelations of the whistleblower as disloyal to the organisation, especially when they are revealing entrusted information that the employer does not want revealed [Uys & Senekal 2008: 40].

Organisational loyalty is a complex issue. It is often understood as flowing from the employee's relationships within the organisation as well as their identification with the organisation as members. In terms of the social contract existing between employers and employees the latter is expected to act in ways that demonstrate their good faith and enhances the best interests of the organisation. This entails that reasonable instructions should be carried out, their actions should be consistent with the values and norms of the organisation, they should defend the organisation's reputation and confidentiality should be maintained [Uys 2008: 907].

The way in which the majority of organisations worldwide respond to whistleblowers demonstrates that they place organisational loyalty above any considerations of public interest or corporate governance. Whistleblowing is regarded as a violation of trust, a form of betrayal, which threatens its profitability and damages its reputation. Whistleblowers are therefore victimised in various ways [Glazer & Glazer 1989: 133-166; Gummer 1985:97; Hunt 1995: 155-156; Rothschild & Miethe 1994: 265; Uys 2008: 909-916].

In South Africa the adherence to the value of *ubuntu* does not seem to favour whistleblowers. *Ubuntu* implies that "we can only be persons in and through other persons" [Prozesky 2007: 54] or "a person is a person through other persons" [Metz 2007: 323]. The emphasis that *ubuntu* places on the concrete principles of communal relations, harmony and consensus and by implication loyalty to significant others, seems to preclude the generally individualistic act of whistleblowing where perceived organisational wrongdoing is exposed in the interest of the more abstract ideal of promoting the public interest. The distinction between the public and private spheres has become blurred. The ability of power-holders to separate the public and private spheres is particularly important in order to combat corruption [Doig & McIvor 1999: 9].

Ubuntu conflicts strongly with whistleblowing when viewed as "the obligations of mutual support, the imperatives of reciprocity, the importance of gift exchange, the payment of tribute, the need to redistribute, even the habits of cattle rustling" [Chabal & Daloz 1999: 100]. In these terms condemnation of corruption only follows if "its fruits are [not] deemed to have been suitably and vigorously redistributed according to the logic of patronage" [Chabal & Daloz 1999: 100]. Whistleblowing that goes against this understanding would be denounced.

A third and final concern is related to the power struggle that the act of whistleblowing engenders. When management attempts to silence whistleblowers through victimisation, this attack on their credibility and reputation forces them into a situation where they believe they have no choice but to fight back. From a loyal employee the whistleblower develops into a political activist which may result in the initial internal disclosure escalating to a public exposure [Rothschild & Miethe 1994: 262-267; Uys 2000: 265].

The power relations impacting on whistleblowing demonstrate another important distinction compared to informers. While informers are the lackeys of the powerful, whistleblowers curb the abuse of power. As the speakers of truth to power, whistleblowers disrupt the status quo; they always find themselves at the losing end as the playing fields are never level. In South Africa this implies that the exposure of the abuses of the apartheid government in the past would now translate into exposes of the transgressions of the liberation movement that has become the ANC government of the new South Africa.

5. Conclusion

Some researchers pose the question whether it is at all possible for a developing country to successfully protect whistleblowers. William de Maria [2005] identifies a number of prerequisites that should be in place to ensure that whistleblowing achieves its goal of challenging wrongdoing in the workplace: The presence of a stable state, the general acceptance of the rule of law, a general belief in the effectiveness of state anti-corruption agencies, public confidence in the effectiveness of disclosure in combating corruption, guarantees of the freedom of expression, a separation of judicial, regulatory and state powers and the overarching importance of the public interest when it comes to state revenue collection and spending. While South Africa through its liberal constitution strives to achieve these goals, our democracy is still very fragile. The King Commission into Corporate Governance in South Africa [King 2002] encouraged a culture of openness in the corporate environment by promoting whistleblowing practices in organisations. The South African whistleblowing legislation is a step in the right direction, but it needs a stronger political will on the part of the power holders to ensure that whistleblower protection achieves its goals. As Lewis and Uys [2007: 88] put it:

> In a situation where the facts are not available, owing to a lack of investigation, and the whistleblower is unable to defend him/herself properly owing to lack of resources, the Act amounts to little more than a collection of praiseworthy principles. It offers a solution to the problems of whistleblowers but it lacks foundation. In view of the above considerations, we are of the opinion that there is much more to be done before South African whistleblowers can dare to disclose irregularity in the workplace.

The numerous stories that regularly appear in South African newspapers about the ongoing sacrifices that South African whistleblowers are expected to make without any real and concrete support compel me to agree with Matebello Moutloung's [2007] conclusion that South Africa has no "Deep Throat" culture (a reference to the pseudonym given to the whistleblower who provided Bob Woodward of *The Washington Post* with information about President Richard Nixon's administration's involvement in the Watergate scandal).

Notes

1. See Lewis and Uys (2007) for a detailed analysis of the provisions and shortcomings of PDA 2000 as well as PIDA 1998.
2. This discussion relies heavily on the more detailed discussion of PDA 2000 in Lewis & Uys (2007).

References

Auriacombe, C. J., 2005, What happens when one blows the whistle? Recent South African cases, *Politeia* 24(1): 85-100.

Beresford, D. & Van Niekerk, P., 1996, Inkathagate's whistleblower, In Manoim, I. (Ed.), *You have been warned: the first ten years of the Mail and Guardian:* 142-155. London: Viking.

Calland, R., 1999, Let's encourage the whistle-blower, *Mail and Guardian,* October. 12. 1999.

Camerer, L., 1996, Ethics and the professions: blowing the whistle on crime, *Africa Security Review,* 5(6), 48-54.

Camerer, L., 2001, Protecting whistle blowers in South Africa: The protected disclosures Act no. 26 of 2000, *Anti-Corruption Strategies, Institute of Security Studies,* Occasional Paper No. 47-2001. http://www.iss.co.za/pubs/paper/47/paper47.html.

Camerer, S., 2004, Fair treatment of Tshishonga: a test case, The Democratic Alliance web site, available at: www.da.org.za/da/Site/Eng/News/Article.asp?ID=4130 (accessed 12 December 2006).

Chabal, P. & Daloz, J., 1999, *Africa works: Disorder as political instrument,* London: Villiers Publications.

Daily Dispatch, 1999, Editorial opinion: The Pagad phenomenon, 2 March. Accessed on 14 May 2009 from http://www.dispatch.co.za/1999/03/02/editoria/EDITORIA.HTM.

De Maria, W., 2005, Whistleblower protection: Is Africa Ready?, *Public Administration and Development,* 25:217-226.

De Maria, W., 2006, Common law - common mistakes? Protecting whistleblowers in Australia, New Zealand, South Africa and the United Kingdom, *International Journal of Public Sector Management,* 19(7):643-658.

Doig, A. & Mclvor, S., 1999, Corruption and its control in the developmental context: an analysis and selective review of the literature, *Third World Quarterly,* 20(3): 657-676.

Glazer, M. P. and Glazer, P. M., 1989, *The whistleblowers: Exposing corruption in government and industry,* New York: Basic Books. Gummer, B., 1985, Committing the truth: Whistle-blowing, organizational dissent, and the honourable bureaucrat, *Administration in Social Work* 9(4): 89-102.

Hodgkinson, P., 1997, The sociology of corruption - some themes and issues, *Sociology,* 31(1): 17-35.

Hunt, G., 1995, Conclusion: A new accountability, In *Whistleblowing in the health service: Accountability, law and professional practice,* edited by G. Hunt, London:

Arnold. King, M., 2002, *King Report on Corporate Governance for South Africa: King Committee on Corporate Governance,* Johannesburg: Institute of Directors in Southern Africa.

Lewis, D. & Uys, T., 2007, Protecting whistleblowers at work: A comparison of the impact of British and South African legislation, *Managerial Law* 49(3): 76-92.

Metz, T., 2007, Towards an African Moral Theory, *The Journal of Political Philosophy,* 15(3):321-341.

Moutloung, M., 2007, Out Loud: This is no "Deep Throat" culture, *Marketingweb,* Accessed on 14 May 2009 from http://www.marketingweb.co.za/marketingweb/view/marketingweb/en/page72308?oid=81096.

Orr, L., 1981, Is whistleblowing the same as informing? *Business and Society Review,* Fall: 4-17.

Prozesky, M., 2007, *Conscience: Ethical intelligence for global well-being,* Scottsville: University of KwaZulu-Natal Press.

Rothschild, J. and Miethe, T. D., 1994, Whistle-blowing as Resistance in Modern Work Organizations, In Jermier, J. M., Knights, D. and Nord, W. R. (Eds.), *Resistance and Power in Organizations,* pp 252-273. London: Routledge. *Sunday Independent,* 1999, 27 June.

Uys, T., 2000, The politicization of whistleblowers: A case study, *Business Ethics: A European Review* 9(4): 259-287. Uys, T., 2004, The protection of whistleblowers: Should we and could we?, Paper presented at the Fourth Annual Conference of Ben-Africa held in Zanzibar, 1-3 September 2004.

Uys, T., 2006, "Professional ethics versus corporate loyalty: whistleblowing in the financial sector." In *Whistleblowing: An introduction* edited by CV Krishna Rao, Hyderabad, India: Lemag Books, Magnus School of Business.

Uys, T., 2008, Rational loyalty and whistleblowing: The South African context, *Current Sociology* 56(6): 907-924.

Uys, T. and Senekal, A., 2008, Morality of principle versus morality of loyalty: The case of whistleblowing, *African Journal of Business Ethics* 3(1):38-14.

Van Onselen, C., 2008, *The fox and the flies: The criminal empire of the Whitechapel murderer,* London: Vintage Books.

Welz, M., 1999, Thieves at law: Law societies plot to cover up frauds on road accident victims, *Noseweek* 26: 12-14.

Welz, M., 2004, Protecting whistleblowers, *Noseweek* 60: 7.

World Democracy Audit, 2007, Accessed on 15 May 2009 from http://www.worldaudit.org/corruption.htm.

Whistleblowing at Work: The Polish Perspective

Anna Lewicka-Strzalecka
Institute of Philosophy and Sociology
Polish Academy of Sciences
Warsaw, Poland

1. Introduction

The disclosure by employees of abuses committed by the company, called whistleblowing, has been studied comprehensively in the world literature, both in respect to its theoretical complexity and its far-reaching practical consequences. The ethical and efficient aspects of the phenomenon have been examined, and it has also been studied from the sociological and psychological points of view. In the developed countries some attempts of whistleblowing strategy are undertaken both by the government and by the companies. However, in Poland the discussion and research on the theoretical and practical aspects of whistleblowing is on its beginning. The term of whistleblowing is not familiar and the phenomenon is weakly investigated and poorly known. The whistleblowers are not protected in any way, neither by law nor by the company codes of conduct.

Whistleblowing has become one of the most important and interesting item in the business ethics curriculum. This subject is very difficult as well. Whenever I began to speak generally about whistleblowers the listeners, mainly university students expressed their contempt for such persons quoting negative descriptions and connotations of whistleblowers. As Maria Ossowska (1970) mentions there exists many such pejorative epithets in Polish language and no one word having positive or at least neutral meaning. This is not surprising. Though informing is condemned in many cultures it is especially strongly condemned in our culture on account of historical circumstances and economic realities. In the past centuries the government was an imposed one from outside and was perceived as a foreign body by Poles. There was a clear division between "we" and "they" during the time of three annexations in the nineteenth century and German occupation and then Soviet domination in the twentieth century. Violating order meant violating "their" order not "our's," so disclosing such violations was regarded as treachery.

Contempt for informing the authorities has been enlarged on all kind of informing and is deeply internalized by the Polish people. Because of this the subject of whistleblowing during business ethics classes should be started without using this term. According to my experience the most effective way to teach this topic is to start with presentation of some real cases in which the employees disclosing abuses committed by their companies proved to be the positive heroes. They preserved health and safety of both the workforce and the general public. Then the general notion of whistleblower can be introduced and not till then the ethical appraisal with all its complexity should be done.

2. The Main Characteristics of Whistleblowing at Work

Presentation of the cases is aimed at understanding the essence of the phenomenon of whistleblowing and abstracting its main characteristics from the business practice. In effect we receive a definition of whistleblower as a person who is or was employed by the company and who voluntarily discloses that certain actions of the company are illegal, immoral, or socially harmful for some reasons, e.g., the goods offered are defective or dangerous, the environment is harmed, human rights are violated, etc. Being inside the organization the whistleblower knows its conditioning and quite often has very specialized or unique knowledge and because of it he or she is able to grasp the mechanism of the abuse which can be difficult for the prosecution agency or even the audit department. As Terrance Miethe notes "offenders in work organizations maintain a near immunity against prosecution because of the low public visibility of much organizational crime, its technical complexity, and the strong pressures exerted on employees from both within and outside the organization to remain silent. Fellow employees, acting as whistleblowers, are uniquely situated to increase sharply the public visibility of organizational misconduct" (Miethe, 1999, p. 33). An employee disclosing abuses of the company found out about them in the course of discharging official duties, so this information is confidential and its publication may be perceived as disloyalty to the company. An employee exposing abuses does this in an act of moral protest and is not guided by personal gain. He or she is not obliged to perform this act under the law; the only sanction for desisting from it is his own conscience.

If information about abuses committed by the company was not transmitted outside it, the disclosure is internal. The internal whistleblower expects that his actions will spur the company to take the appropriate measures to counteract the wrongdoing that exists or is about to take place. If such actions are not undertaken the information is made public and the disclosure becomes external. The essential characteristic of this phenomenon is that the whistleblower exhausted the possibility of changing the questionable practices by going through the successive levels of the official hierarchy and sees the final solution in disclosing the information outside the institution. The addressees of external disclosing are government agencies of the appropriate level, control institutions or mass media, which often broadcast such information in sensational form. The exposure of abuses is a serious matter, and it may have serious consequences both for the society and for the image of the company. These two kinds of disclosures are interrelated as many companies induce their employees to internal disclosure to avoid publishing information that may prove disadvantageous to the employer.

Not everyone who discloses abuses is a whistleblower. First and foremost, the whistleblower must be an employee or an ex-employee, not someone from the outside. A journalist writing a critical article about the company or a representative of a control institution showing some inaccuracies of the company's activity is not a whistleblower. The phenomenon does not apply to stakeholders other than the employees; it does not encompass the complaints of customers or protests of local communities, etc. At the same time one should stress that a public debate between management and employees of the company on the directions of development of the company or informing the competition of unethical practices in the parent company is not a symptom of the phenomenon of whistleblowing.

3. The Whistleblower's Dilemma

How should an employee behave if he or she is encouraged by his company to violate socially approved moral norms, e.g., lying or concealing the truth, violating the privacy of other persons for the sake of some immediate goal of the company? What should an employee do when he or she knows that production of his company is harmful to the environment or its products are dangerous for users? In many cases the only way of avoiding or reducing the wrongdoing was for an employee to go public with news of abuses committed by his company.

However, an employee going public with news of such or other abuses is generally not highly regarded by the management of the company and other employees. He or she is perceived as “a bird that fouls in its own nest” or as a person violating the principle “dirty laundry has to be washed at home,” as someone who harms his own company. As a result of his actions the company may lose orders, contracts, positive image, customers and other employees may lose their jobs. Examples from real life show that whistleblowers are squelched in various ways, sacked, intimidated, blackmailed, and ostracized at work.

The discussion taken up in the 1990s on the ethical appraisal of whistleblowers is reminiscent of the discussion on civil disobedience of the 1960s, because the essence of these phenomena is similar. The following arguments are presented in the matter of employee whistleblowing (Boatright, 1997; DeGeorge 1990).

On the one hand, it is argued that disclosure by an employee of the abuses of his company violates his relation with his employer, which is a relation between an agent and a principal. The employee is the agent of his employer, formally authorized to represent him and act in his name in contacts with a third party. The agent is employed to act on behalf of the principal in handling matters that the principal cannot or does not want to take care of. Under the contract concluded the agent has the duty to act in the interests of his principal, to meet his requirements and keep confidential information received in the course of performing official duties. On the other hand, the scope of these requirements is not unlimited. The employment contract certainly does not oblige the employee to perform illegal or immoral acts. The question arises whether concealment by the agent of abuses ought to be understood as action in the interest of the principal, hence whether it results from the contract concluded.

In addition to the principle of fulfilling the contract, the other principle to which defenders of whistleblowing refer is freedom of speech, which is the right of every citizen. A person employed in a company does not cease to be a citizen and for this reason retains the right to voice his convictions and opinions publicly. Citizens realize this right by publicly criticizing their elected government officials, bringing charges against them, often with the help of the mass media. Likewise, employees also ought to be able to express publicly critical remarks about their company and its management.

The value most often alluded to, as an argument against whistleblowing is loyalty to the company. The reason why an employee ought to be loyal is thankfulness to the company for giving him a job, which is a precious thing that is not available to everybody. Even if an employee does not feel loyalty, he ought to be aware that the company is an undertaking in which he has placed his stake and the company's loss means his own loss as well. Disloyalty consisting in the disclosure of abuses harms the image of the company, harms its stakeholders, and especially the disloyal employee.

On the other hand, it is argued that loyalty has its limits and the company ought not to expect an employee to tolerate illegal or unethical actions. Extremists even claim that no obligation of loyalty to the employer results either directly or indirectly from the employment contract. The obligation of loyalty was concocted in order to manipulate employees. Loyalty is an empty category in employee-company relations. Loyalty requires the kind of unselfishness one shows to family and friends, but not in business. The goal of business is to make money and as such must be based on the assumption that every person strives to maximize his own benefit and one cannot ask sacrifices of anyone. On the other hand, if loyalty to the company does not mean absolute obedience to superiors but identification with the mission of the company, then certain cases of whistleblowing should not be treated as acts of disloyalty.

Real loyalty to the company requires opposition to practices that in the long run will bring about its downfall, and that is why employees who expose abuses should not be accused of disloyalty. Despite the fact that a better option for them personally would be to leave the company, they do not choose to do so. As Albert Hirschman (1970) notes, it usually is the case that stakeholders dissatisfied with co-operation with the company decide to exit and break off contacts with it rather than to voice their dissatisfaction publicly in order to improve the operations of the company. Although exiting the company is a greater departure from the realization of its mission than the exposure of abuses, the company rarely treats this as disloyalty, because it prefers to get rid of a critical employee than to change its modus operandi. Such a policy may turn out to be unprofitable in the long run. Encouraging critical employees to leave the company limits its development, because it makes it impossible to see potential threats and to counteract them as well as to remove errors and modify the policy of the company in a positive direction.

Yet, it sometimes happens that employees disclose abuses motivated by a desire to gain notoriety, to harm the company or other employees, to exact revenge, or inclined by a passion to legal chicanery. Sometimes their charges are unfair and the consequences of their actions can be destructive for the company: loss of a competitive position on the market, intensified internal and external controls, destruction of friendly relationship. Sometimes it may lead to a company shutdown and mass redundancies which decimate the local community.

Another essential difficulty in the assessment of employees' whistleblowing is difficulty to classify certain conducts as illegal or unethical. The question of the illegality of actions may be decided ultimately by a court, albeit it sometimes requires long months of laborious investigations. The question weather the action is unethical may be much more difficult to judge. The same action can be valued differently from the deontological and consequential points of view. Any event has positive and negative consequences, supports some values and gainsays others and the motivation of an action may be complex. An ethical assessment often depends on estimation of the threat that a given action poses, and in such cases even experts disagree. As Czesław Porebski (1997) points out, the seriousness of the threat may depend on the context in which it is presented. He also shows how the risk of making the same automobile may be interpreted differently, depending on whether it is viewed as a product of a company that brings a profit at the cost of fatal accidents or as a safe automobile whose reliability is not absolute, for there are no such automobiles, but as high as possible.

4. Polish Employees' Attitudes towards Whistleblowing

Although whistleblowing is receiving more and more attention in the academic and public discussion in our country, few empirical researches have been conducted on this topic. The employees' opinions presented below are part of the results of studies conducted under the research project "Ethics in the Polish Economy: Perception, Preferences, Norms" (Lewicka-Strzalecka 1999). The study encompassed employees on all levels of the hierarchy of official responsibility, not only managers or entrepreneurs, as is the usual practice. A total of 945 questionnaires were analyzed. The sample was selected intentionally to investigate the influence of individual characteristics (sex, age, time on the job, position, and education) and of features characterising the respondents as representatives of companies (type of ownership, branch, size, economic condition) on the ethical standards of the company and its employees.

The study was conducted by means of the questionnaire Ethics in the Opinion of Employees. The questionnaire contained several questions on the attitude of employees towards whistleblowing.

As the data presented in table 1 indicate, less than one-third of the respondents hold the conviction that disclosure of abuses is good for the company, 13 percent are of the opinion that it is bad for the company, while more than a half believe that it depends on the situation. If the good of the company is understood as its survival, development or profit maximizing, then these results express the predominant conviction of the respondents that in many situations the concealment of abuses contributes to its success. This view is unquestionably influenced by the conditions in which companies operate in a muddy market. Distorted *competition* and the ease in breaking or avoiding the law cause that it is easier for the company to achieve success by adhering to dishonest methods than by making the effort to improve themselves in response to criticism. For example, it is unlikely that a company will feel a negative market impact because of receiving a license for a bribe. So it will be the company's interest not to reveal the backstage of obtaining the license. The disclosure of informal employment in the company may increase its operating expenses. Situations in which the company improves itself as a consequence of whistle blowing and thanks to this improves its financial results are regarded as rare.

The data presented in table 2 suggest that the percentage of respondents convinced on the positive relationship between the interest of the company and the disclosure of unethical behaviors grows with the hierarchy of the organizational position while most persons believing that it is a negative relationship is among managers.

The data in table 3 is more unequivocal; they show that the percentage of persons expressing the opinion on the positive relationship between the interest of the company and the disclosure of unethical behaviors grows with the education level and respectively the percentage of persons expressing the opinion on the negative relationship between the interest of the company and the disclosure of unethical behaviors diminishes with and education level.

The data in table 4 indicate that the percentage of persons with an unequivocal view on the relationship between disclosure of abuses and the interest of the company increases with the job duration (percentage of persons choosing the answer "sometimes yes, sometimes no" decreases). Although with longer duration of the job the percentage of persons expressing the conviction that this is a positive dependency and those of the opinion that it is negative one increases, the first trend is definitely more pronounced.

To sum up, one can state that the adherents of the positive view on whistleblowing at work are the persons in high managerial positions, with higher education and long professional experience.

Respondents' observations concerning responses to the question: *Do you know persons outside the monitoring system who revealed unethical behavior at work?* are presented in table 6. These data show that whistleblowing is rare among Polish employees in comparison to American ones, among whom every second employee admits to reporting abuses (Goodell, 1994). The attitude of some respondents towards whistle-blowers was expressed by one of them, who responded to the question whether he knows such persons: No, I don't know any such informers. The term informer has in Polish very negative meaning. As one may surmise, the percentage of employees who have encountered whistle blowers increases as responsibility in the official hierarchy grows. This allows one to guess that the managerial staff and managers are the addressees of at least a part of the information disclosed about abuses.

The data shown in table 5 present the attitude of employees surveyed towards the view that every employee has the obligation to disclose unethical practices, a view that companies introducing internal whistleblowing systems are trying to spread. The findings indicate that 15 percent of the respondents are opposed to this view and 53 percent are undecided. The acceptance of this view increases as the responsibility in the official hierarchy rises.

The respondents' views on the reasons for not disclosing unethical behaviors by the employees are presented in table 7. An interesting, although hardly surprising result, is that, in the respondents' opinion, the most important reason (60 percent) for not disclosing is the negative social reaction to this deed, namely, identifying it with snitching. A snitch is most often motivated by personal gain, ill will or bad intention to harm another person. In the case of whistleblowing the other person is a coworker, with whom the informer should be tied by bonds of professional solidarity, or the superior, to whom the whistleblower should be loyal. Polish language does not have a term for a person disclosing abuses and acting unselfishly to remove some evil done to other individuals or society. Notwithstanding the noble intentions and effectiveness of revealing abuses, an ethical appraisal of the whistle blower is not unequivocal. Violation of the socially important norm of the solidarity of fellow-workers has always an important influence on this appraisal.

The second most important reason for not disclosing abuses by employees is the fear of the consequences of this act (56 percent), the third one is the potential harm they can do to themselves by upsetting arrangements that are beneficial for them (54 percent). The last result can indicate the extent of employees enmeshed in the unethical networks. The next to last reason, namely lack of knowledge that certain behaviors are unethical, shows that in the opinion of the respondents most employees are aware of what abuses are. The last reason expresses the conviction that employees who do not disclose abuses do not imitate the behavior of others.

Table 8 shows the distribution of the respondents' opinions on the reactions to disclosing abuses. This distribution shows that respondents do not have a positive opinion on the company's responsiveness to information about abuses; they rarely expect the company to take steps to explain the matter. The report is usually not belittled, but the reaction to it depends on whom it concerns and whose interest it threatens. In some cases the reaction may consist in revenge or retaliation.

The distribution of respondents' opinions on the best ways to limit unethical behaviors shows that they believe that the most important one is the ethical behavior of managers. This view conforms to the findings of many studies confirming that the behavior of managers has a greater influence on everyday decisions made by employees than any other factor (Ferrell, Gresham, 1985). It has been confirmed that a lot of man's ethical or unethical behaviors are behaviors learned in the course of interactions with other people, among whom managers play an important role. Managers convey ethical standards directly - in words and by being a personal pattern of the desired behavior, and indirectly - by exerting a decisive influence on the culture of the company.

The second most effective way to limit unethical behaviors, according to the respondents, is training employees. Data obtained earlier show that ethics training in companies is quite rare in the Polish companies. For this reason the respondents' conviction on the effectiveness of training as a way of limiting unethical behaviors is more an expression of their expectations than a result of experience. American studies, which show a positive influence of training on employees' ethical standards and behaviors, confirm the correctness of those expectations. Polish employees expressed at the same time the view that methods based on lack of trust employees are ineffective. According to them, greater control is the least effective method of limiting unethical behaviors. This was to some extent an expression of lack of faith in the effectiveness of control.

5. Conclusion

Well-managed companies pursuing a far-sighted policy try not to allow publication of abuses committed in the company. To this end they attempt to create an internal system for the discovery and prevention of abuses. However, apart from benefits a company whistleblowing policy has its dangers precisely reasoned from a theoretical point of view and verified by the empirical study.

The employees' opinions on whistle blowing presented above suggest great caution should be exercised when introducing an internal system of disclosing abuses in the company. Given the historically determined aversion of Poles to informing, the direct transfer of such systems from Western companies, especially American ones, may fail and do more harms than good. The project of an internal system of disclosing abuses ought to consider the attitude of the company's employees towards whistle blowing and the means of influencing that attitude. Creating an internal system of disclosing abuses in the company as the only element of the ethics program may prove especially harmful. Lack of employees' understanding of the essence of this system would make it as serving to pay off old scores and not to eliminate abuses from the company activity. The opinions expressed by the surveyed employees suggest the decision about introducing an internal system of disclosing abuses in the company should be preceded by some important steps. The first one is preparing an adequate code of conduct and the second - is carrying out an ethics training. The code of conduct and ethics training will allow the employees to learn with ethical standards of the company and the necessity to comply with them. They should know which abuses should be disclosed, how to do it and what for. And first of all they should be convinced that the managers will be the first to comply with company ethical standards.

References

Boatright J. R. 1997. *Ethics and the Conduct of Business*. Englewood Cliffs, NJ: Prentice-Hall.

DeGeorge R. T., 1990, *Business Ethics*. Englewood Cliffs, NJ: Prentice-Hall.

Ferrell O. C., Gresham L. G. 1985. "A Contingency Framework for Understanding Ethical Decision Making in Marketing." *Journal of Marketing* 49, 87-96.

Goodell R. 1994. *Ethics in American Business: Policies, Programs and Perceptions*. Washington, DC: Ethics Resource Center.

Hirschman A. O. 1970. *Exit, Voice, and Loyalty*. Cambridge, MA: Harvard University Press.

Lewicka-Strzalecka A. 1999. *Ethical Standards of Firms and Employees* (in Polish). Warsaw: IFiS PAN.

Miethe T. D. 1999. *Whistleblowing at Work*. Boulder, CO: Westview Press.

Ossowska M. 1970. *Moral Norms* (in Polish). Warsaw: PWN.

Porebski C. 1997. *Does Ethics Pay?* (in Polish). Krakow: Znak.

Building Legal Protection to Whistleblowers in Poland[1]

Anna Wojciechowska-Nowak
Stefan Batory Foundation
Warsaw, Poland

1. Introduction

Each organization has its own history of how it began to deal with a particular problem and so Anticorruption Program had its own path which led its team to thinking of how to build legal protection to whistleblowing and whistleblowers. Unlike, however, other non-governmental organizations such as Government Accountability Project or Public Concern at Work, who devote all their capacities to the issue, whistleblowing in the work of Anticorruption Program has been set in wider context of various activities directed to preventing and fighting corruption.

Anticorruption Program was set up at the beginning of 2000, the time when Poland was constantly falling down in the Corruption Perception Index table, when the social acceptance for bribes reached 40 percent, and the belief in personal capacity to make change in this area was very low (nearly 70 percent of respondents believed they cannot contribute to curbing corruption). It was also the moment when Commission of the European Union initiated the monitoring of Poland's progress towards accession and among other problems it took a closer look at measures undertaken to prevent the corruption risks. Given the context accompanying the launch of Anticorruption Program, its work initially was to be focused on education *sensu largo,* i.e., raising public awareness about all aspects of corruption phenomenon.

Soon after the program started its daily work, however, it turned out that legal support was needed. The Program became one of the few places in the country where individuals who faced corruptive practices believed they could address and ask for advice or an intervention. In response to the incoming letters and phone-calls legal counseling project was set up. Some of the stories described by those seeking help fit a specific and repetitive scenario. These were stories of people who refused to turn a blind eye to the abuses occurring in their workplace and as a result had to struggle with consequences of their attitude. Each story, apart from being an example of the infringement of employment rights, showed that whistleblowing could be an efficient tool of detecting and preventing abuse of power, misuse of public funds, corruption, nepotism but also risks to safe working conditions or environmental protection. On a grass-roots level and based on the first-hand experience we had a chance to see the practical meaning of Article 9 of the Civil Law Convention obliging the member states to provide for "appropriate protection against any unjustified sanction for employees who have reasonable grounds to suspect corruption and who report in good faith their suspicion to responsible persons or authorities."

The support we offer in whistleblowers' cases is monitoring of court trials through *amicus curiae* procedure. Based on that experience we have gathered knowledge allowing us to depict the legal situation of a whistleblower at the employment court and the barriers to the efficient protection of professional careers.

2. Legal Status of a Whistleblower in Poland

Poland belongs to countries which do not provide specific protection against employer's retaliation to an employee, who acting in good faith brings wrongdoing to light. Unlike whistleblowing statutes in Great Britain, the United States, New Zealand, or Australia to mention but a few examples, Polish law does not offer protection which would take into consideration and reflect the specificity of this type of cases. What is offered is general rules of labor law which protect any employee against unlawful dismissal, i.e., "groundless or unlawful termination of the employment agreement". General rules however do not for instance shift the burden of proof in whistleblowers cases. This does not mean the shifted burden of proof is a new concept in Polish law. According to the amendments implemented to Labor Code in January 2002, the burden of proof in discrimination cases lies upon the employer. Since whistleblowing is inexistent term in the legislation and in vast majority of cases cannot be interpreted as a form of discrimination, whistleblowers cannot benefit from this particular solution.

The Group of States Against Corruption found the standard of legal protection in Poland satisfactory. Having examined Polish legislation in the course of the second evaluation round (2003-2006), covering general anti-corruption measures applicable to the administration and public officials, GRECO did not find it necessary to make recommendations to Poland to improve its whistleblowing measures. Just like in Finland, France or Spain, the assessment carried out concluded that general rules under Labor Code offer a satisfactory alternative to whistleblowing laws.

This was also our guess when we initially took a closer look into the problem. We assumed that despite the fact there is no specific protection mechanism as such, the ban of unfair dismissal is flexible enough to cover the situation where an employee is fired in the aftermath of the activities undertaken in order to reveal an abuse in the workplace. We believed the employment courts, understanding the role of an active attitude of a member of the given community in preventing the occurrence of harmful phenomena, would establish protection based on the ban. Consequently, each *amicus curiae* submitted to the employment court explained, based on our observations, the role of a whistleblower, showed Poland's obligations resulting from the international law and described trends in laws of other countries.

The above assumption was interrelated with another one, which very soon proved to be false, the flexibility of the employment courts' judicature. The expectation that employment courts would be more open to a new approach seemed to be justified given the fact that Poland is not a common law country. The judgments of the Supreme Court or circuit courts, the latter having jurisdiction over cases on appeal, are binding only within the scope of a case being the subject matter of the given proceedings. In practice however lower courts do follow standpoints reflected in the body of rulings of upper courts even if such rulings are not binding in the particular case. Apart from the influence resulting from the recognized authority of the Supreme Court, employment courts are formally bound by resolutions adopted by the Supreme Court (the entire Supreme Court bench, a joint bench of chambers or a bench of one chamber), so called legal principles.

Below are presented trends in the judicature of the Supreme Court, which make the struggle for whistleblower's protection difficult, and are commonly cited by lower courts. What should be stressed is the fact that none of presented rulings was held in the context of whistleblowing.

Termination notice as a regular way to dissolve the employment agreement. Under Polish law the employment agreement can be put to an end either with a termination notice or without it, the latter solution being applicable to cases where the gross violation of basic duties occurred either on the part of the employer or the employee. Dissolving the employment relationship with a termination notice is perceived as regular way to end an agreement. "Therefore the cause for the employment termination does not need to carry any particular weight or extraordinary importance."[2]

Given the fact that termination notice is usually used to end employment with a whistleblower, no significant reason, no grave trespasses need to be evidenced to suffice legitimate termination or the agreement.

Verifying the existence of economic basis for redundancy. In whistleblowing cases the cause of termination, which is most often exploited, is the redundancy. The reason why employers call upon reorganization is that the jurisdiction of employment courts leaves much freedom to the employers within the scope of decisions of reducing workforce. The employment courts are not entitled to verify whether the redundancy was a justified decision in terms of economics, e.g., whether the difficult financial standing or inefficient internal structure required downsize or reorganization. It is an established judicial practice, resulting from the Supreme Court resolution, to assume that the assessment on what internal structure and organization best suits the needs of employer belongs to the employer's domain. As the Court held: "Reducing the staff numbers is manifested in the necessity to dismiss a certain number of employees and those employees who hold job positions being made redundant. The decision whether reducing employment would be justified shall be taken by the bodies of the enterprise (...). Decisions pertaining to this matter belong to the organizational sphere of an employer and for this reason are not subject to the verification in the dispute over the groundless dismissal."[3] Furthermore, the Supreme Court puts the stress on „the necessity to leave the employer an appropriate margin of appreciation, the lack of which could make the human resources policy excessively difficult to be run."

The above-cited reasoning of the Supreme Court is reaffirmed in subsequent decisions. In 2007 for instance the Court recalled "According to the long-lasting and well-established judicature redundancy carried out within the framework of genuine organizational changes justifies termination of employment agreement, as the decisions on the purpose and efficacy of marinating the given position fall within the range of employers' exclusive competence and are not subject to the verification by employment court."[4]

3. (Un) fair Redundancies

In the light of the above-cited judicial decisions it is very difficult for a whistleblower to prove the employer used redundancy to cover up the real reason for ending their employment. The strategy to argue that dismissal was fictitious, as it was not justified in the light of economic standing or needs, would fail in the employment court.

The experience gathered until now by the Batory Foundation suggests there is only one situation which opens a chance for a whistleblower to be restored to the job. In unfair dismissal cases it is required that the cause of termination is genuine. If the employer for instance recruits new employees after downsizing, the court will not find the reorganization genuine. In this context the condition of genuine cause form employment termination seems to be relatively easy to satisfy.

The fictitious redundancy argument was successfully raised by one of whistleblowers whose case was monitored by Batory Foundation. Former inspector in the State Forests—National Forest Holding have not had questioned the dismissal until the employer recruited two new inspectors in the regional branch he used to work for. The court found the reorganization fictitious and held the dismissal was unfair. Consequently compensation was awarded.

One cause to justify legitimate termination. In cases where more than one cause for termination is indicated, in order to sustain the termination it is sufficient to establish that any of the causes was legitimate.[5] In such case the court will find the termination justified and effective as such. For this reason, if an employer indicates redundancy as a cause for the employment termination, the task of the court is narrowed merely to verify, as mentioned above, whether downsizing was genuine. Provided this test is satisfied, the employment court will not verify the question whether the primary cause of the decision to downsize a given position was the intent to get rid of a trouble-making employee.

The above-mentioned trends in judicial practice leave an employer with a wide margin of freedom. The Batory Foundation monitored cases where employers included the whistleblower's position into the larger restructuring as well as cases where only the whistleblower's position was downsized. The employment termination was found in each of those cases effective as the possible primary reason, i.e. interventions undertaken by a whistleblower, had never been the subject of the court's consideration.

Loss of trust as the cause of terminating agreement with an employee holding a managerial position. The Supreme Court held in the previously-cited resolution that: "Employees holding managerial or independent positions should be confronted with higher standards than the rest of the staff. Those employees should serve as an example both of good job and appropriate attitude. They are also responsible for low effectiveness of departments they are heading. For this reason their behavior must be assessed according to more severe criteria which are also applicable to minor and singular failures."[6]

The above ruling—let us recall—having the effect of a binding legal principle, has a significant impact in whistleblowers' cases. The ruling is often referred to by employers calling upon the lost of trust, which next to the redundancy is the most often exploited cause for termination in whistleblowers cases. Employers argue that revealing the problems by a whistleblower to an external forum undermined the trust necessary to continue the employment.

The observations made by the Batory Foundation show that this argument can also be successfully raised in cases where whistleblowers try to raise their concerns internally. In one of the monitored cases the employer informed the employee upon the termination of the agreement due to "the loss of trust to you as a member of the management staff, who by disseminating false information about the work organization and relations in the company acted to its detriment." *Dissemination* in this case referred to the activities of the whistleblower, who having undertaken unsuccessful trials to solve the problems internally, notified the owner of the enterprise and finally, given the continuing threats to the safety co, the prosecutors' office.

The judicial practice referred to in above again has the implications in whistleblowers' cases. It is quite often that whistleblowers recruit from management staff or held independent positions. It seems reasonable that better knowledge and access to information about how the company operates allows an employee to detect the problems or abuses within the company.

Conflict between an employer and an employee as a cause for employment termination. There is a well established judicial practice to perceive a conflict, specifically the one provoked by an employee as legitimate cause for the employment termination. In particular this predominant point of view refers to misunderstandings which make it impossible for a superior to coordinate work and to fulfill his/her management responsibilities effectively.

The above trend is vivid in the context of whistleblowers' cases as well. Where a whistleblower reveals information undermining honesty or even merely the competences of his/her superior, conflict of a personal nature becomes very probable.

Another aspect of conflicts between an employer and an employee was pointed out by the Supreme Court in the following ruling: "The loss of trust to an employee is perceived as a legitimate cause for the employment termination. The lack of employee's enthusiasm or his/her disapproval to the superior's decisions, even resulting from the employee's genuine concern about the interest of the company and the deepest conviction as his/her righteousness, may lead to the situation where the mutual understanding is impossible, and finally cause the loss of trust."[7]

Does winning a case mean being a winner? Whistleblowers who initiate the court trial hoping to be restored to work may still have to face the problem to achieve their goal once the battle is over. Winning the trial in the employment court does not necessary mean being restored to work. Should the court trial establish the termination notice was groundless or unlawful, there can be two optional judgments: either the court will rule the termination is inefficient and restore a whistleblower to work or the court will only adjudicate damages. As a rule the court will follow the option chosen by an employee. However, should the court assess reemployment would be *impossible* or *pointless,* the whistleblower will be only adjudicated damages and refused to be restored to work.

In practice, given the fact that the complete court proceedings usually take a few years, the position previously held by a whistleblower by the time the trial is over will have been usually occupied by a new employee, while the whistleblower's professional skills will have been degraded.

One of the reasons for *impossible* or *pointless* reemployment which is most often called upon by employment courts is the conflict with the superior and bad atmosphere in the workplace. This point of view is reflected by the Supreme Court in the following ruling: "In case of serious a long-lasting conflict between the employer and the employee, which negatively affects not only other employees but also the image of the employer the purpose of restoring the employee to work is doubtful".[8] It is assumed that bad relations between the employer and the employee will affect the appropriate cooperation. Especially with regard to places like school judicial practice tends to perceive conflicts between a regular teacher and his/her headmaster as serving a bad example to pupils. The interest of pupils requires that their attention is focused on education and not dispersed on conflicts within the teaching staff.

Following the above line of thinking, in cases where the court finds the employment termination inefficient, usually damages are adjudicated. Whistleblowers can seldom expect to be reemployed. No matter the concerns were raised in the interest of pupils, financial or other interests of school or other employer. Sadly, the Batory Foundation has never had a chance to monitor a case where a transfer to another position, the position which would not be subordinated to the person whose activities were questioned by a whistleblower, would be considered and thus the risk of potential conflict excluded.

Lack of a unified approach to issues typical to whistleblower cases. Running the legal counseling project we have had an opportunity to observe that, when it comes to some aspects typical to whistleblowing trials, the judicial practice varies from case to case and no unified approach has been worked out. The two questions are the most common examples: (i) should a whistleblower make a disclosure to the employer first? and (ii) must the concerns raised be confirmed?

In one of the monitored cases the court accepted an argument of an employer that skipping the internal disclosure by the whistleblower and addressing the police directly infringed the employer's trust to the extent which made the employment termination legitimate. The court however did not take into consideration circumstances indicating the whistleblower could have been risking his employment by making a disclosure to his employer. In another case, where the whistleblower raised his concern firstly to the employer, secondly to the owner of the company and as the last resort to the police, the court focused exclusively on the fact that problematic issued were revealed at the external forum.

Analogically, there is no unified approach to the actual occurrence of the concerns raised. Generally the employment courts avoid checking on the stage of criminal investigation, should one be in process, and also the probability the whistleblower could have been perceived as a threat to dishonest executives. Employment courts usually refuse to look upon the files of criminal investigation. On the opposite, should the criminal investigation be extinguished, the judgment will usually include that argument that appropriate proceedings did not confirm that the concerns raised did actually occur.

4. Conclusions

The observations gathered by the Batory Foundation while monitoring whistleblowing trials in the employment courts made it clear that based on general rules of Labor Code the protection can be executed only in rare and rather accidental cases. We saw that proceedings run in front of employment courts very seldom lead to the heart of the issue—the genuine reason for employment termination, i.e., bringing problems to light. Not only Polish whistleblowers need specific law, but also employment courts and employers. These should be provisions which on the one hand would take into consideration the specificity of whistleblowers situation, help to unify judicature and on the other hand carefully balance the interests of both parties to the employment agreement, clarify to an employee what conditions must be satisfied to make a protected disclosure and help employers see potential in whistleblowing as a tool to protect their interests.

Notes

1. Based on Works of Anticorruption Program at the Stefan Batory Foundation.
2. Judgment of the Supreme Court of 6.12.2001, case reference no I PKN 715/00.
3. Supreme Court Resolution of 27 June 1985, case reference no III PZP 10/85, published in OSNC 1985/11/164.
4. Judgment of the Supreme Court of 4 September, 2007, case reference no I PK 92/07.
5. Judgment of the Supreme Court of 5.10.2005, case reference no I PK 61/05.
6. Supreme Court Resolution of 27 June 1985, case reference no III PZP 10/85, published in OSNC 1985/11/164.
7. The judgment of the Supreme Court of 23.09.2004, case reference number I PK 487/03.
8. The judgment of the Supreme Court of 4.01.2008, case reference number I PK 179/07.

Notes about the Authors

Marek Arszulowicz is a scientist and an entrepreneur. Has earned his Ph.D. in Management Science at the Kozminski University, Warsaw, Poland in 2005 (*Whistleblowing in Organizations*). His main research is in the business ethics as well as in determinants of success in small and medium entreprices. He holds a position of a lecturer at the School of Marketing and Management. Associate of Business Ethics Center at the Kozminski University. He published articles on whistleblowing.

A. J. Brown is a Professor at Griffith University Law School in Brisbane, Queensland, Australia. He was the project leader of the recently completed Whistling While They Work research project. He is a former Senior Investigation Officer with the Commonwealth Ombudsman. Email: A.J.Brown@griffith.edu.au

Wojciech W. Gasparski is Professor of Humanities, Dr. Sc., Director and founder of the Business Ethics Centre (ajoint unit of Kozminski University & Polish Academy of Sciences Institute of Philosophy and Sociology). Immediate past vice rector for research of the Kozminski University. Professor emeritus of the Institute of Philosophy and Sociology, Polish Academy of Sciences (PAS) where he chaired the Academic Board and headed the Department of Praxiology as well as the Research Group for Ethics in Business and the Economy. His publications on human action theory (praxiology), business ethics, methodology, science studies, and systems theory. are numerous. He is a member of the Warsaw Learned Society, Learned Society of Praxiology (Founder and Honorary President), Polish Philosophical Society, International Society of Business, Economics and Ethics, Academy of Management (USA), Science Studies Committee PAS (Honorary Member), Management Science Committee PAS. Editor-in-chief of *Praxiology: The International Annual of Practical Philosophy and Methodology* (Transaction Publishers, USA).He recently published *Responsible Management*

Education (2008). In 2006 he was nominated to the European Faculty Pioneer Award for Business in Society by Aspen Foundation (USA) and the European Academy of Business and Society. He was awarded The Tadeusz Kotarbinski Medal by the Polish Academy of Sciences for his achievements in management science (2008).

W. Michael Hoffman, Ph.D, is the founding Executive Director of the Center for Business Ethics at Bentley University in Waltham, Massachusetts, a 33 year-old research and consulting institute. He is also the Hieken Professor of Business and Professional Ethics at Bentley. He received his Ph.D. in Philosophy at the University of Massachusetts/Amherst and has been a professor for 40 years in higher education. He has authored or edited 16 books, including Business Ethics: Readings and Cases in Corporate Morality (4th edition), The Ethical Edge, and Ethics Matters: How to Implement Values-Driven Management, and has published over 95 articles. He consults on business ethics for corporations and other organizations, and serves as an expert witness in litigation. Dr. Hoffman was co-founder and the first Executive Director of the Ethics & Compliance Officer Association and the Advisor to its board of directors for ten years. He was co-founder and President of the Society for Business Ethics, served on the advisory board of the U.S. Sentencing Commission, and is frequently sought out globally for professional lectures and media interviews. Dr. Hoffman was named the 2007 Humanist of the Year by The Ethical Society of Boston.

Paul Latimer is an Associate Professor in the Department of Business Law and Taxation at Monash University, Melbourne, Victoria, Australia. He was one of the researchers in the recently completed Whistling While They Work research project. Email: Paul.Latimer@buseco.monash.edu.au.

Aaron Levine is the Samson and Halina Bitensky Professor of Economics at Yeshiva University. A Phi Beta Kappa at Brooklyn College, he earned his Ph.D. at New York University. He was ordained in Jewish civil and ritual law at the Rabbi Jacob Joseph School.

A noted authority on Jewish commercial law, Professor Levine's research specialty is the interface between economics and Halakhah, especially as it relates to public policy and modern business practices. He has published widely on these issues, including five books and numerous monographs. His books include *Free Enterprise and Jewish Law* (1980); *Economics and Jewish Law* (1987); *Economic Public Policy and Jewish*

Law (1993); *Case Studies in Jewish Business Ethics* (2000), and *Moral Issues of the Marketplace in Jewish Law* (2005).

An associate editor of *Tradition,* Dr. Levine also serves on an ad hoc basis on the *Bet Din* (rabbinical court) of the Rabbinical Council of America for disputes in monetary matters.

Dr. Levine is a member of the World Jewish Academy of Science and the recipient of the Irving M. Bunim Prize for Jewish Scholarship. In 1982, he was respondent to Milton Friedman in the Liberty Fund symposium on the Morality of the Market.

Anna Lewicka-Strzalecka Ph.D. is a Professor at the Institute of Philosophy and Sociology, Polish Academy of Sciences, Warsaw, Poland. Her primary research interests include praxiology, practical philosophy, science studies and business ethics. She published several books and almost a hundred articles and conference papers. She is a founder and vice-president of EBEN Poland.

David Lewis is Professor of Employment Law at Middlesex University, London, UK. He has a first degree in law, a masters degree in Industrial Relations and is a member of the Charter Institute of Personnel and Development. For many years his main research interest has been employment protection for whistleblowers. He has published widely in the field and his output since 2005 includes the following articles: 'Whistleblowers and the law of defamation: time for more statutory privilege?'(2005) 3 Web Journal of Current Legal Issues 1-13; 'Providing rights for whistleblowers: would an anti-discrimination model be more effective?'(2005) Industrial Law Journal 34(3),239-252; 'The contents of whistleblowing / confidential reporting procedures in the UK: some lessons from empirical research'(2006) Employee Relations 28(1),76-86; (with Tina Uys, T) 'Protecting whistleblowers at work: a comparison of the impact of British and South African legislation' (2007) Managerial Law 49(3,76-92; 'A survey of whistleblowing/ confidential reporting procedures used by persons prescribed under the Public Interest Disclosure Act 1998'(2007) Communications Law. 12(4),124-130; 'Ten years ofpublic interest disclosure legislation in the UK: are whistleblowers adequately protected?' (2008) Journal of Business Ethics. 82(2),497-507.

Tobias Louw is currently Professor in Philosophy at the University of Fort Hare in the Eastern Cape, South Africa. He completed his initial studies at the University of Stellenbosch where he obtained the following degrees: BA (Philosophy and Psychology), BA Honours (Philosophy) and MA (Philosophy). He obtained his D Litt et Phil (Philosophy) at the University of Fort Hare under the supervision of Gerhard Rauche. He has edited and introduced the book, GA Rauche—Selected Philosophical Papers, and has published several articles and book-chapters in national and international publications. Current work includes the forthcoming three books namely, Holding on to the Vision (including the autobiography of Gerhard Rauche), Reluctant Witness—the Story of the Hogsback United Church Fellowship, and The Sciences of the Text. He is the current chairman of the Philosophical Society of South Africa. His fields of interest are hermeneutics, ethics, ancient Greek philosophy and philosophical consultation

Robert E. McNulty is the director of programs at the Center for Business Ethics (CBE), Bentley University. He joined CBE after many years in both business and academia.

At CBE, Dr. McNulty is responsible for managing many aspects of CBE's various programs and overseeing the Center's research activities. Besides Bentley, he has taught at Columbia University and at the State University of New York at New Paltz. Prior to entering academia he had a lengthy career in international business, specializing in the application of strategic communications to assist countries in their economic development efforts. He has also served as a consultant to many Fortune 500 and foreign based firms. For the last decade and a half, the focus of his work has been ethics, both in its theoretical and applied forms. Dr. McNulty founded and heads Applied Ethics, Inc., a nonprofit organization with the mission of seeking ethical solutions to significant social issues through projects, education, counseling, and advocacy.

Some of his recent publications include "Business Ethics Perspectives on International Negotiations" and "International Business, Human

Rights and Moral Complicity: A Call for a Declaration on the Universal Rights and Duties of Business," both co-authored with W. Michael Hoffman.

Dr. McNulty received his Ph.D. in philosophy and education from Columbia University and Master of International Affairs degree also from Columbia. He received his bachelor's degree magna cum laude from the University of Massachusetts, Amherst.

An American by nationality and an internationalist by disposition, he has traveled extensively and has lived and worked overseas in France, Taiwan, Indonesia and Singapore.

Guido Strack is a jurist with two German state exams in law and a LL.M. of the University of Cologne. For almost ten years he worked as an official with the European Commission. Most of that time with the Publications Office in Luxembourg being responsible for a project consolidating the texts of European laws in all official languages of the European Union. There he blew the whistle to the European Anti-Fraud Office (OLAF). OLAF launched an investigation which was closed after 18 months with no findings and no follow up. Mr. Strack went to the Court of the European Union asking that decision to be annulled but his case was turned down as non admissible (T-4-05, C-237/06P) despite the fact that by blowing the whistle he fulfilled an obligation of the EU staff regulation. He won some other court cases against the European Commission while others are still pending. The European Ombudsman based on complaints of Mr. Strack found maladministration by the European Commission and OLAF in eight cases. Mr. Strack became sick and was found unfit to work for job related issues. After returning to Germany in 2006 he became co-founder and president of the Whistleblower-Netzwerk e.V. (http://whistleblower-net.de). This NGO tries to council and support whistleblowers and promote whistleblo-wer culture and whistleblower protection in Germany. Mr. Strack was expert witness at the German Bundestag concerning a whistleblower protection law proposal in 2008.

Tina Uys is currently Professor of Sociology and Chairperson of the department at the University of Johannesburg. She is a past president of the South African Sociological Association (SASA) and of the International Sociological Association's (ISA) Research Committee on Social Psychology (RC42). She is a member of the Executive Committee of the ISA (2006-2010). The main focus of her research is on whistleblowing and South African sociology. She has also published on HIV/Aids, relative deprivation and developments in higher education. As project leader of an NRF project titled: "Citizenship and Social Capital: Exploring struggles over social space and inclusion" she is presently exploring broader understandings of citizenship, in particular the issue of academic citizenship as well as the link between organizational citizenship, family resilience and whistleblowing. She has published the following articles on whistleblowing: 'Whistleblowing: Fighting fraud in organisations.' (with Nico Alant In *Fraud and the African renaissance,* edited by Deon Rossouw and Dee Carabine 1999); 'The politicization of whistleblowers: A case study.' (*Business Ethics: A European Review* 2000); 'Preempting whistleblowing with ethics.' (with Deon Rossouw In *Business ethics* by Deon Rossouw and Leon van Vuuren 2004); "Professional ethics versus corporate loyalty: whistleblowing in the financial sector." (In *Whistleblowing: An introduction* edited by CV Krishna Rao. 2006); 'Rational loyalty and whistleblowing: The South African context.' (*Current Sociology* 2008); Morality of principle versus morality of loyalty: The case of whistleblowing. (with Anton Senekal *African Journal of Business Ethics* 2008).

Wim Vandekerckhove is a post-doctoral researcher at the Research Foundation Flanders (FWO) and assistent professor of practical ethics at Ghent University, Belgium. He holds a Master degree in Moral Philosophy (Ghent University), a Postgraduate degree in Business Administration (OUBS) and a Doctoral degree in Ethics (Ghent University). He is a founding member of the International Global Ethics Association and of the Belgian chapter of the European Business Ethics Network. He coordinates the Responsible Investment Interest Group of EBEN.
In 2006, he published the book *Whistleblowing and Organizational Social Responsibility: A Global Assessment* with Ashgate, in which he analyses the shifts in moral argumentation with regard to protecting whistleblowers in numerous countries around the world. He is also the editor of 6 books and 7 special journal issues on global ethics, human trafficking, business ethics, and socially responsible investment. He has published 15 chapters in books and 22 papers in academic journals on globalisation, business ethics, socially responsible investment, and whistleblowing, such as *Whistleblowing and Rational Loyalty* (2004, Journal of Business Ethics) and *Whistleblowing and Moral Autonomy in Organisations* (2008, Journal of Business Ethics). He regularly writes columns on issues in business ethics for Belgian newspapers.

Wang Nan is a post doctorate of the College of the Humanities and Social Sciences, Graduate University of Chinese Academy of Sciences in Beijing, China. Her Ph.D. is in Philosophy (Philosophy of Science &Technology) received in the same university. Her main research area is philosophy of technology and philosophy of engineering. Her magisterial thesis was on *The Modern Explanation of Ernst Kapp's "Organ-Projection Theory"* and doctoral thesis was on *Tadeusz Kotarbinski and the 100-Year History of Praxiology.* She published the following articles: "The Development of Praxiology and the Comparison Between Praxiology and the Philosophy of Engineering" (*Engineering, Technology and*

Philosophy: Research Yearbook of Philosophy of Technology in China, 2008), "On Human Action From The Efficiency Perspective: A Book Review of Tadeusz Kotarbinski's Praxiology" (*Engineering Studies,* 2008), "Design in Praxiology" (*EngineeringStudies,* 2009), "Engineering Rationality" (*with Li Bo-cong, The Paper Collection of The 13th International Congress of Logic, Methodology and Philosophy of Science,* 2009), "The Modern Explanation of Ernst Kapp's 'Organ-Projection Theory'" (*with Wang Qian, Studies in Dialectics of Nature,* 2005), "A General Review on The Chinese Study of Philosophy of Technology in Europe and America" (*Engineering, Technology and Philosophy: Research Yearbook of Philosophy of Technology in China,* 2004), The History and Present Condition of German Philosophy of Technology: Interviewing Professor Li Wen-chao (*Philosophical Trends,* 2003).

Anna Wojciechowska-Nowak is a graduate of Warsaw University, Faculty of Law. Since the beginning of her professional career as a lawyer she has been involved in human rights issues and works of non-governmental sector. Initially she was gathering her experience in the field of women's human rights, specifically reproductive rights and equal status on labor market. In 2003 she joined the team of Stefan Batory Foundation, Anticorruption Program and expanded the scope of her interests into interrelations between corruption, transparency of public life and human rights. She has been responsible for legal counseling project focusing on whistleblowers' legal protection, access to public information, and freedom of speech. She has been advising on internal anticorruption strategies operating within organizations. As a trainer she has been participating in a number of trainings for public administration and non-governmental sector. She is the author of "How to Expose A Swindle. A Short Manual to Whistleblowing" (Warsaw: Stefan Batory Foundation, 2008) and co-author of "Transparent Local Government. Handbook of Good Practices" (Cezary Trutkowski, ed., Warsaw: Scholar, 2006).